COOKERY AMERICANA

COOKERY AMERICANA is a series of 27 cookbooks in 15 volumes that chronicles a fascinating aspect of American social life over the past 150 years. These volumes provide unique insight into the American experience and follow the movement of pioneer America from the original colonies to the Great Plains and westward to the Pacific. More than cookbooks, these works were manuals for daily living: household management, etiquette, home medicinal remedies, and much more. See the last pages of this volume for a complete listing of the series.

LOUIS I. SZATHMARY, Advisory Editor for this series, is an internationally known chef, food management consultant, owner of the renowned Chicago restaurant, The Bakery, and author of the best selling *The Chef's Secret Cookbook* (Quadrangle Books, 1971). As a serious student of the history of cookery, he has collected a library of several thousand cookbooks dating back to the 15th century. All of the works in *Cookery Americana* are from his private collection.

GATHERING WATERCRESS—FRESH WATERCRESS WAS
ONE OF THE FAVORITE GARNIHES OF SOUTHERN COOKS

MRS. M. E. PORTER

MRS. PORTER'S
NEW SOUTHERN
COOKERY BOOK

Introduction and Suggested Recipes

by

LOUIS SZATHMÁRY

ARNO PRESS

A NEW YORK TIMES COMPANY

New York • 1973

LIBRARY OF CONGRESS CATALOGING IN PUBLICATION DATA

Porter, Mrs. M   E
    Mrs. Porter's new southern cookery book.

    (Cookery Americana)
    Reprint of the 1871 ed.
    1.   Cookery, American—Southern States.
I. Szathmáry, Louis. II. Title. III. Series.
TX715.P844 1973   641.5   72-9802
ISBN 0-405-05053-4

Reprint Edition 1973 by Arno Press Inc.

Introduction Copyright © 1973 by Louis Szathmáry

Reprinted from a copy in the private collection of Louis Szathmáry

COOKERY AMERICANA
ISBN for complete set: 0-405-05040-2
See last pages of this volume for titles.

Manufactured in the United States of America

Introduction

f one looks here for what is generally called Southern cooking or for Southern dishes, he will do so in vain. There are few recipes for hominy grits, hush puppies, gumbos, and red-eye gravies, in this "New Southern" cookbook. It was published only a few years after the Civil War, during a period in history when at least some Southerners wanted to change their image. Therefore, recipes from all over the country are included.

Mrs. Porter's *New Southern Cookery Book,* written in Virginia and published in Philadelphia, is easy to read, easy to understand, and easy to follow. The title is justified because the recipes are rather frugal. The publisher's comments in the preface, although not exactly like those of a Madison Avenue adman, tell us that "those who examine this New Cookery Book cannot but acknowledge that we have no call to apologize for offering it to the public and expecting a large sale."

In the first section on *Soups,* there is a recipe for Southern Gumbo (p. 30) which is worth a try and which should bring good results. It uses, besides okra (which makes a gumbo) some rice and a dozen oysters. The Corn Soup (p. 33) is unusual and good. Like many other authors of the time, Mrs. Porter includes a Portable Soup (pp. 35-36). Her Crab Soup (p. 42) is simplicity, elegance and good taste all in one short recipe. It is unique, with the addition of a half-dozen yolks of hard-boiled eggs and the heart of a green lettuce cut into small pieces.

Her *Fish* recipes are very plain and sensible, while her many and varied oyster and clam recipes indicate the abundance, 100 years ago, of good fresh seafood.

The general remarks on beef are instructive, and her Roast Beef (pp. 72-73) is what we today know as roast beef—it is cooked in an oven, not next to an open fire. Her Stuffed Beefsteak (pp. 77-78) is tempting, as are her Beef Cakes and Beef Patties (p. 79). The pork recipes, like those for the fish, are plain, and the information and instructions for the Roast Pork, prepared on a spit (pp. 99-100) are outstanding. The recipe for Sausage Dumplings (p. 104) is an early forebear of today's "pigs-in-the-blanket," but it is more curious reading than a recipe to follow. Mrs. Porter does not include much information in her recipes for chicken, goose and duck, and perhaps the only unique recipe of this section worth trying today is the one for Chicken Puffs (p. 115).

We can see that game was not just a delicacy for the rich in those days, for in this "frugal cookbook" we find recipes for pigeon, canvas-back duck, widgeon and teal duck, partridge (prepared in in seven different ways), woodcock, lark and pheasant.

A significant move forward from earlier cookbooks is found in the excellent, large chapter on *Vegetables*. Earlier books had only four or five such recipes, while Mrs. Porter has six recipes just for cooking potatoes! She roasts, steams, boils, stews, fries, and mashes them. She also includes recipes for Potato Fritters and Potato Salad (pp. 134-135), and finds many other uses for potatoes throughout the book.

The slaws are called either "cold" or "hot" in Mrs. Porter's time. Recipes for spinach, asparagus, stewed green pumpkin, squashes, egg-plant, parsnips, turnips, beets, corn, succotash, and many others are listed in the *Vegetable* section. She not only has three tomato recipes, but includes a Raw Tomato recipe (p. 147) which we suggest trying.

Shrimp Sauce and Cranberry Sauce are among her fine sauce recipes. For Celery Sauce she has two recipes listed, but don't look for celery in the first (p. 156) for it seems that the printer's devil placed this title over the wrong recipe! If you do want to try a very tasty recipe for Celery Sauce, look on page 160.

Mrs. Porter is very American in her choice of adjectives. On pages 166 and 168 she includes recipes for "Good" Yeast, but between them, on page 167, she gives a recipe for "Unrivaled" Yeast.

"Unexcelled" describes her Milk Rolls (p. 179). One of her recipes for Arrowroot Biscuits (p. 190) is called "Fine," and among her breakfast cakes is one which is called "Excellent." Her Maryland Biscuits are "delicious" according to us, if one has the time and elbow grease.

Almost one-half of the book is devoted to cakes, puddings and sweets, and among her "Good," "Better," and "Best" gingerbreads is one so good that she calls it "Imperial" (p. 198). But the most delicious cakes are her Georgia Marble Cake and her Hickory-Nut Cake (pp. 220 and 221), the latter of which she calls "Very Fine."

Her book is among the first with a Potato Bread recipe (which includes wheat flour). Right next to it she also has a Wheat and

THE TYPE OF STOVE USED IN MRS. PORTER'S TIME

Sweet Potato Bread recipe (pp. 171-172). She lists many breads and rolls made with corn meal, though sometimes calls it Indian Meal.

Without calling any special attention to it, Mrs. Porter lines up several pages of cake recipes. Upon further study, we soon see that each cake's name could be a chapter heading in a large Victorian novel printed in monthly installments in *Harper's, Leslie's,* or some other literary monthly of the time. The "story" begins on page 236 with a Bachelor's Cake, followed by:

Ancient Maiden's Cake,
Introduction Cake,
Acquaintanceship Cakes,
Sweet Drops,
Flirtation Cakes,
Love Cakes,
Kisses,
Rival Cakes,
Jealousy Puffs,
Engagement Cake,
Wedding Cakes,
Very Rich Wedding Cake,
The Little Folks' Joys.

Although written 100 years ago, Mrs. Porter includes, believe it or not, an Ice Cream Cake (p. 259). Her Pioneer Cake (p. 262) would keep well for the road as would many of the other cakes, cookies and biscuits. She even remarks that some of these baked goods "last long and are suitable for travel."

After a Real Cheesecake recipe (p. 287), she includes a variety of others—Brandy-Wine, Egg-Cocoanut, Rice, Lemon and Cream Cheesecakes (pp. 288-289). Following an assortment of pie recipes (Pumpkin, Marmalade, Almond, Sweet Potato, etc.), she adds some tempting new twists—a Banana Custard Pie (p. 296), Tomato Mince (p. 308) and even a Potato Pie (p. 308). Mrs. Porter is neither selfish nor jealous when she gives a pumpkin pie recipe entitled A Jersey Girl's Recipe—Unrivaled (p. 292).

Among her numerous puddings, she has an Ice or Frozen Pudding (p. 335) which she simply tells us to "put in the freezer." Someone today would think that she is talking about the frozen food holding cabinet which stands in kitchens forming Siamese twins with the refrigerator, or standing alone, proud and cool. Not

OYSTERING IN FLORIDA (*See* oyster recipes, pp. 62-65)

TERRAPIN—ONE OF THE GREAT DELICACIES OF THE SOUTH
(*See* Terrapin Stew, p. 59)

so! What she calls a freezer is a wooden bucket, filled with ice. Mother purchased a large block of ice in the morning, the children then hammered it to chips, mixed it with salt, and pressed it firmly around a turning metal container inside the bucket. The premixed ingredients were then poured into this tightly sealable container, and children, grownups and servants alike took turns turning the handle of the clever gadget until the liquid inside froze.

Since Mrs. Porter cannot go further with adjectives in her *Pudding* section, she simply calls one Honest Plum Pudding, not to confuse it with the Best Christmas Pudding next to it (pp. 338-339). Her Apple Pudding (p. 340) is nothing but "Excelsior" and not far from the Wine Sauce (p. 346) she includes a Temperance Foam Sauce (p. 345) for those beginning to gather under the ever-threatening flag of temperance.

Among the *Light Desserts* she has a very tasty Green Corn Delight (p. 351), but we suggest trying this recipe only in the beginning of the fresh corn season. She has recipes for Floating Islands (p. 356), Balloon (p. 357), Custards (p. 358), Syllabub (p. 359), Cup Custards—not cooked (p. 360), Raspberry Fool (p. 361) and Snow Cream (p. 364). Of course, she continues to use the word "freezer" in her Frozen Custard and Fine Ice-Creams

THE FAMILY CHERRY-STONER.

A practical machine for removing the stones from cherries without mashing the fruit has long been needed, and can now be supplied in a limited quantity.

THIS HANDY GADGET HELPED THE HOMEMAKER PREPARE CHERRY PIE (p. 302) AND CHERRY BOUNCE (p. 386)

recipes. Besides ices, recipes for frozen fruits are also included in the book.

Her Poached Eggs with Ham Sauce (p. 375), which we recommend trying, offers a delightful alternative to ordinary Sunday breakfast and brunch dishes.

In her *Beverage* chapter, she not only gives instructions for making Coffee (p. 378), but also includes Substitutes for Coffee: roasted acorns, chick peas, beans, rye, cocoa shells, burned wheat bread, dried and roasted turnip, carrot and dandelion root. After suggesting all this, she adds: "We do not recommend any substitute."

We have all heard of lemonade and orangade, but have you ever made Appleade or Cranberryade? Mrs. Porter includes recipes for each (pp. 381 and 382), and also gives a recipe for Cherry Bounce (p. 386). We made this some years ago, and can guarantee that whoever tries it will know why it is called "bounce."

Mrs. Porter doesn't refer to preserving as "preserving" as was the case in earlier cookbooks. She uses the word "canning" and in her general instructions she explains that "the best method to preserve fruit with all its original flavor is by hermetically sealing it from the air in cans prepared for the purpose." She then lets everyone know that she favors the "Valve Jar," the "Mason," and the "Hero."

**GEORGIA STRAWBERRIES,
SIMILAR TO THE ONES MRS. PORTER PRESERVED**

After *Preserves, Jellies, Etc.,* she has an instructive chapter on *How to Make Pickles.* Besides such delicacies as pickled peaches, red cabbage, mushrooms, and walnuts, she has a recipe for Chou Chou (p. 408) which is nothing more than a "peck of green tomatoes" with onions, peppers, vinegar and spices.

This book is very dynamic, with short, no-nonsense recipes which assume a general cooking knowledge, understanding and skill. It is a great step forward from previous cookbooks, mainly because it is designed not for a special group, but for a large, mass audience.

Louis Szathmáry
CHICAGO, ILLINOIS

SUGGESTED RECIPES

*The following recipes have been tested and adjusted to today's
ingredients, measurements, and style of cooking
by Chef Louis Szathmáry.*

CHICKEN PUFFS (p. 115)

INGREDIENTS FOR 8:

Filling

2 cooked chicken breast halves, (10 to
   12 ounces total)
4 ounces sliced ham
½ teaspoon anchovy paste
1 teaspoon parsley flakes or 1 tablespoon
   fresh chopped parsley
1 tablespoon chopped shallots or onion
   The zest of ½ lemon, scraped or grated
   (the yellow part only)
½ teaspoon salt
   Pinch black pepper
   Pinch cayenne pepper or 1-2 drops of Tabasco
   Pinch mace
½ can (10½ ounce size) undiluted cream of
   chicken soup

"Express" puffpaste

8 ounces (2 sticks) lightly salted butter
8 ounces cream cheese
12 ounces sifted flour

METHOD: *To prepare filling:* Finely mince the chicken breast and
sliced ham. Combine with the remaining ingredients for the filling.
   To prepare the dough: Place the flour in a mixing bowl. Place
cold (refrigerated temperature) butter and cream cheese into the
flour. Cover both with flour and, alternating between butter and
cream cheese, break into pieces, first into halves, then fourths, etc.,
being careful that always *floured* and never the *naked hand* touches
the shortening. Continue breaking until both the butter and cream
cheese are in pieces the size of a kernel of corn. Press entire mixture
quickly into a ball, place on plastic wrap, form into a square ½

inch thick, wrap and refrigerate for 15-20 minutes.

To finish the chicken puffs, roll out the dough on a lightly-floured pastry board until double in size, then fold ⅓ of it from the top toward you, then ⅓ of it from the part closest to you up over the first fold. Repeat this with the left and right sides, making one one-third folds from both ends. Turn over, roll out immediately. Cut 2¼ inch squares; divide chicken filling among the squares. Pull all the edges together, press firmly; turn each puff over and let it rest on pinched side.

Heat 2 cups of shortening of your choice in a small heavy pan, drop the puffs, 3 to 4 at a time, into the shortening and fry them until they are golden brown. Serve on a napkin-covered plate; decorate with parsley. Yield: Approximately 48 puffs.

ROAST PORK (pp. 99-100)
(ROASTED ON A SPIT)

INGREDIENTS FOR 8:

3-4	pound porkloin
1	tablespoon salt
2	thick (ranch style) slices of bacon
1	teaspoon caraway seeds
¼	teaspoon black pepper
½	teaspoon paprika
	Pinch garlic salt
	Cooking time: 3-3½ hours

METHOD: With a small, sharp knife, cut ¼ inch deep slashes, ½ inch from each other, into the top fat part of the loin, first in one, then in the other direction, so that the cuts crisscross. Combine all the spices and rub well into the roast. Tie with string into a roll, then secure it on a rotating spit, over a charcoal broiler.

Have it approximately 7-8 inches from the coals and place a loaf cake pan under the roast so that the drippings fall into the pan. When it begins to brown, or after approximately 1 to 1½ hours, secure 1 slice of bacon at a time on a fork with a long handle and gently rub the surface of the roast. Repeat this every 10 minutes for the next hour, then every 5 minutes for the rest of the third hour. Remove from the spit, and let the roast stand for 15-20 minutes in a warm place before serving.

SOUTHERN GUMBO SOUP (p. 30)

INGREDIENTS FOR 8:

- 1 3-pound chicken
- 1 pound picnic, shoulder ham, smoked butt, or ½ pound ham, shank part only
- 2 quarts boiling water
- 1 whole onion, including skin
  In a cheesecloth:
- ½ teaspoon chervil, ½ teaspoon tarragon,
- ½ teaspoon basil, ½ teaspoon parsley, chopped
- 4 tablespoons shortening
- ½ cup rice
- 1 No. 2 can okra, drained and rinsed
- 1 8-ounce can oysters
- ½ cup white wine or sherry
  Salt

METHOD: Cut up the chicken into 2 drumsticks, 2 thighs, 2 wings; cut the breast into 2 halves and split the back into 2 pieces. In a frying pan heat the shortening until it begins to smoke. Sprinkle chicken pieces with salt and fry the pieces until brown on the outside but still raw on the inside, about 6-8 minutes. Place the pieces of fried chicken in a large soup pot with the picnic ham (or whatever other type of ham is used), the onion and the spice bag. Pour in boiling water to cover. Cover the pot, and over low heat, simmer for 2 hours.

Remove from fire and strain. Let the chicken and ham cool, discard onion and herbs. Skim the fat from the soup. Cut chicken and ham into small pieces, about ½ inch in size. Bring the liquid to a boil. Add the rice and the canned okra. Cook for 30 minutes over low heat. Add the cut up chicken, ham, and the canned oysters along with their liquid, and the wine or sherry. Serve hot.

NEW

SOUTHERN COOKERY BOOK

THE

Southern Cookery Book

Mrs. Porter's

New

Southern Cookery Book,

and

COMPANION FOR FRUGAL AND ECONOMICAL HOUSEKEEPERS;

CONTAINING

CAREFULLY PREPARED AND PRACTICALLY TESTED RECIPES
FOR ALL KINDS OF PLAIN AND FANCY COOKING.

By Mrs. M. E. PORTER,

PRINCE GEORGE COURT-HOUSE, VIRGINIA.

PHILADELPHIA:

JOHN E. POTTER AND COMPANY,

617 SANSOM ST.

PREFACE.

MUCH money has been squandered in misdirected efforts of well-meaning, painstaking housewives to supply their tables with palatable necessaries as well as luxuries of life; in vast numbers of instances, health has been impaired and the comfort and happiness of families marred by the ignorance of those who have the supervision of the culinary department. Quite a large number of books have been written and published with the commendable design of correcting this fault; some of these have been carefully prepared by competent writers, and have been excellent so far as they went, and yet they have not been so complete and perfect as to render improvement difficult or impracticable.

Those who examine this New Cookery Book cannot but acknowledge that we have no call to apologize for offering it to the public and expecting a large sale. Its intrinsic merits and superiority will readily be seen by those who critically analyze the recipes, and will certainly be proved by putting them to practical test. The recipes are from the pen of a lady whose experience and skill as a housekeeper would have justified us in publishing them without question, but to insure perfect reliability we have had them severally tested by competent housewives and successful cooks. But in addition to their reliability, we claim for these recipes that they are written in plain English, concisely yet clearly, so that none can mistake their meaning. In many cases, while giving the more elaborate and expensive mode of making certain articles, we have added cheaper and scarcely inferior methods.

One fact will impress those who use this book : it is that we have studied the interests of the user by giving the modes of making the most tempting luxuries, as well as the commoner necessaries, with the least possible outlay ; in other words, our study has been to give the most economical as well as best methods of preparing the various viands.

Hoping that our efforts and care may tend to lighten the labors and anxieties of the painstaking housewives throughout our land, and be appreciated by them, and also by those whose tables are in consequence better and more economically supplied than before,

Respectfully,

THE PUBLISHERS.

CONTENTS.

HOW TO MAKE SOUPS.

HOW TO DRESS FISH.

HOW TO DRESS FISH.—Continued.

HOW TO COOK MEATS.

4 CONTENTS.

HOW TO COOK MEATS.—Continued.

POULTRY AND GAME.

POULTRY AND GAME.—Continued.

1 *

6 CONTENTS.

POULTRY AND GAME.—Continued.

HOW TO PREPARE VEGETABLES.

CONTENTS.

8 CONTENTS.

HOW TO MAKE BREAD.—Continued.

HOW TO MAKE BREAD.—Continued.

HOW TO MAKE CAKES.

HOW TO MAKE CAKES.—Continued.

HOW TO MAKE CAKES.—Continued.

HOW TO MAKE CAKES.—CONTINUED.

HOW TO MAKE CAKES.—Continued.

HOW TO MAKE CAKES.—Continued.

HOW TO MAKE CAKES.—Continued.

HOW TO MAKE PASTRY.

HOW TO MAKE PASTRY.—Continued.

2 *

HOW TO MAKE PASTRY.—Continued.

HOW TO MAKE PUDDINGS.

HOW TO MAKE PUDDINGS.—Continued.

HOW TO MAKE PUDDINGS.—Continued.

PRESERVES, JELLIES, ETC.—Continued.

HOW TO MAKE PICKLES.

COOKERY FOR THE SICK.

MRS. PORTER'S

NEW

SOUTHERN COOK-BOOK.

HOW TO MAKE SOUPS.

GENERAL REMARKS.

GOOD meat is essential to good soup. It should be well boiled by the long and slow process, that the essence of the meat may be drawn out thoroughly, and the liquor should be carefully skimmed to prevent it from becoming turbid. When no more scum accumulates, and the meat is softened so as to readily separate with the use of the fork, the vegetables should be put in, the seasoning done, and the necessary amount of hot water added if too much has boiled away. A common camp-kettle will be found an excellent utensil for making soups, as the lid is heavy and will keep the steam in. An earthen pipkin or jar, if of a long and narrow make, widening a

3

little at the centre, is perhaps one of the best **ves-**
sels for soups, and is universally used by foreign
cooks, who insist that "it renders the gravy
clearer and more limpid, and extracts more savor
from the meat, than when made in tin or copper." The glutinous matters contained in the
bones render it important that they should be
boiled with the meat, as they add to the strength
and thickness of the soup, although the meat
should be cut off the bone and divided into small
pieces, removing the fat. The following thickening is indispensable to all rich soups : A tablespoonful or more of flour, mixed to a smooth
paste, with a little water and enriched with a
teaspoonful of good butter or beef dripping ; it
should be well stirred in. If making a rich
soup that requires catsup or wine, let it be added
immediately before the soup is taken from the
fire. Soup may be colored yellow with grated
carrots ; red with tomato juice ; green with the
juice of powdered spinach, and brown with carefully scorched flour kept ready for the purpose.
The use of any of these is undoubtedly some improvement, both as to look and flavor. The soups
contained in the following pages have been thoroughly tested, and their merits contrasted with

numerous others of a similar character. They were found to be more palatable, nutritious, easily made and superior as a whole; they but need good ingredients.

FARMER'S AND PLANTER'S SOUP.

THIS soup can be made from trimmings of beef or other meats. Put the bones, skin and all the rough residue of any joint into a saucepan, with a quart and a half pint of cold water, one large carrot cut and scraped, two large onions sliced and fried brown in one ounce of butter, and one very small head of celery washed and cut up. Let it stew two hours; take two potatoes peeled and sliced, a salt-spoonful of salt, a half salt-spoonful of black pepper, and a half salt-spoonful of mixed mustard. Let it simmer slowly three-quarters of an hour longer. Remove the bones and strain all through a sieve.

BEEF SOUP.

SELECTING a small shin of beef of moderate size, crack the bone, then remove the tough outside skin, wash, and place it in a kettle to boil with six or eight quarts of water and two table-

spoonsful of salt. Let it boil about four hours,
until it becomes perfectly tender, then take it out
of the liquid. If necessary, add more salt to the
liquid; then two onions cut in small pieces, eight
turnips cut in quarters, one carrot sliced small, one
large tablespoonful of sugar, a little sweet marjoram and thyme rubbed fine, and one red pepper
cut in very small pieces. Thicken this moderately
with flour and water made into the consistency of
thick cream, and stir in while boiling. Care must
be taken not to make the soup too thick with this
mixture. About three-quarters of an hour before
the soup is served put in eight potatoes cut into
quarters. Then make some very small dumplings
with a quarter of a pound of flour, two ounces of
butter, a little salt, and sufficient water to make
a dough. These dumplings require about ten
minutes to boil. When put into the soup, they
must not be much larger than a nutmeg. When
all are done, just before going to table, add some
parsley chopped very fine. If noodles should be
preferred to dumplings, take a quarter of a pound
of flour, a little salt and as many yolks of eggs as
will make it into a stiff dough. Roll it out very
thin, flour it well, and let it remain on the pie-
board to dry; then roll it up as you would a sheet

of paper, and cut with a sharp knife into slips as thin as straws; after all are cut, mix them lightly together, and to prevent them from adhering keep them well floured.

A very nice relish for either breakfast or tea can be made as follows: Before adding the vegetables, remove the meat (either beef or veal) from the kettle, and, mincing tolerably fine, put it into a stew-pan with a piece of butter; season with salt, black or cayenne pepper, mixed with vinegar, to taste; set over a slow fire, stir well together, and send to the table hot.

CHICKEN SOUP.

Cut up the fowl, cutting each joint, and wash the parts; boil one hour, then stir in thickening, pepper, salt and parsley enough to season; put in a few dumplings, made of half a pound of flour mixed with a quarter of a pound of butter; divide this dough into equal portions, and roll them in your hands into little balls the size of a nutmeg; let it then boil a quarter of an hour, or until the flesh of the fowl becomes loose on the bones; the yolk of three or four eggs, stirred in, will add richness to the taste; boil ten minutes longer, and then take it up; remove the flesh from the bones of the fowl, and divide into pieces of a size to suit, mincing the livers and gizzards; place the parts of the fowl in a tureen, pour in the soup and serve.

SOUTHERN GUMBO SOUP.

CUT up one chicken, and fry it to a light brown, also two slices of bacon; pour on them three quarts of boiling water; add one onion and some sweet herbs tied in a bag; simmer them gently three hours and a half; strain off the liquor, take off the fat, and then put the ham and chicken (cut into small pieces) into the liquor; add half a teacup of okra, also half a teacup of rice. Boil all half an hour, and just before serving add a glass of wine and a dozen oysters with their juice.

LAMB SOUP.

PUT into a stew-pan the leg or neck and breast of lamb after washing; add water (according to the quantity of soup you wish to make), a large teacupful of rice, six or eight turnips pared, washed and cut into small pieces, two onions cut fine, a little sweet marjoram, salt, black and red pepper. Boil over a slow fire about one hour; then add six or eight white potatoes, cutting them into quarters and washing them; put in a tablespoonful of white sugar, and when nearly done add a little parsley minced fine; place the meat on a dish, garnish with parsley, put the soup in a tureen and serve hot.

VEGETABLE SOUP.

TAKE two quarts of yellow split peas, or two quarts of dried white beans; soak them in cold water all night, and drain them in the morning; add a small quantity of salt and pepper, with a head of celery cut fine, and place them in a soup-pot with four quarts of water, and boil them slowly till they are all dissolved; stir them frequently. Have ready a large quantity of fresh vegetables such as turnips, carrots, parsnips, potatoes, onions, cauliflowers and asparagus tops. The vegetables requiring the longest boiling should be put in first, cutting them all into small pieces; the addition of some bits of fresh butter rolled in flour will give richness and flavor to the soup. When the vegetables are boiled quite tender put the soup into a tureen and serve up hot.

PEA SOUP.

TAKE a quart of split peas, wash them, and put
them into the soup-kettle with two quarts of cold
water.   Boil one hour, then add a piece of lean
salt pork, about three-quarters of a pound, and
boil two hours longer.   When nearly done, add a
few thin slices of ham, a few split crackers and
some pepper and salt.   Stir the soup frequently
while boiling to prevent its burning.   Should
it become thicker than is desirable, pour on boiling water and stir.   Put the soup into a tureen
and serve hot.   A more simple method is to
take the liquor in which a joint of beef has been
boiled, and, after skimming it well, put in the peas,
which have been soaked and boiled.   Flavor with
a little mushroom sauce.

BEAN SOUP.

PUT into a kettle, containing three quarts of
water, three pints of dried white beans ; let them
simmer, and when they begin to shrink drain
them in a colander; put them again into the
kettle with three quarts of boiling water, then
add two pounds of pickled pork after washing;
cook slowly, and if necessary add a little salt
and pepper, and send to the table hot.

CORN SOUP.

Put into a soup-pot, with some bits of boiled ham, a knuckle of veal and a set of calf's feet, adding a little pepper, allowing a quart of water to each pound of meat; let it boil until the meat is ready to fall from the bone; strain and pour the liquid into a clean pot. If you have plenty of milk at hand, use no water. Take a tough fowl, and, cutting it into pieces, let it boil with the veal and feet. When the soup is well boiled and the shreds all strained away, have ready some young and tender ears of sweet corn, which have been cooked by themselves in another pot; cut the grains from the cob, mix the corn with fresh butter, season with pepper, and stir it in the strained soup; boil a little longer, and serve.

PEPPER-POT.

Cut into small strips about a half pound of good white tripe which has been thoroughly boiled and skimmed in a pot by itself; boil in another pot a neck of mutton and a pound of lean ham, with a gallon of water; boil slowly, and when skimmed sufficiently, add two large onions sliced, four potatoes quartered and four

c

sliced turnips; season with a very small piece of red pepper, taking care not to make it too hot; then add the boiled tripe. Make a quart bowlful of small dumplings of butter and flour mixed with a very little water, put them into the pepper-pot and boil about three-quarters of an hour; take out the meat, letting the tripe remain, and pour the soup into a tureen.

CURRY SOUP.

SEASON two quarts of strong veal broth with two onions, a bunch of parsley, salt and pepper; strain it, and have ready a chicken cut in joints and skinned; put it in the broth with a table-spoonful of curry powder; boil the chicken till quite tender. A little before serving add the juice of a lemon and a teacupful of boiling cream. Serve boiled rice to eat with this soup. Always boil cream before putting it in soup or gravy. (A recipe for making Curry Powder will be found under the head of Sauces.)

MACARONI SOUP.

TAKE a quart of gravy soup, break two ounces of Naples macaroni into pieces of little more than

an inch long, putting them, by degrees, into a
small portion of the boiling soup, to prevent them
from sticking together, and let them boil until
quite tender, but not soft or pulpy—from fifteen
to twenty minutes if quite fresh, but nearly half
an hour if at all stale. Vermicelli is used in the
same manner. Either will improve the consistency
of the soup if the quantity above stated be added;
but it is useless and does not look well to see, as
at some tables, only a few strings of it floating in
the tureen.

PORTABLE SOUP.

PUT on, in four gallons of water, ten pounds of
a shin of beef, free from fat and skin, six pounds
of a knuckle of veal, and two fowls; break the
bones and cut the meat into small pieces; season
with one ounce of whole black pepper, quarter
of an ounce of Jamaica pepper, and the same of
mace; cover the pot very closely, and let it simmer
twelve or fourteen hours, and then strain it. The
following day take off the fat and clear the jelly
from any sediment adhering to it; boil it gently
upon a stove without covering the sauce-pan,
and stir it frequently till it thickens to a strong
glue. Pour it into broad tin pans, and put in

a cool oven. When it will take the impression of a knife, score it in equal squares. Stand it in a south window or near a stove. When dry, break it at the scores. Wrap it in paper, and put it closely up in boxes. There should always be a large supply of this soup, as with it and catsup no one will ever be at a loss for dressed dishes and soups.

HARE OR RABBIT SOUP.

Cut up two hares, put them into a pot with a piece of bacon, two onions chopped fine, a bundle of thyme and parsley, which must be taken out of the soup before it is thickened; add pepper, salt, pounded cloves and mace; put in a sufficient quantity of water, stew it gently three hours, thicken with a large spoonful of butter, brown flour or glass of red wine; boil a few minutes longer, and serve with the nicest parts of the hare.

Squirrels make equally as good soup, prepared in the same way.

FRENCH SOUP.

Take the nicest part of a thick brisket of beef, about eight pounds; put it in a pot with everything directed for other soup; make it exactly in the same way, only put it on an hour sooner, that you may have time to prepare the *bouilli* (*i. e.*, the beef which has been boiled in the soup). After it boils five hours, take out the beef, cover up the soup, set it near the fire to keep hot. Take the skin off; have the yolk of an egg well beaten, dip a feather in it and wash the top of your beef; sprinkle over it the crumbs of stale bread grated, put it in an oven previously heated, put the top on with coals enough to brown it, let it stand nearly an hour, and prepare your gravy thus: Take sufficient quantity of soup and vegetables boiled in it, add a tablespoonful of red wine and two of mushroom catsup, thicken with a little butter and brown flour; make it very hot, pour it in your dish, and put the beef on it; garnish with green pickle cut in thin slices, serve up the soup in a tureen with bits of toasted bread.

TURTLE SOUP.

Kill the turtle at night in winter, and in the morning in summer. Hang it up by the hind fins, cut off the head and let it bleed well. In dressing, separate the bottom shell from the top

4

with great care, lest the gall-bladder be broken.
Put the liver in a bowl of water; empty the
entrails and lay them in water; if there be eggs,
lay them in water also. It is proper to have a
different bowl of water for each. Cut the flesh
from the bottom shell and lay it in water; then
break the shell in two, put it in a pot, having
washed it clean; pour on water enough to cover
it; add one pound of middling, with four onions
chopped, and set it on the fire to boil; let it boil
steadily three hours; if the water boils away too
much, add more. Wash the top shell nicely after
taking out the flesh, cover it and set it by. Parboil the fins, clean them nicely, taking off all the
black skin; put them in water; cut the flesh taken
from the bottom and top shell in small pieces;
cut the fins in two, lay them with the flesh in a
dish, sprinkle salt over, and cover them up.
When the shell, etc., is done, take out the bacon,
scrape the shell clean and strain the liquor,
one-third of which put back in the pot, reserve
the rest for the soup; take out all the nice bits,
strain, and put them in the gravy; lay the fins,
cut in small pieces, in with them, and as much of
the flesh as will be sufficient to fill the upper
shell; add to it (if a large turtle) one bottle of

wine, cayenne pepper and salt to your taste, one gill of mushroom catsup, one gill of lemon pickle, mace, nutmegs and cloves pounded, to season high. Mix two large spoonfuls of flour in one pound and a quarter of butter, put it in with thyme, parsley, marjoram and savory, tied in bunches; stew all these together till the flesh and fins are tender; wash out the top shell; put a puff-paste around the brim; sprinkle the shell over with pepper and salt; then take the herbs out of the stew. If the gravy is not thick enough, add more flour and fill the shell. If there are no eggs in the turtle, boil six new-laid eggs for ten minutes, put them in cold water a few minutes, peel and slice them and place them on the turtle; make a rich forcemeat, fry the balls nicely, and put them also in the shell; set it in a dripping-pan, with something under the sides to keep it steady; have the oven heated as for bread, and let it remain till nicely browned. Fry the liver and send it in hot.

To prepare the soup, commence early in the morning; put on eight pounds of coarse beef, some bacon, onions, sweet herbs, pepper and salt. Make a rich soup, strain it and thicken with a bit of butter and brown flour; add to it the water left from boiling the bottom shell; season very high with wine, catsup, spice and cayenne; put in the flesh you reserved, and if it is not enough, add the nicest parts of a well-boiled calf's head, but do not use the eyes or tongue; let it boil till tender, and serve it up with fried forcemeat balls in it. If you have curry powder (see receipt for it in remarks for Sauces), it will give a higher flavor to both soup and turtle than spice.

MOCK-TURTLE SOUP.

SCALD a calf's head, and wash it clean; boil it in a large pot of water for half an hour, then cut all the skin off by itself; take the tongue out; take the broth made of a knuckle of veal, put in the tongue and skin, with one onion, half ounce of cloves, and half ounce of mace, half a nutmeg, all kinds of sweet herbs chopped fine, and three anchovies; stew it till tender; then take out the meat, and cut it in pieces two inches square; cut the tongue, previously skinned, in slices, strain the liquor through a sieve, melt half a pound of butter in a stew-pan, put in it half a pound of flour; stir it till smooth—if at all lumpy strain it; add the liquor, stirring it all the time;

then put to the meat the juice of two lemons, and one bottle of madeira wine if you choose; season with pepper, salt and cayenne pepper pretty high; put in five meat-balls, eight eggs boiled hard. Stew it gently one hour, serve in a tureen; if too thick, add more liquor before stewing last time.

LOBSTER SOUP.

To boil a lobster put it in a fish-kettle and cover it with cold water, cooking it on a quick fire. Remove the small bladder found near the head, and take out a small vein found immediately under the shell all along the back of the lobster, and use the rest. Two lobsters will make soup for six or eight persons, and salad also. All the under shell and small claws are pounded in a mortar to make the soup; when pounded, put it into a pan and set it on the fire with broth or water. The meat is cut in small pieces, to be added afterward. The soup is left on the fire to boil gently for half an hour; then pour it in a sieve and press it with a masher to extract the juice. To make it thicker, a small piece of parsnip can be added and mashed with the rest into a pan, so that all the essence is extracted in that way from

4 *

the lobster. When you have strained it, put a
little butter with it, and add as much broth as is
required. Put some of the meat in the tureen and
pour the soup over it.

CRAB SOUP.

BOIL in three quarts of milk the meat of two
dozen crabs cut in bits; add a little cayenne, nutmeg and powdered mace; thicken with butter
mixed in flour; just before taking it from the
fire, crumble into the soup half a dozen yolks
of hard boiled eggs, and after pouring into the
tureen strew over the surface the heart of a fresh
green lettuce cut small.

OYSTER SOUP.

PUT two quarts of oysters, liquor and all, in a
pan, taking care to remove any particles of shell
that may adhere to the oysters; set them on a
stove to heat, but don't let them boil or come
very near to it. Drain all the liquor into your
soup-kettle, and put in a pint of water and two
quarts of new milk, half a pound of butter, a
little whole allspice, pepper and a few blades
of mace. When it boils, break up some crackers

fine and put into the soup. Then add the oysters, which have been kept warm. Oysters should never be allowed to boil, as it makes them tough and shrinks. them up; they should be scalded only. Salt should be the last thing to add in any soup where milk is used, which it is apt to curdle. Serve up hot.

CLAM SOUP.

HAVING put your clams into a pot of boiling water to make them open easily, take them from the shells, carefully saving the liquor. To the liquor of a quart of opened clams allow three quarts of water. Mix the water with the liquor of the clams, and put it into a large pot with a knuckle of veal, the bone of which should be chopped in four places. When it has simmered four hours, put in a large bunch of sweet herbs, a beaten nutmeg, a teaspoonful of mace and a tablespoonful of whole pepper, but no salt, as that of the liquor will be sufficient. Stew slowly an hour longer, then strain it. When you have returned the liquor to the pot, add a quarter of a pound of butter divided in four, and each bit rolled in flour. Then put in the clams (having cut them

in pieces), and let it boil fifteen minutes. Send
to table with toasted bread cut in dice. This
soup will be greatly improved by the addition of
small forcemeat balls. Make them of cold veal
or chicken, mixed with equal quantities of chopped suet and sweet marjoram, and a smaller proportion of hard-boiled egg, grated lemon peel and
powdered nutmeg. Pound all the ingredients
together in a mortar, adding a little pepper and
salt. Break in a raw egg or two (in proportion
to the quantity), to bind the whole together and
prevent it from crumbling to pieces. When
thoroughly mixed, make the forcemeat into small
balls, and let them boil ten minutes in the soup,
shortly before you send it to the table. If you
are obliged to make them of raw veal or raw
chicken, they must boil longer. It will be a
great improvement to cut up a yam and boil in
the soup. Oyster soup may also be made in this
manner.

HOW TO DRESS FISH.

GENERAL REMARKS.

FISH are dressed in a variety of ways, according to taste. They are boiled, broiled, baked, stewed and fried, but the most common methods are broiling and frying—broiling when required to be done in a plain way, and frying when a high relish or flavor is to be given. In all modes of preparing fish for the table much care is required to prevent them from being broken or disfigured. In determining the signs of freshness and good condition the utmost caution must also be exercised. In a wholesome state the eye of the fish will appear bright, the gills of a fine, clear red, the body stiff, the flesh firm and the odor not unpleasant. They should be well cleaned, scraped and rinsed, care being taken not to let them soak longer than necessary, as fish, like meat, lose flavor by remaining too long in the water. In opening and removing the entrails of the fish, be very careful not to

45

allow the smallest particle of offensive matter to remain inside. Wash out the blood, scraping it carefully from the back-bone. A fish can be dressed without splitting it entirely down from head to tail. Smelts and other small fish are drawn or emptied at the gills. It is very desirable to have boiled fish served with the flesh as firm as possible; this can be accomplished by putting a small piece of saltpetre with the salt into the water in which it is boiled: a quarter of an ounce is enough for a gallon. Fish should never be left in the water after they are done, but taken up and laid upon a sieve to drain. Salt fish must always be well soaked in plenty of cold water for a night, or until the flesh is well softened.

FRIED HALIBUT.

SELECT a choice piece of this large and delicate-looking fish, and, after carefully washing and drying with a soft towel, cut it into thick fillets, remove the bone with a sharp knife, cut the fillets into slices, place them upon a suitable dish and take off the skin. Season with a little salt and pepper, and place upon each slice a piece of good butter.

Dip the slices into a pan of beaten yolk of egg seasoned with grated nutmeg and powdered mace (already prepared); having ready another pan of grated bread-crumbs, dip the slices into it also, then place them in a hot frying-pan of boiling lard. When one side becomes fried sufficiently, turn the slices, and when all are done remove them from the frying-pan and drain. Send to the table hot.

BOILED HALIBUT.

TAKE a piece of the fish weighing from four to six pounds; score the back deeply, and lay it on the strainer in your kettle, with the back undermost. Cover it with cold water and throw in a handful of salt. Do not let it come to boil too fast. Skin carefully when the fish becomes hard; hang the kettle higher or diminish the fire under it, so as to let the liquor simmer twenty-five or thirty minutes. Strain it, and send the fish to the table garnished with grated horseradish in alternate heaps, and curled parsley, accompanied with a boat of egg sauce.

What is left of the halibut prepare for the supper-table by mincing it when cold, and seasoning it with a dressing of salt, cayenne, sweet oil, hard-boiled eggs and a large proportion of vinegar.

HALIBUT CUTLETS.

CUT your halibut steaks an inch thick, wipe them with a dry cloth, and season with salt and cayenne. Have ready a pan of yolk of eggs well beaten and a dish of grated bread-crumbs. Put some fresh lard or beef drippings in a frying-pan, and hold it over the fire till it boils. Dip your cutlets in the egg, and then in the bread-crumbs. Fry a light brown; serve up hot, with the gravy in the bottom of the dish. Salmon or any large fish may be fried in the same manner.

BROILED SHAD.

SCRAPE, split, wash and dry the shad on a cloth; season with pepper and salt; grease the gridiron well; as soon as it is hot, lay the shad on to broil. One side being well browned, turn it. It should broil a quarter of an hour or more, according to thickness. Butter well, and send to table hot.

The roes of the shad are relished by many persons as a great nicety. They should be carefully washed, and then parboiled in salted water. Season with salt and cayenne pepper, dredge with flour and fry in fresh lard. When they are nicely browned on both sides, dish, and send to table hot.

BAKED SHAD.

MANY people are of the opinion that the very best method of cooking a shad is to bake it. Stuff it with bread-crumbs, salt, pepper, butter and parsley, and mix this up with beaten yolk of egg; fill the fish with it, and sew it up or fasten a string around it. Pour over it a little water and some butter, and bake as you would a fowl. A shad will require from an hour to an hour and a quarter to bake.

PLANKED SHAD.

PROCURE at a house-furnishing store a shad-board of oak. It is better to purchase one ready made, the cost being only about seventy-five cents. These boards are very strong and smooth, and furnished with thick wires crossing the board

5   D

diagonally. These secure the fish without nailing. The plank should be well seasoned. Cut off the head and tail of the finest shad you can get, split it down the back, and, after a good washing, wipe it dry. Scatter upon it some salt and pepper. Having placed the plank before the fire until it has become very hot and ready to char, place the shad (spread open) within the wires crossing the hot board, with the back next to the plank, the head downward. Roast, and in a little while turn the other end of the board, placing the tail downward. That the juice of the fish may be well absorbed, turn the board frequently up and down. When sufficiently roasted, add some fresh butter, and send to the table on the board, under which place a large tray or dish. Shad cooked in this way are greatly relished by parties, who in the shad-season frequently repair to the banks of our rivers where there are shad-fisheries, and purchase of the fishermen the shad fresh from the water.

PICKLED SHAD.

DIVIDE fine fresh shad into halves, fry them a nice brown, and set them away till cold, having, of course, salted and peppered them properly. Make a pickle of a quart of good vinegar, a blade of mace, the rind of a lemon, a few pepper-corns and a pepper; simmer all together, then pour it over the shad hot, cover down close, and stand for a day or more before using.

POTTED SALMON.

Skin the salmon, and clean it thoroughly by wiping with a cloth (water would spoil it); cut it into small pieces, which rub with salt; let them remain till thoroughly drained; then lay them in a dish, and season with powdered mace, cloves and pepper to taste. Add a quarter of a pound of butter, and bake; when quite done drain them from the gravy, press into pots for use. and when cold pour over them clarified butter.

DRIED SALMON.

Cut the salmon into layers; have ready some eggs boiled hard and chopped; put both into half a pint of thin cream, and two or three ounces of butter rubbed with a teaspoonful of flour; skim it, and stir till boiling hot; make a wall of mashed potatoes round the inner edge of a dish, and pour the above in it.

BOILED SHEEPSHEAD OR TURBOT.

As much of the excellence of this most delicate and delicious fish depends upon the manner in which it is dressed, great care should be taken to properly prepare it. After having thoroughly cleaned and washed the fish, soak it an hour or two in salt and water to draw off the slime; let it remain three-quarters of an hour in cold water, after which drain and wipe it dry; then score the back deeply with a knife. By rubbing the fish over with a cut lemon its color will be greatly improved. The fish-kettle should be large and very clean. Lay the fish on the strainer of the kettle, with its back downward; cover well with equal proportions of milk and water, adding a small spoonful of salt. Do not let it come to a boil too fast, and skim carefully; when the scum has ceased to rise, diminish the heat under the kettle, and let it simmer for about half an hour or more, not allowing it to boil hard. When the fish is done, take it up carefully with a fish-slice, and pour over it a sauce prepared in the following manner: Mix together very smoothly with a broad-bladed knife a quarter of a pound of fresh butter and two tablespoonfuls of flour; put them into a clean sauce-pan and hold it over the fire, and stir them till melted. Then add a large salt-spoonful of powdered mace, and as much cayenne as will lay on a sixpence. It will be much improved by the addition of some boiled lobster, chopped small. When the sauce has simmered five minutes, add very gradually half a pint of rich cream, and let it come almost to a boil, stirring all the time. The hot sauce may either be poured over the fish, or it may be sent to the table in a sauce-boat; in which case you may ornament the fish with the coral of the lobster, put on in a handsome figure.

STURGEON STEAKS.

REMOVE the skin; cut from the tailpiece slices half an inch thick; rub them well with salt, and broil them over a clear fire of bright coals. Butter, sprinkle with cayenne pepper, and send them to the table hot, garnished with slices of lemon.

Another way is to make a seasoning of bread-crumbs, sweet herbs, pepper and salt. First dip

5 *

the slices of sturgeon in a beaten yolk of egg,
then cover them with seasoning; wrap them up
closely in sheets of white paper well buttered, and
broil them over a clear fire. Send them to the
table either with or without the paper.

BOILED ROCKFISH.

AFTER the fish has been nicely cleaned, put it
into a pot with water enough to cover it, and
throw in salt in the proportion of half a teaspoonful to a pound of fish. Boil it slowly until
the meat is tender and easily separates from the
bones. A large fish will require an hour to cook.
When done, serve on a hot dish, and have a few
hard-boiled eggs, cut in thin slices, laid around it
and over it. Have egg-sauce in a boat to eat
with it.

FISH CHOWDER.

THE best fish for chowder are haddock and
striped bass. Cut the fish in pieces about one
inch thick and two inches long. Cut five or
six good slices of the best salt pork, lay them
in the bottom of an iron pot and fry till crisp;
take out the pork, leaving the fat; chop the pork

fine; put into the pot a layer of fish, a layer of split crackers and some of the chopped pork, a little red and black pepper, a little chopped onion, then another layer of fish, split crackers and seasoning, and so on till all the fish is used. Then just cover all with water, and stew slowly till all is tender. Thicken the gravy with cracker-crumbs and catsup if you like; take out the fish, boil up the gravy once, squeeze in the juice of a lemon, and pour the gravy over the fish. Add salt if necessary.

FRIED PERCH.

When the fish are scaled and thoroughly cleaned, brush them over with egg and cover with bread-crumbs. Have ready some boiling lard, put the fish in, and fry a nice brown. Serve with melted butter or anchovy sauce.

FRIED SMELTS.

They should not be washed more than is necessary to clean them. Dry them in a cloth; then lightly flour them, but shake it off. Dip them into plenty of egg, then into bread-crumbs grated fine, and plunge them into a good pan of boiling lard; let them continue gently boiling, and a few minutes will make them a bright yellow-brown. Take care not to remove the light roughness of the crumbs, or their beauty will be lost.

FRIED CATFISH.

CATFISH must be cooked quite fresh—if possible, directly out of the water. The larger ones are generally coarse and strong; the small-sized fish are the best. Wash and clean them, cut off their heads and tails, remove the upper part of the back-bone near the shoulders, and score them along the back with deep gashes or incisions. Dredge them with flour, and fry them in plenty of lard, boiling fast when the catfish are put into the pan. Or you may fry them in the drippings or gravy saved from roast beef or veal. They are very nice dipped in a batter of beaten egg and grated bread-crumbs, or they may be done plain, though not in so nice a way, with Indian meal instead of bread-crumbs. Drain off the lard before you dish them. Touch each incision or cut very slightly with a little cayenne before they go to table. Catfish are equally a breakfast or a supper dish.

FRIED EELS.

AFTER skinning, emptying and washing them as clean as possible, cut them into short pieces, and dry them well with a soft cloth; season them with fine salt and cayenne, flour them thickly, and fry them in boiling lard; when nicely browned, drain and dry them, and send to the table with plain melted butter and a lemon, or with fish-sauce. Eels are sometimes dipped into batter and then fried, or into egg and fried bread-crumbs, and served with plenty of crisped parsley.

CODFISH CAKES.

AFTER washing, the fish must remain in water all night to soak; then boil it and remove the bones. Chop and work it until entirely fine; put it in a basin with water; add a large piece of butter, two eggs, and beat it thoroughly until it thickens, without boiling. Have some potatoes ready prepared and nicely mashed; work the fish and potatoes thoroughly together as above, seasoning with cayenne and salt; make the mixture into fine cakes, and fry them in lard, a light brown on both sides.

FISH PUDDING.

Pick any cold fish left from the dinner into fine
bits, carefully removing all the bones. Thicken
some boiling milk with flour wet to a batter with
cold milk, and stir the fish into it; season with pepper, butter and salt. Put it into a pudding-dish,
and spread cracker or bread-crumbs thickly over
the top to prevent the milk from scorching, and
set into the oven to bake just long enough to
brown nicely. This is a good way to use up
cold fish, making a nice breakfast dish or side
dish for dinner.

SALT FISH WITH PARSNIPS.

Salt fish must of course always be well soaked
in cold water at least twelve hours before cooking.
It should then be put on to boil in plenty of cold
water without any salt, and, when thoroughly
done, should be well drained free from any water
and placed on a dish with plenty of well-boiled
parsnips. A sauce may be poured over the
fish; it can be made as follows: Mix two
ounces of butter with three ounces of flour,
pepper and salt, a small glassful of vinegar and
a good half pint of water. Stir this on the fire

till it boils. A few hard-boiled eggs chopped up and mixed in this sauce would add to the excellence of the dish.

STEWED TERRAPIN.

To make a good dish of terrapins it is essential that the terrapins be of the very best quality. Select the largest, thickest and fattest, the females being the best. Put them whole into boiling water, add a little salt, and boil them until thoroughly done; after which, take off the shell, extract the meat and remove carefully the sand-bag and gall, also all the entrails; they are unfit to eat, and are no longer used in cooking terrapins for the best tables. Cut the meat into pieces, and put it into a stew-pan with its eggs, and sufficient fresh butter to stew it well. Let it stew till quite hot throughout, keeping the pan carefully covered, that none of the flavor may escape, but shake it over the fire while stewing. In another pan make a sauce of beaten yolk of egg, highly flavored with madeira or sherry and powdered nutmeg and mace, and enriched with a large lump of fresh butter. Stir this sauce well over the fire, and when it has almost come to a boil, take it off. Send the terrapins to the table hot in a covered dish, and the sauce separately in a sauce-tureen, to be used by those who like it, and omitted by those who prefer the genuine flavor of the terrapins when simply stewed with butter. This is now the usual mode of dressing terrapins in Maryland, Virginia and many other parts of the South, and will be found superior to any other.

BOILED LOBSTERS.

IF purchased alive, lobsters should be chosen by their weight (the heaviest are the best) and their liveliness and briskness of motion. When freshly boiled they are stiff, and their tails turn strongly inward; when the fish appear soft and watery, they are stale. The flesh of the male lobster is generally considered of the finest flavor for eating, but the hen lobster is preferred for sauce and soups, on account of the coral. Throw the lobsters into a kettle of fast-boiling salt and water, that life may be destroyed in an instant. Let them boil for about half an hour. When done, take them out of the kettle, wipe them clean, and rub the shell with a little salad oil, which will give a clear red appearance. Crack the large claws without mashing them, and with a sharp knife split the body and tail from end to end. The head, which is never eaten, should also be separated from the body, but laid so near it that the division is almost imperceptible. Send to table and dress in any way preferred.

SCOLLOPED CRABS.

PUT the crabs into a kettle of boiling water, and throw in a handful of salt. Boil from twenty minutes to half an hour. Take them from the water when done and pick out all the meat; be careful not to break the shell. To a pint of meat put a little salt and pepper; taste, and if not enough add more, a little at a time, till suited. Grate in a very little nutmeg, and add one spoonful of cracker or bread-crumbs, two eggs well beaten, and two tablespoonfuls of butter (even full); stir all well together; wash the shells clean, and fill each shell full of the mixture; sprinkle crumbs over the top and moisten with the liquor; set in the oven till of a nice brown; a few minutes will do it. Send to the table hot, arranged on large dishes. They are eaten at breakfast or supper.

BOILED CRABS.

AFTER boiling the crabs in salt and water about twenty-five minutes, take them out, break off the claws, wipe the crabs very clean, throw away the small claws, but the large ones may be cracked and sent to table. Rub a little sweet oil on the shells, to make them a fine color.

STEWED OYSTERS.

PUT as many good fresh oysters, with their liquor, as you think you will need, into a pan on the stove to heat, but not to boil. Drain the juice off into a saucepan; as soon as it boils add half a pound of butter and some pepper; when this boils add a pint of cream and thicken a little with flour; after this boils up once, put in the oysters, and more salt if necessary. Serve hot.

Many persons prefer oysters stewed in water instead of cream. Make in all respects the same, substituting only the water for the cream.

FRIED OYSTERS.

WHEN fried in bread-crumbs oysters are much the best. Select the largest and finest fresh oysters, and, after freeing them from all the small particles of shell, put them into a colander and pour over a little water to rinse them; then place them on a clean towel and dry them. Have ready some grated bread-crumbs, seasoned with pepper and salt, and plenty of yolk of egg beaten till very light; and to each egg allow a large tea-spoonful of rich cream or of the best fresh butter. Beat the egg and cream together. Dip each oyster first into the egg and cream, and then into the crumbs. Repeat this twice, until the oysters are well coated all over. Have ready boiling, in a frying-pan, an equal mixture of fresh butter and lard. It must come nearly to the edge or top of the frying-pan, and be boiling fast when the oysters go in, otherwise they will be heavy and greasy, and sink to the bottom. Fry them of a yellow brown on both sides. Send them to table hot.

OYSTER FRITTERS.

MAKE a batter of milk, flour, eggs, cream of tartar, saleratus, and salt in proper proportion. Make no thicker than for pancakes. Drop an oyster into each spoon of batter as you dip it out, and fry in hot lard; brown well on both sides.

BROILED OYSTERS.

SELECT the largest and finest oysters. The gridiron, which should be a double one, made of wire, should be well greased with butter; and having placed the oysters so that they will all receive the heat equally, set them over a brisk fire, and broil both sides without burning them. Let them be served hot, adding a small lump of fresh butter, pepper and salt.

PANNED OYSTERS.

TAKE fifty large oysters; remove every particle of shell which may adhere to them, put them into a colander and pour over a little water to rinse them. After letting them drain, put them into a stew-pan with a quarter of a pound of butter, salt, black and red pepper to taste. Put them over a clear fire, and stir while cooking. As soon as they commence to shrink remove them from the fire, and send to table hot in a well-heated covered dish.

SCOLLOPED OYSTERS.

TAKE baker's bread at least three days old. Strain your oysters, put a layer of them on the bottom of your dish, with bits of butter, salt, pepper and a very little mace; spread over them a layer of bread-crumbs, and continue till the dish is full, having bread-crumbs on top. Pour in a cup of the liquor of the oysters. Bake one hour. Be very careful not to have the layers of bread too thick.

OYSTER PATTIES IN BATTER.

Make a batter with three eggs, a little nutmeg, some powdered mace, a little flour, and a little salt; dip in the oysters, and fry them a nice brown in boiling lard or butter. Send to the table hot, garnished with parsley.

OYSTER PUDDING.

Take two dozen nice large oysters, drain them from their own liquor, put a layer of rice, boiled very dry, in your pudding-dish, then a layer of oysters, then a layer of rice, and another of oysters, and a third of rice. Mix two ounces of butter, one gill of cream, half a gill of their own liquor and one well-beaten egg; season with pepper and salt, and pour over the pudding; bake fifteen or twenty minutes.

6 *   E

OYSTER PIE.

STRAIN the liquor from the oysters, and put it on to boil with butter, pepper and a thickening of bread-crumbs and milk well beaten together, and after boiling a few minutes throw in the oysters. Let them remain five minutes, take them off, and when warm add the beaten yolks of three eggs. Line a buttered dish with a rich paste, and fill with white paper or a clean napkin, to support a lid of paste, and bake it. When lightly browned, take off the lid, remove the paper or napkin, pour in the oysters, set a few minutes in the oven and send to table hot.

PICKLED OYSTERS.

TAKE two hundred oysters of the largest size, rinse them in their own liquor, put them in a stew-pan, strain the liquor to them, and let them come to a boil—just and no more. Take them out of the liquor, have ready a quart or more of pure cider vinegar, boiled with whole pepper, a little salt; mace, cloves and nutmeg. When it is cool pour it over the oysters. Before serving add a few raw cranberries and thin slices of lemon.

FRIED CLAMS.

OPEN carefully into a chopping-bowl, saving the liquor, but be careful that no gritty particles from the shell fall in; chop coarsely, and sprinkle over some pepper. Have ready a mixture of egg and grated cracker thickened with a little flour. Take up the clams one by one with a spoon, and dip them into the mixture. Fry slowly in plenty of butter or lard.

CLAM FRITTERS.

TAKE twenty-five clams and chop them fine, leaving out the juice; four eggs beaten, one cup of sour cream (if you have no cream, use one cup of buttermilk and a piece of butter the size of an egg, melted and well mixed); one cup of flour, one small spoonful of saleratus. Then fry in butter, and spread them well with good sweet butter when you take them out of the frying-pan. Serve them up hot.

SCOLLOPED CLAMS.

TAKE a sufficient quantity of small sand-clams, wash the shells thoroughly, put them into a pot of boiling water, and when the shells open take out the clams, drain them, chop into small pieces, throwing aside the toughest portions. Season with black pepper and powdered mace, and mix them with grated bread-crumbs and fresh butter. Have ready some large and well-cleansed clam-shells, and fill them to the edge with the mixture, moistening it slightly with the liquor; cover the surface with grated crumbs, and add to each one a small bit of butter; place them in an oven and bake to a light brown. Send them to the table in the shells they were baked in, nicely arranged on suitable dishes. Scolloped clams are eaten at breakfast and supper.

In this manner oysters are sometimes prepared, and served up in large clam-shells. Boiled crabs are also cooked, minced and prepared in this way, and sent to the table in the back-shell of the crab. The scollops are all improved by mincing among them some hard-boiled eggs minced or chopped, or some raw egg beaten.

How to Cook Meats.

GENERAL REMARKS.

Good fresh beef is of a bright red color, smoothly grained and tender to the touch, the fat more white than yellow, the suet a pure white, and firm. The sirloin, the ribs and the rump are the proper joints for roasting, while, for stewing or boiling, the round or buttock, the shin, the brisket and the shoulder are considered more suitable. The finest and tenderest steaks are cut from the middle of the sirloin.

One of the most useful articles in the economy of the kitchen is the dripping produced from roast beef. It must be taken from the pan under the meat before it becomes overheated or scorched by the fire, leaving sufficient for basting. Dripping is prepared for future use in the following manner: Take it hot from the dripping-pan and pour it into boiling water, that all particles of cinder or other improper matter may fall to the bottom, and leave the pure fat on the surface. Collect these

cakes of fat, and by heating them in a jar placed
in a sauce-pan of boiling water the whole will become a solid mass, and may be thus put aside for
use.   This process not only purifies dripping, but
gives it a clear white color

A well-roasted joint ought to have a nice brown
tinge, and this is to be obtained only by careful
basting, attention to the fire, and removing at the
proper time when experience tells that the joint
is done.   A quarter of an hour for each pound of
meat is generally allowed for solid, heavy joints;
but if required to be thoroughly roasted, a longer
time must of course be given.

The best parts of mutton for roasting are the
leg, the shoulder and the loin; for roast veal, the
fillet, the breast, the loin and the shoulder. Roast
lamb is usually dressed in quarters. All parts
should be well jointed or cut by the butcher
or cook, and the ribs of the forequarter broken
across the centre, in order to accommodate the
carver.

Pork requires a longer time in roasting than
other meats, and, like roast lamb, mutton and veal,
must never be sent to the table in an underdone
state.   All these meats should be nicely browned,
without being burnt.

Frying has the advantage of affording a ready means of dressing in a savory manner many odd pieces of uncooked or cold meat which otherwise might be thrown away as useless. The skillful housewife, with the aid of a frying-pan and a few vegetables, such as onions and potatoes, with a slight seasoning, will make a small portion of meat dine a large family. In frying all meats, excepting those which are sufficiently fat in themselves, some kind of grease should be used, such as beef dripping, lard or butter.

Baked meats are liable to become shriveled for lack of basting, and if done in a baker's oven they are also liable to partake of the flavor of the numerous articles which are there prepared. Perhaps the only dishes which are better baked than roasted are bullock's heart and leg of pork, because, in roasting, they are liable to be scorched on the outside before they are thoroughly cooked in the inner parts.

Broiling has the peculiarity of being applicable only to meat which is to be eaten immediately on being dressed. This is an advantage when expeditious cooking is required, but a disadvantage when an uncertainty exists as to the time at which the meat is to be eaten. The operation of broiling requires a clear, strong fire, with no smoke, and in turning the meat a knife or pair of small tongs should be used; a fork should never be used in turning, as it breaks the skin and allows the gravy to run out. Before placing the meat upon it the gridiron should be heated for a few minutes, and the bars rubbed with a piece of brown paper, to prevent the meat from sticking to them.

In boiling meat there is less waste than in roasting, and in most cases soup may be made of the liquor. There must be a sufficiency of water to cover the meat, and the utensils used must be large, in order to allow the meat perfect freedom. All portions of mutton and lamb may be roasted, but it is only the leg, neck and head that are boiled.

Stewing is a much more savory and nutritious mode of cooking than boiling, because the substance of the meat is partly in the liquor, and is seasoned to have a high relish or flavor.

ROAST BEEF.

TAKE a medium-sized joint, wash it, place it in a roasting-pan, season with pepper and salt, and dredge with a little flour. Pour into the pan three half pints of water, and add a heaping tablespoonful of flour; stir well together, and place in a moderately hot oven; baste frequently. When done and nicely browned, put it on a heated dish, remove a part of the fat from the gravy, and, if not sufficiently seasoned, more may be added. Baste the meat with a few spoonfuls, then pour the gravy into a sauce-tureen and send to table with the meat.

BEEF A LA MODE.

TAKE a fine round of fresh beef, extract the bone and take away the fat. For a round weighing ten pounds make a seasoning or stuffing in the following proportions: Half a pound of beef suet; half a pound of grated bread-crumbs; the crumbled yolks of three hard-boiled eggs; a large bundle of sweet marjoram, the leaves chopped; another of sweet basil; four onions minced small; a large tablespoonful of mixed mace and nutmeg powdered. Season lightly with salt and cayenne. Stuff this mixture into the place from whence you took out the bone. Make numerous deep cuts about the meat, and stuff them also. Skewer the meat into a proper shape, and secure its form by tying it round with tape. Put it into a clean

7

tin oven or bake-pan, and pour over it a pint of port wine. Put on the lid, and bake the beef slowly for five or six hours, or till it is thoroughly done all through. If the meat is to be eaten hot, skim all the fat from the gravy, into which, after it is taken off the fire, stir in the beaten yolk of two eggs. If onions are disliked, you can omit them and substitute minced oysters.

STEWED SHIN OF BEEF.

PUT a shin of beef on to stew in enough cold water to keep it covered until done. When it boils remove the scum, and put one ounce and a half of salt to a gallon of water. Add a few cloves and some black pepper slightly bruised and tied up in muslin, some onions, a root of celery, a bunch of savory herbs, with some carrots and turnips. Gently stew for four or five hours.

STEWED BRISKET OF BEEF.

PUT the part that has the hard fat into a stew-pot, with a small quantity of water; let it boil up, and skim it thoroughly; then add carrots, turnips, onions, celery and a few pepper-corns. Stew till extremely tender; then take out all the flat bones and remove all the fat from the soup. Either serve that and the meat in a tureen, or the soup alone, and the meat on a dish, garnished with some vegetables. The following sauce is much admired served with the beef: Take half a pint of the soup, and mix it with a spoonful of catsup, a teaspoonful of made mustard, a little flour, a bit of butter and salt; boil all together a few minutes, then pour it round the meat.

STEWED RUMP OF BEEF.

TAKE three pounds of tender rump of beef; remove the skin and fat, cut the beef into pieces two inches square, and pour over it a quart of cold broth or gravy. When it boils add salt, if required, and a little cayenne, and keep it just simmering for a couple of hours; then add to it the grated rind of a large lemon, or of two small ones, and half an hour after stir in it a table-spoonful of rice-flour, smoothly mixed with a wineglassful of mushroom catsup and a dessert-spoonful of lemon-juice; in fifteen minutes it will be ready to serve. A glass and a half of port or of white wine will greatly improve this stew, which may likewise be flavored with a sauce made with half a pint of port wine, the same of mushroom catsup, a quarter of a pint of walnut pickle, and a dessert-spoonful of cayenne vinegar, all well shaken together, and poured into a bottle containing the thin rind of a lemon and two fine, mellow anchovies of moderate size. A few delicately-fried forcemeat balls may be put into it after it is dished.

BEEFSTEAK WITH ONIONS.

TAKE a nice rumpsteak, and pound it with a rolling-pin until it is quite tender; flour and season; put it into a frying-pan of hot lard and fry it. When nicely brown on both sides take it up and dredge with flour. Having ready boiled about two dozen onions, strain them in a colander and put them into the frying-pan, seasoning with pepper and salt; dredge in a little flour, and add a small lump of butter; place the pan over the fire and stir the onions frequently, to prevent their scorching. When they are soft and a little brown, return the steak to the pan, and heat all together. Place the steak on a large dish, pour the onions and gravy over it, and send to the table hot.

BEEFSTEAK FRENCH STYLE.

CUT thin steaks from the finest and tenderest part of the rump; sprinkle over them pounded salt, a little cayenne and white pepper combined; lay them in a pan with an ounce of fresh butter cut in pieces, then work half a teaspoonful of flour with three ounces of fresh butter, as much parsley, minced exceedingly fine, as would lay on a shilling; roll it, and cut in large slices, lay it in a dish, squeeze the half of a lemon over the butter, and when the steaks are done lay them upon the butter. Have ready a quantity of raw peeled potatoes cut in thin slices and washed in milk and water; fry them in the butter and gravy left by the steak, and lay them round the dish; they will be done when they are a rich brown. If necessary, add a little more seasoning, and serve.

STUFFED BEEFSTEAK.

TAKE some pieces of bread, scald them soft, mix with plenty of butter and a little pepper and salt. Lay the mixture upon one side of a pound of steak, cover it with the other, and sew it down with needle and thread. Salt and pepper the outside of the steak, and place it in a dripping-pan with

7 *

half an inch of water. When baked brown on one side turn and bake the other.

BEEFSTEAK PUDDING.

PREPARE a good suet crust, and line a cake tin with it; put in layers of steak, with onions, tomatoes and mushrooms chopped, a seasoning of pepper, salt and cayenne, and half a tea-cupful of water before closing it. Bake from an hour and a half to two hours, and serve very hot.

BEEF PIE.

TAKE cold roast beef or steak, cut it into thin slices, and put a layer in a pie-dish; shake in a little flour, pepper and salt, cut up a tomato or onion chopped very fine; then another layer of beef, and seasoning, and so on until the dish is filled. If you have any beef gravy, put it in; if not, a little beef dripping and water enough to make sufficient gravy. Have ready one dozen potatoes well boiled and mashed, half a cup of milk or cream, and a little butter and salt. Spread it over the pie, as a crust, an inch thick; brush it over with egg, and bake about twenty minutes.

BEEF CAKES.

An excellent side-dish can be prepared by pounding some beef that is underdone with a little fat bacon or ham; season with pepper, salt and a little onion; mix them well, and make into small cakes three inches long and half as wide and thick; fry them a little brown, and serve them in a good thick gravy.

BEEF PATTIES.

Shred underdone dressed beef with a little fat; season with pepper, salt and a little onion. Make plain paste; roll it thin and cut it in shape like an apple-puff; fill it with the mince, pinch the edges, and fry them a nice brown. The paste should be made with a small quantity of butter, egg and milk.

BAKED BEEF TONGUE.

Boil and skin the tongue, and season it with pepper and salt; lay it in a pan and pour a rich gravy over it; make deep incisions on the top and put herbs and bread-crumbs into them; grate some bread over it, and bake fifteen or twenty minutes. Garnish with baked tomatoes or mush-rooms.

STEWED TONGUE.

AFTER it has been boiled cut it in thick slices, and stew in rich gravy about three hours, until quite tender. This is a very nice corner-dish.

CURRIED BEEF.

TAKE about two ounces of butter and place them in a saucepan with two small onions cut up into slices, and let them fry till they are of a light brown; then add a tablespoonful and a half of curry powder, and mix it up well. Now cut up the beef into pieces about an inch square; pour in from a quarter to a third of a pint of milk, and let it simmer for thirty minutes; then take it off and place it in a dish with a little lemon-juice. While cooking stir it constantly, to prevent burning. Send it to table with a wall of mashed potatoes or rice round it. This is the Madras style, and a favorite dish at some of the hotels and first-class restaurants.

SPICED BEEF.

TAKE a piece of the round of beef weighing fifteen or sixteen pounds, wash it, remove the bone and skewer the meat into a proper shape;

then rub it well with salt, place it in a clean pickling-tub, sprinkle over it some more salt, close up the tub tightly, and let it remain for a week, turning and sprinkling each day with fresh salt. It should then be well rubbed with two ounces of black pepper, a quarter of an ounce of mace, some powdered nutmeg, and put into an earthen stewing-pan, with a layer of suet under it; add two or three onions sliced and three or four cloves; cover with water, and bake for five hours. When cold it is an excellent standing breakfast or supper dish, being as tender as potted beef. Boiled cabbage and parsnips are an excellent accompaniment to this dish. When the fat has been removed, the liquor in which the beef has been stewed makes excellent stock for soup.

BOILED CORNED BEEF.

Cut four or five pounds of lean from a cold round of beef, and put into a pot that will hold plenty of water. The water should be hot. The same care should be taken in skimming as for fresh meat. It is not too much to allow half an hour for every pound of meat after it has begun to boil. The excellence of corned beef depends

F

very much upon its being boiled gently and long. If it is to be eaten cold, lay it, when boiled, into a coarse earthen dish or pan, and over it a clean board size of the meat; upon this put some heavy weight. Salt meat is much improved by pressing.

ROAST LEG OF MUTTON.

ALL mutton should hang in a cool place till quite tender before being used, but care should be taken that it does not acquire the least rust or taint. After carefully removing from a leg of mutton all the outside skin, put it into a pot of boiling water, with some salt, and cook for an hour before setting in the pan to roast. A second hour in the oven, after dredging with flour, adding three half pints of water to the roasting-pan and basting the meat every ten minutes with the liquor from the pot, will render it perfect. The remainder of the liquor in the pot makes an excellent foundation for soup.

ROAST MUTTON WITH TOMATOES.

TAKE a nice hindquarter of mutton, wash it, rub it with salt and pepper, put it into a baking-pan with a pint of water, and baste it well. Then prepare some tomatoes in the following manner: Take one dozen large, full-ripe tomatoes, slit them into four, but do not sever the pieces entirely at the bottom; make a stuffing of some bread-crumbs, pepper, salt, butter and a very little sugar; mix it well; remove part of the seed from the tomatoes, and fill with the stuffing. Put them in, and roast with the mutton. When done put them in the dish, around the mutton, and pour over some gravy. Tomatoes done in this manner make a delicious accompaniment to all kinds of cooked meats. They also make a nice breakfast dish.

BOILED SHOULDER OF MUTTON.

When the shoulder has hung till tender, bone it and rub the outside with salt. It is better to let it remain for a day or two in a deep dish, turning it over each day and rubbing it with salt. Then sprinkle over the inside one teaspoonful of pepper and half a teaspoonful of powdered mace. Spread twenty oysters over the inside; roll the meat up tightly and tie securely; put it into the stew-pan or boiler, with just enough boiling water to cover it; throw in six pepper-corns, or seeds of the red pepper, and one onion chopped; shut the cover over very closely, and stew; twenty minutes' cooking for each pound of meat is the proper time. Stew twenty-four oysters in a pint of good stock or gravy; add a tablespoonful of butter and enough flour to thicken it. When the meat is done lay it in a good-sized platter and pour the gravy over it.

SPICED SHOULDER OF MUTTON.

TAKE a tender shoulder of mutton, bone it carefully, and for every pound of meat mix two ounces of brown sugar, one salt-spoonful of cloves, one teaspoonful each of mace and pepper and half a salt-spoonful of ginger; rub these spices thoroughly into the meat; lay it into a deep dish, and the next day rub in two teaspoonfuls of salt for every pound of meat, and add one pint and a half of good beef gravy for the whole joint. Turn the meat over; rub it well with this pickle every day for a week or ten days, letting it remain in the pickle, after each rubbing, all the time. At the end of the week or ten days, roll it up tightly, bind with a string and stew gently in beef broth four hours. Serve hot in its own gravy, and eat with any piquante sauce or catsup.

MUTTON STEAKS WITH CUCUMBERS.

QUARTER cucumbers and lay them into a deep dish; sprinkle them with salt, and pour vinegar over them. Fry the chops of a fine brown and put them into a stew-pan; drain the cucumbers and put them over the steaks; add sliced onions, pepper and salt; pour hot water or weak broth on them; stew and skim well.

MUTTON SAUSAGE.

TAKE one pound of a leg of mutton that has been roasted or boiled, chop it very fine, season it with pepper, salt, mace and nutmeg; add six ounces of beef suet, some sweet herbs, a few anchovies and a pint of oysters chopped fine, half pound of grated bread-crumbs, the yolks and whites of two eggs well beaten. When well mixed put in small jars. When used fry in small cakes.

ROAST LAMB.

FROM a forequarter of lamb cut off the scrag one joint from the shoulder; saw off the chine bone, and also the bone of the breast, and joint

8

it thoroughly; crack the ribs in the middle; cut off the thick skin which covers the lower part of the breast, and break the bone of the shoulder, to allow the knuckle to twist around, and secure it in its place with a skewer from beneath the breast right up the knuckle. Put two large skewers at the thin end; pass the spit between the skewers and the ribs through the thick part at the shoulder. The meat should be placed before a clear, brisk fire, but not very near at first. Put a little water in the dripping-pan, and baste with that till the meat begins to cook, adding a little fresh butter. Then place it nearer to the fire, and when more than half done baste the meat frequently with the gravy. Let it roast until thoroughly done and a fine brown is given to it. A forequarter of lamb (comprising the shoulder, neck and breast) weighing eight to ten pounds will require two hours to be well cooked. The hindquarter (the leg and loin) may be roasted in the same manner as the forequarter, the only difference being that in cooking the former requires about one half hour less time than the latter. Before sending to the table sprinkle the meat with the juice of a lemon, and then serve with mint sauce. New potatoes, asparagus, green peas and spinach are the vegetables to be eaten with roast lamb. An excellent recipe for making mint sauce will be found under the head of Sauces.

BOILED LEG OF LAMB.

Choose a ewe leg, as there is more fat on it; saw off the knuckle, trim off the flap and the thick skin on the back of it; soak it in warm water for three hours, then boil it gently (time according to size); pour a little oyster sauce over it.

The loin may be fried in steaks and served round, garnished with dried or fried parsley or spinach; it may also be served with parsley and butter, or with oyster sauce.

LAMB CUTLETS AND SPINACH.

Take six or eight cutlets from a neck of lamb, and shape them by taking the thick part of the chine bone, and trimming off most of the fat and all of the skin, scraping the top part of the bones quite clean. Brush the cutlets over with egg, sprinkle with bread-crumbs and season with pepper and salt. Then dip them into clarified butter, sprinkle over a few more bread-crumbs, fry them over a brisk fire, turning them when required.

Lay them before the fire to drain, and then arrange them on a dish with spinach in the centre, which should be previously well boiled, drained, chopped and seasoned. Peas, asparagus or beans may be substituted for the spinach.

LAMB PIE.

TAKE from two to four pounds of lamb steaks, and after removing the fat and bone cut them in pieces four inches square; season with a little pepper and salt, and put them into a stew-pot with a small quantity of water; let them stew for about three-quarters of an hour. Make a nice paste, allowing half a pound of fresh butter to a pound of flour; mix half the butter with the flour, gradually adding cold water sufficient to make a dough; roll out the dough into a large, thin sheet, and spread over with the knife the rest of the batter; fold it, sprinkle with a little flour, then divide it into two sheets, and roll out each of them; that intended for the upper crust should be the thickest. Cover with the under crust the bottom and sides of a pie dish, and put in the stewed lamb with its gravy; scatter over it a few blades of mace; add some sliced potatoes and boiled turnips sliced. Spread over it a thick layer of the green tops of boiled asparagus, adding a few bits of fresh butter; put on the paste-lid, and close the edges by crimping them. Make a cross-slit on the top; place the pie in the oven and bake it to a light brown. Boiled cauliflower, seasoned with nutmeg, may be substituted for asparagus tops.

ROAST FILLET OF VEAL.

THE best parts of veal for roasting are the fillet, the loin and the shoulder. Select a nice fillet, take out the bone, fill up the space with stuffing, and also put a good layer under the fat. Truss it of a good shape by drawing the fat round, and tie it up with tape. Put it some distance from the fire at first, and baste with butter. It should have careful attention and frequent basting, that the fat may not burn. Roast from three to four hours, according to the size. After it is dished pour melted butter over it; serve with ham or bacon, and fresh cucumbers if in season. Veal, like all other meat, should be well washed in cold water before cooking. Cold fillet of veal is very good stewed with tomatoes and an onion or two.

8 *

BOILED FILLET OF VEAL.

CHOOSE a small, delicate fillet; prepare as for roasting, or stuff it with an oyster forcemeat; after having washed it thoroughly cover it with milk and water in equal quantities, and let it boil very gently three and a half or four hours, keeping it well skimmed. Send it to the table with a rich white sauce, or, if stuffed with oysters, a tureen of oyster sauce. Garnish with stewed celery and slices of bacon. A boiled tongue should be served with it.

BOILED LOIN OF VEAL.

TAKE about ten pounds of the best end of the loin, leave the kidney in with all its fat, skewer or bind down the flap, lay the meat into cold water and boil it as gently as possible from two hours and a quarter to two and a half, clearing off the scum perfectly, as in dressing the fillet. Send it to table with oyster sauce, or with white sauce well flavored with lemon-juice, and with parsley boiled, pressed dry and finely chopped. When the meat is white and small, and it is dressed with care and served with good sauces, this is an excellent dish, and often more acceptable to persons of delicate habits than roast veal.

VEAL STEW.

Cut four pounds of veal into strips three inches long and one thick; peel twelve large potatoes, and cut them into slices one inch thick; spread a layer of sliced salt pork with salt, pepper, sage and onion on the bottom of the pot, then a layer of potatoes, then a layer of veal seasoned. Use up the veal thus. Over the last layer of veal put a layer of slices of salt pork, and over the whole a layer of potatoes. Pour in water till it rises an inch over the whole; cover it close; heat it fifteen minutes, and simmer it two hours.

VEAL CUTLETS.

From a fillet of veal take two or three cutlets; pound, wash, and then dry them on a clean cloth; season with pepper and salt. Beat up two eggs with one gill of milk, and pour over the cutlets; take half a pint of bread-crumbs, or fine crackers; season with pepper and salt, and place them in the cutlets, pressing them with the back of a spoon into the meat. Fry slowly in hot lard, and when well done and nicely browned pour over them some of the gravy, and send to the table hot. Mushroom sauce is considered by many epicures to be an indispensable accompaniment to veal cutlets. The addition of a little cream in frying is also an improvement to the dish.

VEAL CUTLETS WITH HERBS.

CHOP up all sorts of sweet herbs, mushrooms, onions, pepper and salt, with a spoonful of butter; dip the cutlets into this, and reduce the sauce, to make it stick; then dip the cutlets into a mixture of egg and bread-crumbs, and set them into an oven to bake; add a glass of white wine to the sauce, skim it well, and when the cutlets are done lay them on a dish, pour over the sauce, and send to table hot.

VEAL ROLLS.

CUT a few slices from a cold fillet of veal half an inch thick; rub them over with beaten egg; lay a thin slice of fat bacon over each piece of veal; brush these with the egg, and over this spread forcemeat thinly; roll up each piece tightly, egg and bread-crumb them, and fry them a rich brown. Serve with mushroom sauce or brown gravy. Fry the rolls from ten to fifteen minutes. A nice breakfast or supper dish.

SCOLLOPS OF COLD VEAL.

MINCE the meat extremely small, and set it over the fire; season with some grated nutmeg, a little pepper and salt, and a little cream. Then put it into the scollop-shells, and cover them with crumbs of bread, over which put some bits of butter, and brown before the fire. Send to the table hot, accompanied with catsup or mushroom sauce. These scollops form an excellent side-dish at dinner, and are nice at breakfast.

POTTED VEAL AND BACON.

CUT thin slices of veal and the same quantity of bacon; then rub together some dried sweet basil or summer savory very fine, until reduced to a powder; place in a stew-pan a layer of bacon and a layer of veal; then sprinkle over it the powdered herbs, a little grated horseradish, then again bacon and veal, and then herbs and horseradish and a little salt. On this squeeze the juice of a lemon; then cover very tightly and put in an oven. Let it bake two or three hours; take it out and drain off all the gravy; pour over a little catsup, and press down with a heavy weight; then put it away in a pot tightly covered.

STEWED CALF'S HEAD.

REMOVE the hair from a nice large calf's head; take out the brain, wash the head very clean, and soak it for a quarter of an hour. Boil until quite tender in just enough water to cover it; then carefully take out the bones without spoiling the appearance of the head. Season with a little salt and cayenne and a grated nutmeg. Pour over it the liquor in which it has been boiled, adding a gill of vinegar and two large tablespoonfuls of capers or of pickled green nasturtium seeds. Let it stew very slowly for half an hour. Have ready some forcemeat balls made of minced veal suet, grated bread-crumbs, grated lemon-peel, and sweet marjoram, adding beaten yolk of egg to keep the other ingredients together. Put in the forcemeat balls, then stew it slowly a quarter of an hour longer, adding some bits of butter rolled in flour to enrich the gravy. Send it to the table hot.

STEWED CALF'S FEET.

WHEN properly cleaned, rub the feet over with pepper, a very little salt and mace; cut them into moderately-sized pieces and put them into a stew-pan with a little shallot and a beefsteak, also cut into pieces. Cover all with cold water, and let them simmer together for three hours. When quite tender take them off the fire; strain the gravy through a sieve. The next day, when cold, take off all the fat; boil a small quantity of saffron in cream, and a little cayenne pepper; mix it with the gravy, and warm the whole without boiling; one foot and one pound of steak will make a dish for a small family.

POTTED CALF'S FEET.

AFTER a thorough cleansing, boil the feet five hours. Take half a pint of the jelly in which they are boiled and flavor it with nutmeg, garlic and pounded ham, and let them simmer together a few minutes. Cut up the feet into small pieces, and season them; dip a mould into cold water and put in the meat, mixed with a little grated lemon-peel and minced parsley. Some persons add beet-root, baked or boiled, cut in slices and mixed with the meat. When this is arranged in the mould, fill up with the flavored jelly. Turn out when quite cold. The remainder of the jelly in which the feet were boiled can be used as a sweet jelly.

ROASTED CALF'S LIVER STUFFED.

TAKE a nice, fresh liver, make a hole in it lengthways with a large knife, but do not cut the hole entirely through; fill the opening with forcemeat made of some of the liver parboiled, and some fat bacon minced fine, with some powdered sweet herbs, and some spice and grated bread-crumbs, pepper and salt. Lard the liver well with fat bacon, and flour it; roast it and baste it well with butter. Serve hot with gravy sauce.

FRIED CALF'S LIVER.

CUT it in slices, season with pepper and salt, dredge with flour, and fry brown in lard. Have it perfectly done. Serve in its gravy.

Calf's heart dressed in this way is also very nice.

STEWED KIDNEYS.

CUT them through the centre, take out the core, pull the kernels apart, pour them into the sauce-pan without any water, and set them on the fire, where they may get hot; they should not be allowed to boil. In half an hour put the kidneys into cold water, wash them clean, and put them back into the sauce-pan, with just enough water to cover them. Boil one hour, then take them up and clean off the fat and skin; put into the frying-pan some butter, pepper and salt, dredge in a little flour, and add a pint of hot water; then put in the kidneys, let them simmer twenty minutes, stirring them often. Do not let them dry, as it hardens them. This is a very nice breakfast dish.

BAKED SWEETBREADS.

In this and every other method of dressing sweetbreads they should be prepared by blanching or whitening and then parboiled. Take two large sweetbreads, and after having followed the above directions lard them with very thin slips of bacon. Put them into a shallow pan, and place under each sweetbread a piece of good fresh butter with a little flour mixed into it. Mix the juice and grated yellow rind of a lemon with a glass of good white wine, and pour into the pan; season also with grated nutmeg; or for sauce you may use mushroom catsup with a little salad oil stirred into it.

Sweetbreads spoil very rapidly, and should

never be used unless they are perfectly fresh; never attempt to keep them until next day, except in cold weather, and then on ice. Those taken from the breast of the calf are the best.

FRIED SWEETBREADS.

LAY the sweetbreads in warm water, with a half teaspoonful of salt in it, for an hour, to make them white, then put them into cold water, and let them remain over the fire until they have boiled ten minutes. Cut them into slices, brush them with egg and sprinkle over with bread-crumbs. Fry them in butter; each sweetbread will require three-quarters of an ounce of butter. Serve with some good gravy, such as you would prepare for a fowl.

STEWED SWEETBREADS.

PARBOIL two nice sweetbreads; when cold, lard them down the middle with bits of bacon, then with slices of lemon-peel on each side, and then with small pieces of pickled cucumber. Stew them gently in rich gravy thickened with flour; add a little mushroom catsup to the taste, and the juice of a lemon.

SWEETBREADS AND OYSTERS.

Soak and blanch three large and fine sweetbreads, cut them into quarters and remove the
pipe. Take three dozen large fresh oysters, strain
off the liquor, season it with powdered nutmeg
and mace and a little cayenne. Put the quartered sweetbreads into a stew-pan, and pour over
them enough of the oyster-liquor to cover them
well, adding, if you have it, three large spoonfuls of the gravy of roast veal and a quarter of
a pound of fresh butter cut into four bits, each
bit rolled or dredged in flour. When the sweetbreads are done put in the oysters, first removing
their gristle or hard part, and take them out
again as soon as they are plumped, which should
be in five minutes. If allowed to boil, the oysters
will shrivel and become hard and tasteless. Add
at the last two wineglasses of cream, and shake
the pan about for a few minutes. Serve up in a
deep dish.

ROAST PORK.

The parts of pork most suitable for roasting
are the loin, the leg, the saddle, the fillet, the
shoulder and the spare-rib. The loins of young

and delicate pork are roasted with the skin on, and this is scored in regular stripes of about a quarter inch wide with the point of a sharp knife before the joints are laid to the fire. The skin of the leg also is just cut through in the same manner. This is done to prevent its blistering and to render it more easy to carve, as the skin or crackling becomes so crisp and hard in the cooking that it is otherwise sometimes difficult to divide it. At first the meat must be placed at some distance from the fire, in order that it may be heated through before the skin hardens or begins to brown, and the basting should be constant; let it cook until thoroughly done and well browned before removing from the spit. A little clarified butter or salad oil may be brushed over the skin at first, particularly should the meat not be very fat, but unless remarkably lean it will speedily yield sufficient dripping to baste it with. Joints from which the fat has been pared will require, of course, far less roasting than those on which the crackling is retained. Brown gravy and apple or tomato sauce are the usual accompaniments to all roasts of pork, except a sucking pig. Cold roast pork, sliced, is very good for breakfast or tea.

ROAST PIG.

TAKE a fat pig three weeks old, wash it thoroughly inside and out; chop the liver fine with bread-crumbs, onions, parsley, pepper, salt and some potatoes boiled and mashed; make it into a paste with butter and egg. Put this stuffing into the body of the pig and sew it up; put it in a baking-pan with some water in the bottom and roast over a clear fire, basting it well with butter; rub it frequently with a piece of lard tied in a clean rag. When well done lay the pig on its knees in a dish, and put a red apple or pickled mango in its mouth. Put some of the stuffing in a bowl with a glass of wine and some of the dripping. Serve some with the roast pig, and the rest in a gravy-boat.

PORK CHOPS.

CUT the chops about half an inch thick, trim them neatly, place a frying-pan on the fire, and put into it a bit of butter; as soon as the pan is hot put in the chops, turning them often until brown all over; they will be sufficiently done in about fifteen minutes. Take one upon a plate and try it; if done, season it with a little finely-

9 *

minced onion, powdered sage and pepper and salt. Serve hot with a dish of apple sauce.

FRESH PORK POT-PIE.

BOIL a spare-rib, after removing all the fat and cracking the bones, until tender; remove the scum as it rises, and when tender season with salt and pepper; half an hour before time for serving the dinner thicken the gravy with a little flour. Have ready another kettle, into which remove all the bones and most of the gravy, leaving only sufficient to cover the pot half an inch above the rim that rests on the stove; put in the crust, cover tight, and boil steadily twenty-five minutes. To prepare the crust, work into light dough a small bit of batter, roll it out thin, cut it in small square cakes, and lay them on the moulding-board until very light; if made with brewers' yeast, the butter should be melted in the wetting of the crust and rolled out before rising, as the first effervescence of brewers' yeast is the strongest; work the dough well before making up the cakes.

PORK APPLE-PIE.

MAKE the crust in the usual way, spread it over a large deep plate, cut some slices of fat pork very thin; also slice some nice, juicy apples, make a layer of apples and then of pork, with a little allspice, pepper and sugar between. Make four or five layers of each, and put a crust over the top. Bake one hour.

BOILED HAM.

SOAK the ham for twelve or fourteen hours, lay it in a suitable vessel and cover plentifully with cold water; bring it very slowly to boil, and clear off the scum. Then draw back the sauce-pan to the edge of the stove, that the ham may be simmered softly, but steadily, until tender. A bunch of herbs, a bay-leaf and a few carrots thrown in will improve it. When sufficiently boiled strip off the skin and strew fine raspings over it. The time required for boiling varies much according to the size of the ham, averaging four hours and a half.

FRIED SAUSAGE.

SAUSAGES are best when quite fresh made. Put a bit of butter or dripping into a clean frying-pan; as soon as it is melted (before it gets hot) put in the sausages and shake the pan for a minute, and keep turning them: be careful not to break or prick them in so doing; fry them over a very slow fire till they are nicely browned on all sides. When they are done lay them on a hair-sieve and place before the fire for a few minutes, to drain the fat from them. The secret of frying sausages is to let them get hot very gradually; they will not burst if they are fresh. The common practice to prevent their bursting is to prick them with a fork, but this lets the gravy out.

SAUSAGE DUMPLINGS.

MAKE one pound of flour and two ounces of drippings or chopped suet into a firm paste by adding water enough to enable you to knead the whole together. Divide this paste into twelve equal parts; roll each of these out sufficiently large to enable you to fold up one pork sausage in it; roll the edge of the paste to fasten the sausage securely in it, and as you finish each dumpling drop it gently into a large sauce-pan containing plenty of boiling water, and when the whole is finished allow them to boil gently by the side of the fire one hour; then take them up with a spoon free from water, place them on a dish, and eat while hot.

POULTRY AND GAME.

GENERAL REMARKS.

POULTRY should invariably be purchased young. If old and tough, fowls are never as savory when cooked as when young and tender. This applies especially to ducks and geese. The flesh of young fowls will be firm and fleshy to the touch, and heavy in proportion to their size; the skin should be clear, white and finely grained, the toes pliable and easily broken when bent back. All kinds of poultry, and turkeys especially, are improved by hanging a day or two, unless the weather should be exceedingly sultry. Dark-legged fowls are best roasted, while the white-legged ones should be chosen for boiling. In dressing poultry, care should be taken not to break the gall: a thorough cleansing in every part is also necessary. The hairs should be singed off with a well-lighted piece of writing paper, holding the fowl before a hot fire. Poultry of all kinds should be thoroughly cooked and handsomely browned.

Game is never good when very fresh, but it does not follow that it should destroy the appetice, when sent to the table, by its offensive odor. The fine flavor and tenderness of the flesh depend almost entirely on its being allowed to hang a reasonable time before cooking. Venison, if kept to the proper time, is the most tender of all meats, but care is necessary to bring it into a fitting state for table without its becoming offensive; a free current of air materially assists in preserving its sweetness, while a close, damp atmosphere is destructive to this as well as all other kinds of meat. Should any moisture appear on its surface, it must be wiped carefully with a soft, dry cloth. The haunch is generally regarded as the prime and favorite joint of venison, although the neck and shoulder are also excellent stewed in various ways or made into pasties. Young hares and rabbits are nutritious and easily digested; when old, the reverse. Partridges, like most birds, should be hung up for a day or two to ripen, and may be chosen by nearly the same tests as poultry. Wild birds need no scalding before being picked. They are much more delicious than domestic fowls, which is owing to the contrast of living. They have free range in the open air, and choose their own food, which produces a delicate texture of flesh.

ROAST TURKEY.

In cold weather a turkey should hang at least a week before it is cooked. Draw and clean it with great care, taking particular pains not to break the gall bladder. Pour cold water plentifully through it, singe with writing paper, dry, and wipe clean. Fill the body with a dressing made with bread-crumbs, a slice of sweet, fat pork (boiled so that it will chop tender), thyme, parsley, pepper, salt, grated lemon-peel and mace. Before putting it in the oven cover the breast with very thin slices of salt pork; roast, and baste frequently, for an hour and a half or two hours, in a not too hot oven. Garnish with a chain of fine fried sausages and green parsley, or with small crimped paper rosettes and celery tops. Serve with cranberry sauce.

BOILED TURKEY.

Select a plump, not too large, hen turkey for boiling; draw, clean and singe the bird smoothly and with great precaution. Cut off the head and neck, cut the skin around the first joint of the legs and draw them off. Fill the breast with raw oysters and a dressing made of bread, chopped celery, a little pork and seasoning. Dress it so as to make it look round and plump as possible. Wrap it in a cloth and place it in boiling water, clear off all the scum which rises, and simmer gently two hours. Garnish with green celery tops and small crisp slices of fried bacon. A ham is often served with boiled turkey. Serve with oyster sauce.

ROAST GOOSE.

SELECT a young, tender and fat goose; draw, clean and wipe thoroughly dry, inside and out: save the giblets for the gravy; fill the body with a stuffing of bread, sage, thyme, one or two par-boiled onions chopped fine, some mashed Irish potatoes and a very little butter. Add salt and pepper and yolk of egg; truss it, and roast it at a brisk fire; baste the same as turkey. Pour off most of the fat that drips from the goose, or the gravy will be too rich. After boiling the giblets in a sauce-pan by themselves, seasoning with salt and pepper and adding a little butter, cut off the neck and chop up the heart, liver and gizzard and serve in the gravy, after it is well skimmed. Unite the two gravies and serve them up in a gravy-tureen. Apple sauce is indispensable as an accompaniment to this dish.

BOILED GOOSE.

AFTER it is well dressed singe it thoroughly. Have ready a dressing prepared of bread-crumbs seasoned with pepper, salt and butter, with the addition of two finely-chopped onions, a little sage and more pepper than would be used for turkey. Fill the body and close it firmly; put it in cold water, and boil it gently an hour if tender, if not, longer; serve with giblet sauce. The onions can be omitted if not relished.

ROAST DUCK.

PREPARE for roasting two fine, fat young ducks in the same manner as for roast goose. Stuff with sage, onion and thyme, bread-crumbs and butter; baste well with salt and water and their own gravy. Roast one hour, or until thoroughly done and finely browned. Serve with cranberry jelly or apple sauce.

10

STEWED DUCK OR GOOSE.

TAKE a couple of young ducks, or a tender fat goose, and after preparing for cooking the same way as roast goose or duck, half roast before a slow fire. Then cut either down neatly into joints, and put them into a stew-pan, with a pint of good beef gravy, a few leaves of sage and mint cut small, pepper and salt and a bit of onion shred as fine as possible. Let it simmer for a quarter of an hour, skimming it thoroughly; then add a pint of green peas or rice mixed with a little port wine; put in a piece of butter and a little flour, and give it one boil. Serve hot in one dish.

ROAST FOWL OR CAPON.

FOWL and capons are roasted and served as turkeys, with the addition of egg sauce, but they require proportionally less time at the fire, and are seldom stuffed. A full-grown fowl will require three-quarters of an hour to be well roasted, a capon an hour and a quarter. A large fowl may be stuffed the same as a turkey.

ROAST FOWL, FRENCH STYLE.

TAKE a fine, plump fowl, fill the breast with a good forcemeat and roast in the usual manner.

When nearly done remove the fowl from the fire, pour tepid butter over it in every part and spread thickly with very fine bread-crumbs; sprinkle these again with butter, and dip the fowl into more crumbs. Place it to the fire, and when of a clear, light brown all over put it carefully into a dish, and serve with lemon sauce and with gravy thickened and mixed with plenty of minced parsley, or with brown gravy and any other sauce usually served with fowls.

BROILED FOWL.

Split it down the back, season well with salt and pepper, and put it on the gridiron with the inner part next to the fire, which must be very clear and brisk. Hold the gridiron at a considerable distance from the fire until the fowl is nearly done; then turn it, taking care that it does not burn. Broil until it is well browned, and serve with stewed mushrooms or a sauce made of pickled mushrooms. If the fowl is very large, half roast it, cut it into four quarters, and then broil it on the gridiron. The time required for cooking is from a half to three-quarters of an hour. A duck may also be broiled in the same way, but it must be young and tender.

BOILED FOWL.

BOILED fowls are prepared in the same manner as boiled turkey. Drawn butter seasoned with parsley or celery is the most common sauce used. Liver sauce is good, but when oysters can be had oyster sauce is generally preferable.

STEWED CHICKEN.

SELECT a pair of young and plump chickens, and after a careful cleansing cut them into joints; season well with pepper and salt and a little powdered mace; put them into the stew-pan with a pint to a pint and a half of water, according to their size; let them simmer over a slow fire, stirring in a little flour mixed with butter. If necessary add more seasoning, and serve hot in a heated dish.

STEAMED CHICKEN.

CLEAN them carefully, split them down the back and lay them in a pan, the inside part down; pour about a half pint of water into the pan and cover them with another pan; let them steam twenty minutes, and bake. When nearly done pepper them nicely, and grate some bread-crumbs over them. Make a rich gravy, and serve hot.

FRIED CHICKEN.

TAKE two fine young chickens, clean them carefully, and wipe them thoroughly dry. Put them into the frying-pan, season with pepper and salt and dredge them with flour. Fry in lard till richly browned on both sides; take them out and keep them near the fire; skim the gravy carefully in which the chickens have been fried, mix with it half a pint of cream, season with mace, pepper, salt and parsley; pour it over the chickens, and serve hot.

CHICKEN BAKED IN RICE.

CUT two small, tender chickens into joints, as for a fricassee; season well with pepper and salt, and lay them in a pudding-dish lined with slices of ham or bacon; add a pint of veal gravy and an onion finely minced, fill up the dish with boiled rice well pressed; fill the dish to its utmost capacity; cover it with a paste of flour and water. Bake one hour, and serve before taking off the paste.

FRICASSEED CHICKEN.

CUT off the wings and legs of three small chickens; separate the breasts from the backs;

10 * H

divide the backs crosswise; cut off the necks and clean the gizzards; put them with the livers and other parts of the chickens (after being thoroughly washed) into a sauce-pan. Add salt, pepper and a little mace; cover with water, stew till tender, and take them up. Thicken a half pint of water with two spoonfuls of flour rubbed into four ounces of butter; add a tumbler of new milk; boil all together a few minutes, then add eight spoonfuls of white wine, stirring it in carefully, so as not to allow it to curdle. Put in the chickens, and shake the pan until they are sufficiently heated. Green peas, lima beans, asparagus tops or mashed potatoes are excellent accompaniments. Chicken fricassee is a nice side-dish for company.

CHICKEN PIE.

TAKE a pair of nice, tender chickens, clean them thoroughly and cut up into small pieces; wash well and let them cook for twenty minutes in water sufficient to cover them. Mix a table-spoonful of flour in cold water to a thin paste, and stir in the gravy; add a lump of butter, and season thoroughly with pepper and salt; let all cool. To make a paste, mix together equal quantities of lard and flour, adding a little salt; roll out thin; line a deep pie-dish; after rolling out the top crust to half the size required spread over it butter to the depth of one quarter of an inch; roll up and roll out again, and repeat the operation two or three times; put in the chicken, and put on the top crust, and pinch the edges well together; cut a slit in the top crust. Bake till the crust is slightly browned.

CHICKEN PUFFS.

MINCE up together the breast of a chicken, some lean ham, half an anchovy, a little parsley, some shalot and lemon-peel, and season these with pepper, salt, cayenne and beaten mace. Let this be on the fire for a few minutes, in a little good white sauce. Cut some thinly-rolled-out puff paste into squares, putting on each some of the mince, turn the paste over, fry them in boiling lard and serve them up on a salver. These puffs are very good cold, and they form a convenient supper-dish.

CHICKEN GUMBO.

PREPARE two young chickens as for a fricassee. Mix a tablespoonful of good butter with a teaspoonful of flour, and put into a stew-pan with an onion minced finely; brown over a brisk fire, and then add a quart of water and a quarter of a peck of ochras, first sliced thin and then chopped; season with a very little salt, cover the pan, and let the whole stew together till the ochras are entirely dissolved; then put in the pieces of chicken, and cook for half an hour, or until they are thoroughly done. Serve up hot in a deep dish. An equal quantity of tomatoes cut small may be added to the ochras; no water will be required if tomatoes are used, as their juice will supply ample liquid.

ROAST PIGEONS.

PIGEONS lose their flavor by being kept more than a day after they are killed. They may be prepared and roasted or broiled the same as chickens; they will require from twenty to thirty minutes' cooking. Make a gravy of the giblets, season it with pepper and salt and add a little flour and butter.

BOILED PIGEONS.

TRUSS the pigeons the same as boiled fowls; put them into boiling water, season with a little salt, and in about fifteen minutes lift them out, pour over them parsley and butter, and send a tureen of it to the table with the pigeons.

PIGEON PIE.

CUT into quarters four young pigeons and sprinkle them with pepper, salt and herb seasoning; cut also into four pieces a pound or less of sweet salt pork, and lay them at the bottom of the dish. Boil four eggs ten minutes, take out the hard yolks, and lay them between the pigeons upon the steaks; pour in a gill of gravy or water; cover with puff paste.

STEWED GIBLETS.

AFTER very nicely cleaning goose or duck giblets, stew them for several hours with a small quantity of water, onion, black pepper and a bunch of sweet herbs till nearly done; season them with salt and pepper and a very small piece of mace. Before serving give them one boil with a cup of cream and a piece of butter rubbed in a teaspoonful of fine flour.

GIBLET PIE.

WASH and clean your giblets; put them in a sauce-pan; season with pepper, salt and a little butter rolled in flour; cover them with water and stew till very tender. Line a pie-dish with paste and put in the giblets. If the gravy is not thick enough, add a little more butter rolled in flour; let it boil once, pour in the gravy, put on a top crust, leaving a square hole in the centre. Ornament the pie with leaves of paste. Set the pie in an oven, and when the crust is done take it out.

ROAST HAUNCH OF VENISON.

To prepare a haunch of venison for roasting, wash it slightly in tepid water, and dry it thoroughly by rubbing with a clean, soft cloth. Lay over the fat side a large sheet of thickly-buttered paper, and next a paste of flour and water about three-quarters of an inch thick; cover this again with two or three sheets of stout paper, secure the whole well with twine, and lay the haunch to a clear, steady fire; baste the paper immediately with butter or clarified dripping, and roast the joint from three to four hours, according to its weight and quality. Doe venison will require half an hour less time than buck venison. About twenty minutes before the joint is done remove the paste and paper, baste the meat in every part with butter, and dredge it very lightly with flour; let it take a pale brown color, and serve hot, with unflavored gravy in a tureen and good current jelly. Venison is much better when the deer has been killed in the autumn, when wild berries are plentiful, and it has had abundant opportunities to fatten upon this and other fresh food.

BAKED SADDLE OF VENISON.

IN ordering the saddle request the butcher to cut the ribs off pretty close, as the only part that is of much account is the tenderloin and thick meat that lies along the backbone up to the neck. The ribs which extend from this have very little meat on them, but are always sold with the saddle. When neatly cut off they leave the saddle in a better shape, and the ribs can be put into your stock-pot, to boil for soup. Wash the saddle carefully. See that no hairs are left, dried on to the outside. When ready in the oven cover with some buttered white paper, put some boiling water, with a little salt, into the bake-pan, set the saddle on the rack, and while baking baste often. When two-thirds done remove the paper, that the top may be nicely browned. Venison should not be over-done, and should be eaten hot.

BROILED STEAKS OF VENISON.

HEAT the gridiron, grease it well, lay on the steaks cut from the neck; broil quickly, without scorching, turning them two or three times; season with salt and pepper. Have the butter melted in a well-heated platter, into which the steaks must be laid hot from the gridiron, turning them over three times in the butter, and serve hot with currant jelly laid on each steak. It is well to set the platter into another in which you have some boiling water.

STEWED SHOULDER OF VENISON.

AFTER carefully removing the bone from the shoulder season it with cayenne, salt and pounded mace, with a little allspice. Lay over it thin slices of the fat of a loin of well-fed mutton; roll and bind it tightly; lay it into a vessel nearly of its size, and hardly cover it with some good stock made of equal parts of beef and mutton. Stew it slowly from three to four hours, according to size and weight, and turn it when it is half done. Dish, and serve it with some of the gravy in which it has been stewed, thickened with rice flour, mixed with a glass or more of claret or of port wine, and seasoned to taste.

ROAST HARE OR RABBIT.

A VERY close relationship exists between the hare and the rabbit, the chief difference being in the smaller size and shorter legs and ears of the latter. The manner of dressing and preparing each for the table is therefore pretty nearly the same. To prepare them for roasting, first skin, wash well in cold water and rinse thoroughly in lukewarm water. If a little musty from being emptied before they were hung up and afterward neglected, rub the insides with vinegar and afterward remove all taint of the acid by a thorough washing in lukewarm water. After being well wiped with a soft cloth put in a filling of force-meat, sew the animal up, truss it, and roast for a half or three-quarters of an hour, until well browned, basting it constantly with butter and dredging with flour. Serve with fine red currant jelly.

STEWED RABBIT.

CUT up a young rabbit and soak it an hour in water; lay it in the stew-pan with half a dozen mushrooms, a bunch of parsley, a teaspoonful of salt, half as much pepper and two blades of mace; pour over a pint of port wine, stew gently for

11

half an hour. Then take out the rabbit, strain the sauce, reduce it a little over the fire, add two tablespoonfuls of thick cream, put in the rabbit, and heat over the fire, without boiling, for a quarter of an hour. Serve in the sauce, with sliced lemon.

CANVAS-BACK DUCK.

It will generally be conceded that the best canvas-back ducks are to be found along the Potomac River. Having picked, singed and drawn it well, wipe it carefully, so as to have it clean without washing it. Truss it, leaving the head on, to show its quality. Place it in a moderately hot oven for at least three-quarters of an hour; serve it hot, in its own gravy, on a large chafing-dish. Currant jelly should be on the table.

COMMON WILD DUCK.

These are prepared like canvas-back ducks, except the heads are taken off, also the toes, but not the feet. They are sometimes skinned, which is hardly advisable. To free the fowls from a "fishy" taste, first parboil them, with a carrot

placed inside them, which absorbs the "sedgy"
taste; throw it away, and lay the duck in cold
water for a time. Wild fowls should not be
stuffed. Flour them well, baste plentifully with
butter and roast briskly three-quarters of an hour.
Serve with currant jelly.

WIDGEON AND TEAL.

A WIDGEON is a water-fowl of the duck per-
suasion, as is also the teal, although smaller than
the common duck. They are dressed precisely
like the duck, only less time in cooking is required
for the widgeon, and still less for the teal.

ROAST PARTRIDGE.

PLUCK, singe, draw and truss them; roast about
twenty minutes; baste them well with butter, and
when the gravy begins to run from them they are
done. Put them on dishes, three in each dish,
with some bread-crumbs fried a nice brown and arranged in small heaps. The gravy should be served
in a tureen separately. Orange sauce is a nice
accompaniment. If these birds have a bitter taste
when cooked, do not eat them. It is produced by
their feeding on laurel berries in winter, when

their food is scarce. Laurel berries are poisonous, and people have died from eating birds that
have fed on them.

FRIED PARTRIDGE.

TAKE a pair of cold partridges that have been
roasted or broiled; cut them into quarters and dip
them into beaten and seasoned yolks of eggs; put
some butter into the frying-pan, and when the fat
becomes very hot drop the birds into it, and cook
them over a moderately hot fire until nicely
browned.

BROILED PARTRIDGE.

SPLIT them down the back; wash and wipe
them inside and out with a soft towel; dip them
into melted butter, then roll them in bread-
crumbs; repeat this; lay them, inside down, upon
a well-heated gridiron, turning them once; season
with a little salt and cayenne; when done serve
them with piquante sauce.

STEWED PARTRIDGE.

CUT them up, after preparing properly; slice
an onion, pull it in rings and put into the stew-

pan with a piece of butter rolled in flour and a tablespoonful of water, one of wine and another of vinegar; boil once, and then put in the partridge; simmer very gently till done. Garnish with slices of toast, and pour the gravy over them.

BOILED PARTRIDGE.

CLEAN and wash them well, cut off the heads and truss like boiled fowls; then put them into boiling water; boil them quickly for fifteen minutes. Make a rich sauce by adding an ounce of butter to half a pint of thick cream; put in a little salt; stir one way over the fire till hot, and pour it into a dish with the partridges. Serve immediately.

POTTED PARTRIDGE.

CLEAN them nicely, and season with mace, allspice, white pepper and salt in fine powder; rub every part well, then lay them breast downward in a pan, and pack the birds as close as you possibly can; put a good deal of butter on them, then cover the pan with a coarse flour paste and a paper cover. Tie it close, and bake in a slow oven for seven or eight hours. Remove the paste, take the bones from the partridges and

11 *

beat them to a proper consistency; put the beaten paste into pots and pour butter over.

PARTRIDGE PIE.

PREPARE and truss them as for boiling; pound in a mortar the livers of the birds, a quarter of a pound of fat bacon and some shred parsley; lay part of this forcemeat at the bottom of a raised crust, put in the birds, add the remainder of the forcemeat and a few mushrooms; put some slices of fat bacon on the top, cover with a lid of crust, and bake it two hours and a half. Before serving the pie remove the lid, take out the bacon and add sufficient rich gravy and orange juice.

ROAST WOODCOCK.

WOODCOCKS should not be drawn, as the trail (the intestines) is considered the most delicious part of the bird; truss their legs close to the body, and run an iron skewer through each thigh close to the body, and put them on a small bird-spit feet downward; place them to roast at a slow fire; cut as many slices of bread as you have birds, toast or fry them a delicate brown, and lay them in the dripping-pan under the birds to catch the trail;

baste them with butter and froth them with flour; lay the toast on a hot dish and the birds on the toast; pour some good beef gravy into the dish, and send some up in a boat; twenty or thirty minutes will roast them. Garnish with slices of lemon.

Snipes differ little from woodcocks, unless in size; they are to be dressed in the same way, but require about five minutes less time to roast.

A good broth may be made of the trimmings and parings of the birds used, by stewing them with some vegetables and proper seasoning.

ROASTED LARKS.

THESE are considered the most delicate of the small birds. When cleaned and prepared for roasting, brush them with the yolk of an egg, and roll in bread-crumbs; spit them on a small bird-spit, and tie that on a larger spit; ten or fifteen minutes at a quick fire will cook them; baste them with fresh butter, and sprinkle them with bread-crumbs till they are quite covered, while roasting. Sauce, grated bread fried in butter, which set to drain before the fire that it may harden. Serve the crumbs under the larks when you dish them, and garnish them with slices of lemon.

A SALMI OF PHEASANTS OR PARTRIDGES.

THIS is a nice mode of serving the remains of roasted game, but when a superlative salmi is desired, the birds must be scarcely more than half roasted for it. In either case, carve them very neatly, and strip every particle of skin and fat from the legs, wings and breasts; bruise the bodies well, and put them with the skin and other trimmings into a very clean stew-pan. If for a simple and inexpensive dinner, merely add to them two or three sliced onions, a bay-leaf, a small blade of mace and a few peppercorns; then pour in a pint or more of good veal gravy, or strong broth, and boil it briskly until reduced nearly half; strain the gravy, pressing the bones well, to obtain all the flavor; skim off the fat, add a little cayenne and lemon juice, heat the game very gradually in it, but do not on any account allow it to boil; place pieces of fried bread round a dish, arrange the birds in good form in the centre, give the sauce a boil, and pour it on them.

How to Prepare Vegetables.

GENERAL REMARKS.

VEGETABLES are more healthy and better flavored when fresh; the summer varieties, particularly, should be cooked soon after being gathered, as much of their delicately-fine flavor becomes lost if they are the least withered. If purchased at the markets or of the provision-dealers, they should be washed and allowed to soak for some time in cold water before cooking. To destroy the small snails and other insects which cluster in the leaves of cabbage, cauliflower, lettuce and similar plants, put them in a pan of strong brine, with the stalk ends uppermost, and in about twenty or thirty minutes the insects will fall out and sink to the bottom. A pound and a half of salt to the gallon of water will answer for this purpose, and if strained daily it will last for some time. When the vegetables are properly prepared for cooking, boil them quickly in hot water until they are sufficiently tender, probing them with a fork to ascertain this, and if quite done dish them immediately, draining them well through a colander, taking care that they do not become broken. In cooking vegetables too much salt must not be used, as it renders them hard and is apt to impair their taste. Half-cooked vegetables are exceedingly indigestible and unwholesome, and those who regard health as of the first importance will very sensibly prefer to have them thoroughly cooked.

ROAST POTATOES.

SELECT the largest and finest potatoes for roasting. Wash them thoroughly and put them in a stove or oven with their skins on. Let them roast about two hours, turning them with a fork. When well done, send them to the table hot in their skins. Sweet potatoes are roasted in the same manner, but require a little longer time to be well done. To roast potatoes with beef, poultry and other meats, peel the potatoes, and when the meat is nearly roasted lay the potatoes in the pan and cook them in the gravy. It is generally customary to roast both varieties of the potatoes in the same dish.

STEAMED POTATOES.

PUT them, clean washed, with their skins on, into a steam sauce-pan, and let the water under them be about half boiling; let them continue to boil rather quickly till they are done. If the water once relaxes from its heat, the excellence of the potato is sure to be affected, and to become soddened, be the quality ever so good. A too precipitate boiling is equally disadvantageous, as the higher part of the surface of the root begins to crack and open, while the centre part continues unheated and undecomposed. When cooked sufficiently tender, dish them, throw over a clean napkin and send to the table immediately.

BOILED POTATOES, IRISH METHOD.

WASH the potatoes well, leaving the skins on, and put them into boiling water. As soon as they are boiled sufficiently tender to allow a fork to penetrate easily, pour some cold water into the pan; let the potatoes remain two or three minutes, and then pour off the water. Half remove the lid of the pot, and let the potatoes remain over a slow fire until the steam is evaporated; then peel and send to the table in an open dish.

STEWED POTATOES.

POTATOES are unquestionably more nutritious and delicious to the taste when cooked raw. Cold potatoes re-cooked become hard, tough and indigestible. The experienced and thrifty housewife, however, suffering nothing to be lost, and with the aid of proper seasoning and flavoring, will know how to prepare the scraps of potatoes, as well as those of other vegetables, which remain after each meal, imparting to them an agreeable, savory taste and attractive guise well calculated to tempt the most delicate and fastidious appetite.

To stew potatoes, take perfectly sound raw ones; divide each potato into four parts, and put them into the stew-pan; add salt and pepper, and a piece of fresh butter; pour in milk (adding a little cream if at hand) just sufficient to keep the potatoes from burning. Place the lid on the sauce-pan, and allow the potatoes to stew until soft and tender throughout. Stewed potatoes should always be thoroughly cooked; if otherwise, they are tough and unpalatable.

To stew potatoes that have been either boiled or steamed, cut them into thin slices, season well and dredge them with flour; put them into a stew-pan with some fresh butter or olive oil. Fry them slightly on both sides for five minutes, drain off the fat, pour upon them half a pint of good gravy, nicely flavored, and let them stew by the side of the fire twenty minutes. Serve with the sauce in which they were cooked.

FRIED POTATOES.

BOIL some nice, large potatoes; set them aside a few minutes, and when sufficiently cold slice them; sprinkle over them pepper and salt, fry them in butter or fresh lard until both sides are of a light brown.

Another way is to mash the potatoes immediately after boiling, seasoning with cayenne and salt and some finely-chopped ham; make them into small cakes, dip them in egg sauce ready prepared, and fry both sides a nice brown.

To fry cold boiled potatoes, grate them and season with pepper and salt; beat some eggs very light, mix well with the potatoes, and fry them in butter.

MASHED POTATOES.

AFTER boiling some fine raw potatoes, pare them and mash fine, adding a mixture of butter,

12

rich milk or cream, and some salt. Sprinkle pepper over the top, and serve while hot.

Another method is to prepare them as above, placing them in a dish, smoothing them on the top, and spreading over the beaten yolk of an egg. Place them in an oven, and cook until they are of a light brown.

POTATO FRITTERS.

BOIL three or four large potatoes and mash them fine. Beat up four yolks and three whites of eggs, adding one large spoonful of cream, another of sweet wine, a little lemon juice and powdered nutmeg. Beat together this batter until very light, dip the potatoes into it, and then place them upon the griddle and fry until nicely browned.

POTATO SALAD.

BOIL three or four nice potatoes, cut them up into small pieces and pass them through a sieve. Have ready a dressing made as follows: One spoonful of mustard, two spoonfuls of salt, three spoonfuls of sweet oil, one spoonful of vinegar, the yolks of two hard-boiled eggs, one small onion chopped fine and one teaspoonful of anchovy sauce. Mix the whole well with the potatoes, and garnish with parsley and hard-boiled egg sliced.

BOILED CABBAGE.

To destroy any insects that may lie concealed in the cabbage, follow the plan suggested in the General Remarks on Vegetables; after which strip off the loose or faded leaves, and wash well; then split in two, or if very large into four, pieces, and put it into boiling water with some salt; let it boil slowly, skimming it carefully. When done, strain it through a colander. Place it in a vegetable-dish, lay inside, among the leaves, some bits of cold fresh butter; season with pepper, and serve while hot.

Cauliflowers are cooked in a similar manner.

COLD AND HOT SLAWS.

To make cold-slaw, take a nice, fresh cabbage, wash and strain it (after submitting it to the insect-destroying process); cut off the stalk, shave down the head into very small strips with a cabbage-cutter or very sharp knife. It must be done evenly. Put it into a deep china-dish and prepare for it the following dressing: Melt in a sauce-pan a quarter of a pound of butter, with half pint of water, a large tablespoonful of vinegar, a saltspoonful of salt and a little cayenne. Give this a boil, and pour it hot on the cabbage. Send to the table cold.

To prepare warm-slaw, cut the cabbage as for cold-slaw (red cabbage is best); put it in a deep dish, cover closely, and set it on the top of the stove for half an hour or till warm all through; do not let it boil. Then make a dripping as for cold-slaw. Boil this mixture in a sauce-pan, and pour it hot over the warm cabbage; send to table immediately.

DRESSED SALAD.

TAKE tender lettuce leaves, carefully wash and half blanch, cutting them slightly. Make a dressing of the yolk of hard-boiled eggs, mixed mustard, pepper, butter and vinegar. Boil two or three eggs more than are needed for the sauce; slice the whites and yolk together; lay them on the lettuce. Then pour the sauce over the whole. Beet-roots, baked or boiled, blanched endive, celery, with any ready vegetable, will supply salads through the winter.

CHICKEN SALAD.

SELECT one or two nice, fresh lettuces; pick, wash, drain, cut them small, and spread them evenly on a large, deep dish. Having ready a pair of cold fowls, skin them, take away the fat, and cut up as if for eating. Cut all the flesh from the bones and mince it; mix with a little grated smoked tongue or cold ham. Place the minced chicken and grated tongue in the centre of the dish containing the lettuce. For the dressing, mix together the following ingredients, in the proportions of the yolks of four eggs well beaten, a teaspoonful of powdered white sugar, a salt-spoonful of cayenne, two spoonfuls of made mustard, six tablespoonfuls of salad oil and five of vinegar; stir this mixture well; put it into a small sauce-pan, set it over the fire, and let it boil exactly three minutes, stirring all the time. Then set it to cool. When quite cold, cover with it thickly the heap of chicken in the centre of the salad. Ornament it with half a dozen or more hard-boiled eggs, which, after the shells are removed, must be thrown directly into a pan of cold water, to prevent them from turning blue. Cut each egg lengthways, the white and yolk together, into four long pieces of equal size and shape; lay the

12 *

pieces upon the salad all round the heap of chicken and close to it, placing them so as to follow each other in a slanting direction, something in the form of a circular wreath of leaves. Arrange in a circle upon the lettuce, outside of the circle of cut egg, some very red cold beet cut into small cones or points, all of equal size. In helping those at table, give a portion of everything to each person, and it can be mixed together on the plate. The salad should be eaten entirely cold, but standing too long will injure it.

LOBSTER SALAD.

PREPARE a sauce with the coral of a fine, new lobster boiled fresh for about half an hour. Pound and rub it smooth, and mix very gradually with a dressing made from the yolks of two hard-boiled eggs, a tablespoonful of English mustard, three of salad oil, two of vinegar, one of white powdered sugar, a small teaspoonful of salt, as much black pepper, a pinch of cayenne and two fresh yolks of eggs. Next fill your salad bowl with some shred lettuce, the better part of two, leaving the small curled centres to garnish your dish with. Mingle with this the flesh of your lobster, torn, broken or cut into bits. Pour your sauce over the whole, put your lettuce hearts down the centre, and arrange upon the sides slices of hard-boiled eggs.

SPINACH.

It must be carefully picked and washed in several waters, to prevent its being gritty. After draining in a colander, put it into a large saucepan, with only the water that adheres to it. Let it simmer slowly for about an hour; then drain and dish it. Spread over the spinach a lump of butter, and season with pepper and salt. Slice a couple of hard-boiled eggs, and place the pieces over the top. Serve hot.

ASPARAGUS.

Scrape the stems of the asparagus lightly, but very clean, throw them into cold water, and when all are scraped and very clean, tie them in bunches of equal size; cut the large ends evenly, that the stems may be all of the same length, and put the asparagus into plenty of boiling water, with a little salt. While it is boiling cut two slices of bread half an inch thick, pare off the crust, and toast it a delicate brown on both sides. When the stalks of the asparagus are tender, lift it out directly, or it will lose both its color and its flavor, and will also be liable to break; dip the toast quickly into the liquor in which it was boiled, and dish the vegetable upon it, with the points meeting in the centre. Pour over rich melted butter, and send to table hot.

STEWED GREEN PUMPKIN.

TAKE a large pumpkin, not too old, cut it in half and take out the seeds; then cut the pumpkin into thin slices, pare them, and put them into a pot with just water enough to prevent them from burning; slice a small onion, and stew with the pumpkin. When quite tender throughout, take them up, and drain, wash and press them through a colander; season with black pepper. Prepared in this way, stewed pumpkin is very nice when eaten with boiled corned beef or corned pork.

STEWED CYMLINGS OR SQUASHES.

AFTER carefully selecting squashes that are not too old or beginning to harden, wash them, cut into slices, remove the seed, and stew them three-quarters of an hour or until quite tender. Take them up, drain and press out the water thoroughly. Mash them with a little fresh butter, pepper and salt. Then put them into the stew-pan, set it on hot coals, and stir till the squashes become dry. Be careful not to burn them.

STEWED EGG PLANT.

PURPLE egg plants are better than the white. Put them whole into a pot with plenty of water; let them simmer till quite tender. Take them out, drain, peel and mash them smooth in a deep dish. Mix them with grated bread-crumbs, powdered sweet marjoram, a large piece of butter, and a few pounded cloves. Grate a layer of bread-crumbs over the top, put in an oven and brown; send to table on the same dish.

FRIED EGG PLANT.

Do not pare the plant; slice it half an inch thick, and lay the slices an hour or two in salt water. Take them out, wipe them, and season with pepper and salt. Beat up some yolk of egg, and in another dish grate some bread-crumbs. Have some lard and butter boiling hot in a frying-pan.

Dip the slices first in the egg and then in the bread-crumbs till both sides are covered; fry them brown, being careful to have them well cooked throughout.

PARSNIPS.

SCRAPE off the outside, wash and boil them in a little salt and water. When done they may be dressed with butter and a little pepper, or drawn butter, if desired. They are very nice when fried. After they are boiled, split open the largest ones, season with pepper and salt, dredge a little flour over them, and fry them a light brown. Another method is to prepare them the same as above, and let them boil till very tender, after which, press them through a colander, then mash them very fine, and season with butter, pepper and salt.

BEETS.

SELECT small-sized, smooth roots. They should be carefully washed, but not cut before boiling, as the juice will escape and the sweetness of the vegetable be impaired, leaving it white and hard. Boil them until tender in clear water; do not probe them, but press them with the finger, to ascertain if they are sufficiently done. When satisfied of this, take them up and put them into a pan of cold water, and slip off the outside. Cut them into thin slices, and while hot season with butter, salt, a little pepper and very sharp vinegar. To bake beets, boil and peel them, slice them thin, and put them into a baking-dish, forming a layer of sliced beets and a layer of grated bread-crumbs; make a gravy of butter, pepper and salt and pour over them. Bake ten or fifteen minutes. Dish them, and send to table.

TURNIPS.

Turnips should be pared, cut into thin slices, and put into a plenty of boiling water, with a lump of salt and a small quantity of dripping. Boil them very fast. In a quarter of an hour take them up, drain them in a colander, and pour melted butter over them; garnish the top of each with a spot of black pepper. If the turnips are to be mashed, they must be boiled exceedingly tender and well drained; mash them with a wooden spoon, turn them into a basin, add a little milk, cover the basin, heat them in the oven, turn them into a warm dish, and serve them hot.

INDIAN CORN.

SELECT full-grown but young and tender ears. If young, the grains will be soft and milky. The corn is much sweeter and more nutritious when cooked with the leaves or husks on, although a longer time is required. Remove only the outside leaves, and carefully take out the silk; put the corn into a pot of fast-boiling water; when done, take up, drain and place in a covered dish, or cover them with a napkin, and serve up hot. Just before eating, rub each ear with salt and pepper, and then spread over some butter. Corn is unquestionably sweeter when eaten off the cob. But fastidious people, before company, dislike to be seen holding an ear of corn with their hands and biting off the grains with their teeth. For this reason it is perhaps more frequently cut off the cob into a dish and mixed with salt, pepper and butter.

SUCCOTASH.

TAKE one dozen ears of nice, tender corn, cut off the grains from the cob, and mix with them one quart of lima beans. After boiling them well in salt and water, drain them through a colander and place them at once into a pan, covering to keep them hot. Have ready two eggs well beaten, with two ounces of butter; pour this mixture over the corn and beans, adding pepper and salt to taste; serve hot.

MOCK OYSTERS OF CORN.

TAKE one dozen and a half of young corn and grate off the grains as fine as possible; mix with the grated corn three large tablespoonfuls of sifted flour, the yolks of six eggs well beaten, two table-spoonfuls of melted butter and a little pepper and salt. Have ready in a frying-pan equal portions of lard and butter boiling hot. Put a dessert-spoonful of the mixture at a time into the pan and fry to a light brown, making each as near the size of an oyster as possible. They must be half an inch thick. Send to table hot.

HOMINY.

AFTER washing and soaking the hominy over night, early the next morning put it on to cook, in plenty of water, with a little salt; it absorbs, like rice, much water, and must be cooked with care, and be perfectly white and soft. When quite

13 K

done, stir in some new milk and butter, and let it stew for ten minutes; serve hot. It is very nice fried for breakfast, and is a necessary accompaniment to pork.

STEWED TOMATOES.

SELECT large, sound and thoroughly ripe tomatoes; scald them in hot water, and when sufficiently cool remove the skins; drain and put them into a stew-pan. An iron pot lined with block tin is the most suitable, but by all means avoid using a copper vessel, as the acid in the tomatoes will render it poisonous, especially if the enamel is a little worn off. When the stew-pan is nearly filled with the tomatoes, add one or two boiled onions minced fine and some powdered white sugar, to lessen the extreme acrid taste; add also a piece of fresh butter dredged with flour, and a little salt and pepper. Then put in some bread-crumbs, and stew for at least three hours. Tomatoes require a long cooking, otherwise they will have a raw, acrid taste. The cooking should be commenced at least three hours before dinner. The juice of the tomatoes is sufficient without any water. Send to the table hot.

TOMATOES BAKED WHOLE.

Take one dozen large ripe tomatoes, peel them, cut slits in the sides, and stuff them with a mixture of bread-crumbs, yolk of egg, pepper, salt and butter. Place them in shallow baking-dishes and bake them till done. Pour a little drawn butter over them, and serve hot.

BROILED TOMATOES.

Wash and wipe the tomatoes, put them on a gridiron over live coals, with the stem part down; when that side is done, turn them and let them cook through. Place them on a hot dish and send to the table quickly, to be there seasoned to taste.

RAW TOMATOES.

Select large and fully ripe tomatoes, remove the skins without scalding, and slice them. Make a dressing of half a cup of cider vinegar, one tablespoonful of mixed mustard, one tablespoonful of salad oil, with a little pepper and salt, and pour over the tomatoes. Another method of dressing raw tomatoes is as follows: After peeling and slicing them put them in a glass dish, and make a sauce with one gill of wine, half cup of white sugar, quarter of a cup of cream and some grated nutmeg. Pour this over the tomatoes.

STEWED ONIONS.

PEEL off the outer skin, trim the ends, and arrange the onions in a sauce-pan of sufficient size to contain them all in one layer; just cover them with good beef or veal gravy, and stew them very gently for a couple of hours; they should be tender throughout, but should not be allowed to fall to pieces. Send to table hot. The savor of this dish is heightened by flouring lightly, and frying the onions of a pale brown before stewing.

BOILED ONIONS.

PEEL and wash the onions, and lay them in a broad-bottomed pan or kettle, so that the onions may not be piled one upon the other. Cover them with milk and water, and let them simmer slowly until done.

FRIED ONIONS.

PEEL and slice them evenly, and fry them in a pan of hot butter till slightly browned.

STEWED CUCUMBERS.

SLICE them thick, or halve, and divide them in two lengths; strew over some sliced onions; add salt and pepper, a little butter, and dredge in a little flour. Simmer slowly until done, and serve them up hot, at breakfast, or as a side-dish at dinner.

FRIED CUCUMBERS.

PEEL them, and cut them lengthways, and in slices about as thick as a silver dollar. Dry them on a cloth, season with pepper and salt, and sprinkle them thick with flour. Put some butter into a frying-pan; when it boils, put in the slices of cucumbers, and fry a light brown; serve hot.

DRESSED CUCUMBERS.

AFTER paring and slicing them very thin sprinkle some fine salt over them, and let them stand for a few minutes; then drain off the water; add more salt and some pepper, with two or three tablespoonfuls of the purest salad oil; turn the cucumbers well, that the whole may receive a portion of the seasoning. Then pour over them very strong vinegar; transfer into a clean dish, and serve.

13 *

STEWED MUSHROOMS.

REMOVE the skins and ends of the stalks, wash them very clean, and place them in a sauce-pan without water except what adheres to them. Season with pepper, salt and a piece of butter. Dredge over them a little flour. Cook slowly over the fire, stirring them often. Send to the table hot. The best mushrooms grow on uplands, or in high, open fields, where the air is pure.

BAKED BEANS.

HAVING soaked the beans over night in soft water, in the morning parboil them, adding salt to suit the taste. Then place them in a pan and set in the oven to bake, putting in a piece of good sweet butter: the size of a butternut will answer. Bake until tender and nicely browned over on top. Beans are very nutritious, and cooked in this way are palatable, digestible, and can be eaten by any one. It is a very common custom to cook them with a chunk of fat pork. The grease bakes out into the beans, making a most unwholesome and indigestible mess, destroying all the good flavor of the beans. If you want the pork, cook it in a dish by itself.

BOILED BEANS.

Soak over night any small white beans in soft water, put them in a strong bag, leaving room to swell; let them boil in a potful of water until done; hang them up, to let all the water drain off, and season with butter, pepper and salt to the taste.

BOILED GREEN PEAS.

Wash and drain the peas, which should be young and freshly shelled; put them into plenty of fast-boiling, salted water; when quite tender, drain them well, dish them quickly and serve very hot, with good melted butter, in a tureen.

BOILED RICE.

Pick the rice, and wash it thoroughly in cold water; after the second washing do not drain off the water till you are ready to put the rice on to cook. Prepare a sauce-pan of water with a little salt in it, and when it boils sprinkle in the rice. Boil it hard for twenty minutes, keeping the pan covered. Then take it from the fire and drain off the water. Afterward set the sauce-pan aside, with the lid off, to allow the rice to cool and the grains to separate. Rice, if properly boiled, should be soft and white, and every grain stand alone.

BAKED RICE.

BOIL one cup of rice in half pint of milk; when done take it out, place it in pudding-dish, and season with pepper and salt, and a quarter of a pound of butter.

FRIED RICE.

POUR your boiled rice into a shallow pudding-dish, having first seasoned it with pepper, salt and butter. Allow it to remain until cold and stiff; cut it in slices two inches thick, and fry in butter until it is of a nice brown.

SAUCES AND GRAVIES.

GENERAL REMARKS.

In making a good sauce but little merit can be claimed when the housekeeper or cook has plenty of good and proper materials on hand; but it is when a fine flavor has been produced from an inadequate supply that praise is justly due; as, for instance, giving a rich flavor of meat to a mess of potatoes or some other plain dish when no meat has been employed. But to do this it is necessary to know the qualities of the various vegetables, and how these may be made to resemble the juice of animal food. The vegetable products of which by far the most can be made by a skillful housekeeper are onions, mushrooms and carrots, which may be dressed so exquisitely as hardly to be distinguished from the gravy of beef.

Gravies should always be well adapted in flavor to the dishes they are to accompany. For some, a high degree of savor is desirable, but for delicate white meats this should be avoided, and a soft, smooth sauce of refined flavor be used. The bones of undressed meats will supply almost as good gravy stock as the meat itself, if well boiled down. Vermicelli or rasped cocoa-nut, lightly and very gently browned in a small quantity of butter, will both thicken and enrich gravies, if about an ounce of either of them to the pint of gravy be stewed gently in it half an hour to an hour, and then strained out. Too much thickening should be avoided. Before sending gravies to table see that they are all well skimmed; no particle of fat should ever be perceptible upon them.

FISH SAUCE, TO KEEP A YEAR.

CHOP twenty-four anchovies, bones and all, ten shalots (a species of small onion or garlic), a handful of scraped horse-radish, four blades of mace, one quart of white wine, one pint of anchovy liquor, one pint of claret, twelve cloves and twelve peppercorns; boil them together until reduced to a quart; strain and bottle for use. Two spoonfuls will be sufficient for a pound of butter.

SHRIMP SAUCE.

Wash a half pint of shrimps clean, put them into salted boiling water; when cold, cut off the heads and peel off the shells. Then place them in a stew-pan with a spoonful of anchovy liquor, and thicken some good drawn butter with the shrimps; boil up the whole five minutes, and squeeze in half a lemon. Shrimp sauce is eaten with salmon and other fine fish.

OYSTER SAUCE.

Scald a pint of oysters and strain them through a sieve; then wash some more in cold water, and take off their beards; put them in a stew-pan and pour the liquor over them; then add half a lemon, two blades of mace, and thicken it with good butter rolled in flour. Put in some more butter, boil it till it is melted; take out the mace and lemon, and squeeze the lemon-juice into the sauce; boil it, and stir it all the time. Put into a boat and simmer. For fish, add a large spoonful of anchovy liquor.

If your oysters are salt, and you can get no others, boil a pint of milk instead of the oyster liquor, seasoning with powdered nutmeg and mace, and enriching it with fresh butter dredged with flour.

CAPER SAUCE.

TAKE two large spoonfuls of capers and a little vinegar, stir them in a half pint of melted butter. This sauce is for boiled mutton. If you have no capers, pickled cucumbers chopped fine, or pickled radish pods or nasturtions, may be stirred in the butter as a substitute.

EGG SAUCE.

BOIL four eggs a quarter of an hour; dip them in cold water to prevent them looking blue; peel off the shell, chop all the yolks and the whites of two; stir them in melted butter. Serve with boiled fish or poultry.

CELERY SAUCE.

WASH a bundle of parsley in cold water. Then boil it six or seven minutes in salt water, drain, cut the leaves from the stalks, and chop them fine. Have ready some melted butter and stir in the parsley. Allow two small tablespoonfuls of leaves to half pint of butter. Serve with boiled fowls, rock fish, sea bass, and other boiled fresh fish. Also with knuckle of veal and calf's head boiled plain.

APPLE SAUCE.

PARE, core and slice some nice, juicy apples that are not too sweet; put them in a stew-pan with some lemon-peel, grated, and water enough to keep them from burning. Stew them till soft and tender, mash them to a paste, and sweeten well with brown sugar, adding a little butter and some nutmeg. To be eaten with roast pork, roast goose or roast duck.

PEACH SAUCE.

TAKE a quart of dried peaches (the richest are those with the skins on), soak them in cold water till tender; then drain and put them in a covered pan with very little water. Set them on the coals and simmer till entirely dissolved, then mash them with good brown sugar, and send to the table cold. To be eaten with roast meat, poultry and game.

CRANBERRY SAUCE.

PICK the cranberries over carefully, put a pound of broken lump sugar to a quart of the fruit; let them simmer down for a long time, add a little lemon-juice, pour into wetted moulds, and it will turn out in form.

14

ONION SAUCE.

SELECT some nice small onions, and boil them whole in milk, adding a very little salt and pepper, and some butter rolled in flour; let them boil till tender all through, but not till they lose their shape. Eat them with any sort of boiled meat.

MUSHROOM SAUCE.

WASH a pint of small button mushrooms, remove the stems and outside skins, stew them slowly in veal gravy or milk or cream, adding an onion, and seasoning with pepper, salt and a little butter rolled in flour. Their flavor will be heightened by salting a few the night before, to extract the juice. In dressing mushrooms, only those of a dull pearl color on the outside and the under part tinged with pale pink should be selected. If there is a poisonous one among them, the onion in the sauce will turn black. In such case throw the whole away.

VANILLA SAUCE.

SELECT a small stick of vanilla, split and break it up, and boil in a very little milk till all the flavor of the vanilla is extracted; strain it through very fine muslin and stir it into the cream. Give it one boil up in a small porcelain saucepan, and sweeten it well with white sugar. Send to the table hot.

MINT SAUCE.

WASH until entirely free from grit a bunch of spearmint; chop it fine, and mix with it one gill of vinegar and a quarter of a pound of sugar. This sauce is to be eaten with roast lamb.

CURRY POWDER.

To make curry powder, take one ounce of ginger, one ounce of mustard, one ounce of pepper, three ounces of coriander seed, three ounces of turmeric, half an ounce of cardamoms, one quarter ounce of cayenne pepper, one quarter ounce of cinnamon, and one quarter ounce of cummin seed. Pound all these ingredients very fine in a mortar, sift them and cork tight in a bottle.

VENISON SAUCE.

Two spoonfuls of currant jelly, one stick of cinnamon, one blade of mace, grated white bread,

ten tablespoonfuls of water; let it stew, and when
done serve in a dish with venison steak.

SAUCE FOR WILD FOWL.

ONE gill of claret, with as much water, some
grated bread, three heads of shalots, a little whole
pepper, mace, grated nutmeg and salt; let it stew
over the fire, then heat it up with butter, and put
it under the wild fowl, which, being a little roasted,
will afford gravy to mix with the sauce.

CELERY SAUCE.

TAKE a large bunch of celery, wash clean and
pare; cut it very small and boil it softly till
tender; add half a pint of cream, some mace,
nutmeg, and a small piece of butter rolled in
flour; then boil gently. This is a good sauce for
roasted or boiled fowls, turkeys, partridges or
other game.

WALNUT CATSUP.

THE walnuts should be young, freshly gathered
and tender. Keep them in salt and water four
days; then pound them in a marble mortar;

to every dozen walnuts add a quart of vinegar; stir them every day for a week; then press all the juice from them through a bag; to every quart add one teaspoonful of pounded cloves, one of mace, one of grated nutmeg, and a small piece of whole pepper. Let the whole boil for about thirty minutes, and then bottle it, corking each bottle tightly and sealing the corks.

MUSHROOM CATSUP.

TAKE a quarter of a peck of large and freshly-gathered mushrooms. Cut off the ends of the stems, and place them in a deep pan, sprinkling salt over each layer. Let them remain for two days. Then put them in a sieve and strain off the juice; pour it into your preserving kettle. To every pint of the liquor allow one dozen cloves, the same of allspice, two or three pieces of mace, and half of a small nutmeg grated; let it boil for fifteen minutes; then remove it from the fire and let it stand for two or three days. Then, through a funnel, pour it gently from the sediment into small bottles. Finish with a spoonful of sweet oil on the top of each. Cork the bottles tightly and seal the corks.

OYSTER CATSUP.

SELECT large salt oysters, wash them in their liquor, and pound them in a marble mortar, leaving out the parts that are hard. To each pint of pounded oyster add half a pint of vinegar. Let them boil, and as the scum rises skim it off; to every quart of boiled oysters add a teaspoonful of beaten pepper, a small teaspoonful of powdered mace, and cayenne pepper and salt to taste; boil and strain through a sieve; when cool, bottle it up, filling the bottles full. Dip the cork in melted rosin or beeswax.

TOMATO CATSUP.

TAKE ripe tomatoes, scald them and remove their skins; let them stand a day covered with salt; strain them thoroughly to remove the seed. To every quart of tomatoes add three ounces of cloves, two ounces of black pepper, two nutmegs and a very little cayenne pepper, with a very little salt. Boil the liquor half an hour; let it cool and settle. Add one pint of best cider vinegar. Bottle, cork and seal tightly, and keep in a cool place. This catsup, when ready for use, should be very thick and smooth.

MELTED OR DRAWN BUTTER.

NUMEROUS sauces are made with melted butter.
If mixed with too much flour and water, and not
enough of butter, it will be very poor, particularly
if the water is in too large proportion. To prepare it properly allow a quarter of a pound of
nice butter to a heaped tablespoonful of flour.
Mix the butter and flour thoroughly before it
goes to the fire. Then add to it four large tablespoonfuls of milk or hot water, well mixed in.
Hold it over the fire in a small saucepan kept for
the purpose. Take care there is no blaze where
the saucepan is held. Cover it and shake it over
the fire till it boils. Then, having skimmed it,
add three or four hard-boiled eggs chopped small,
and give it one more boil up. None but the
freshest and best quality of butter should be used.
This sauce is usually sent to table with boiled fish
and boiled poultry, also with boiled mutton, lamb
and veal.

GRAVY FOR FOWLS.

TAKE half a pound of lean beef—slice and score
it—and a piece of butter the size of a nutmeg;
sprinkle with flour, add a small onion; then put

it all into a stew-pan. Stir it round over the fire ten minutes; then pour into it one pint of boiling water; skim it carefully; let it all boil together for five minutes; strain it, and it is ready to serve.

BROWN GRAVY.

TAKE a sheep's melt, cut it into slices half an inch thick, flour them lightly, and either fry them a pale brown, or dissolve a small slice of butter in a thick saucepan; lay them in and shake them over a moderate fire until they have taken sufficient color; then pour gradually over them between a half and three-quarters of a pint of boiling water; add a little seasoning of pepper and salt, and stew the gravy very gently for upward of an hour and a half. Strain, and skim off the fat, and it will be ready for the table. When it is to accompany ducks or geese, brown a minced onion with the melt, and add a sprig of lemon thyme.

How to Make Bread.

GENERAL REMARKS.

The importance of this branch of the intelligent, painstaking housekeeper's duties can scarcely be over-estimated. As there is no one article of food that enters so largely into our daily fare as bread, so no degree of skill in preparing other articles can compensate for lack of knowledge in the art of making good, palatable and nutritious bread. Many a case of chronic dyspepsia is attributable primarily to the habitual eating of heavy, sour or ill-baked bread, and in almost every case this is caused by the ignorance or negligence of the maker or baker. A little earnest attention to the subject will enable any one to comprehend the theory, and then ordinary care in practice will make her familiar with the process. To make good bread, the first desideratum is good flour. Be careful to procure the best, as it is the worst sort of so-called economy to buy an inferior article; recollect, by the way, that dampness will soon spoil the best of flour, hence great care must be used to keep it in a dry place. Second only to the quality of the flour in importance is that of the yeast. This should be pure, sweet and lively; the yeast of mild home-brewed beer is frequently used (this requires no purifying, but should be passed through a hair-sieve, first thinning it with warm milk or water), and below will be found some recipes for making excellent yeast. Having secured unexceptionable materials, the rest of the secret of success lies in two words—care and work: care, in mixing the ingredients, in keeping the dough from souring, in having the oven properly heated when the bread is put into it, in baking sufficiently yet not too much, and in handling it while hot to keep it from falling; and work, in kneading it thoroughly.

GOOD YEAST.

Boil four good-sized potatoes; mash or sift fine; to this add a half cupful of sugar, two-thirds cupful of salt, one quart of boiling water, one pint of cold water, one cupful of old yeast; cover the mixture closely and let it rise over-night, when it will be ready for use. One gill will raise three pints of meal.

UNRIVALED YEAST.

On one morning boil two ounces of the best hops in four quarts of water half an hour; strain it, and let the liquor cool to the consistency of new milk; then put it in an earthen bowl, and add a small handful of salt and half a pound of brown sugar; beat up one pound of good flour with some of the liquor; then mix all well together, and let it stand till the third day after; then add three pounds of potatoes, boiled and mashed through a colander; let it stand a day, then strain and bottle, and it is fit for use. It must be stirred frequently while it is making, and kept near a fire. One advantage of this yeast is its spontaneous fermentation, requiring the help of no old yeast; if care be taken to let it ferment well in the bowl, it may immediately be corked tightly. Be careful to keep it in a cool place. Before using it shake the bottle up well. It will keep in a cool place two months, and is best the latter part of the time. Use about the same quantity as of other yeast.

SUMMER YEAST.

BOIL one pint of hops in one quart of water; strain it hot on one pint of flour and one table-spoonful of salt; stir it well, and cool; half a pint of yeast; let it rise; add as much Indian meal as will make a stiff dough. Roll into rolls. When they are light, cut them up in thin cakes and dry them in the shade, turning them several times a day. Keep in a dry place. Use to a baking of four two-pound loaves two cakes soaked in tepid water an hour. It is portable, and every way desirable for warm weather.

GOOD YEAST.

BOIL a small handful of hops in a quart of water. Boil until done five medium-sized pota-toes pared. Now make them smooth with one and a half pints of flour. Pour in the water strained from the hops. Stir this until it is a thin batter, adding hot water if too thick. Let it stand until little more than milk-warm; then add a teacupful of good brewer's yeast. Let it stand in a warm place eight or ten hours, when add a tablespoonful of salt and two tablespoonsful of white sugar. Mix well; set it away in a stone jar or jug, and it is ready for use.

WHEAT BREAD.

CAREFULLY sift sufficient flour for the quantity of bread desired. Put into the bread-bowl, to every quart of flour, two and a half gills of water, a large spoonful of yeast and a teaspoonful of salt; stir well and add a handful from each quart of flour; mix thoroughly, and then combine into it about one-third of the flour. The mixture you now have is called the sponge. Set the sponge in a warm (not hot) place till it becomes very light; then add the remainder of the flour and knead very thoroughly. Make into loaves, and let them rise; as soon as they begin to crack on the top they are ready for the oven, which should be very warm, with tendency to get warmer slowly. A little butter or sweet lard improves the bread, besides making it keep fresher.

WHEAT AND MUSH BREAD.

SPREAD eight quarts of flour in your bread-bowl, so as to leave a large cavity in the centre. Make two quarts of sifted white corn meal into mush by boiling it in either water or milk, and when it becomes cool enough to add the yeast without scalding it turn it into the flour; stir in

15

warm milk or water, mixing in a portion of the flour and a teacupful of good yeast; cover the whole closely, and let it stand over-night. Knead it well in the morning, and make it into loaves. It will rise soon near the fire. Bake it thoroughly, and you will have an excellent article of light, sweet and nutritious bread, which will keep moist longer than any other and make the flour "hold out" wonderfully.

GOOD COUNTRY BREAD.

AT noon pare and wash your potatoes for dinner; have four or five more than you want to eat. When done, drain the boiling water on enough flour to make a stiff batter; mash your extra potatoes, and stir in with a teaspoonful of salt while hot; when cool have your emptying cake soaked soft; stir in; let it stand in a warm room to rise. Before you go to rest for the night take milk (if you have it; if not, warm water), and mix it up hard and let it stand until morning; knead it up again after breakfast; mould and put in tins, and it will soon be ready to bake. Do not burn. If you do not have good bread, it is because your flour is poor.

WHEAT AND RICE BREAD.

1. BOIL half a pound of rice in three pints of water till the whole becomes thick and pulpy. With this, yeast, six pounds of flour and salt to taste, make your dough. It is an excellent summer bread.

2. To make a very palatable and wholesome loaf of bread, take a pint of boiled rice (not overdone); mash it and pass it through a sieve; rub with it two tablespoonsful of butter, and pour in a pint and a half of milk. Mix well, and add sufficient sifted flour to make moderately stiff paste, and bake brown.

WHEAT AND WHITE POTATO BREAD.

TAKE one pint of new milk, one pint of boiling water, and mix with six good-sized potatoes well boiled and mashed; stir in a large spoonful of salt, the same of sugar, and flour enough to make a stiff batter; set it in a warm place to rise, and when it has risen so as to double its first bulk, stir in more flour and knead it slightly; then divide it into three loaves, putting them into deep tins, and when they have again risen as before, bake in a moderate oven.

WHEAT AND SWEET POTATO BREAD.

SAME as preceding, except that instead of six white you use sweet potatoes enough to make about a quart of pulp when mashed and passed through a sieve. Be careful to boil them just enough to mash readily; if they are soft and watery, they will not make good bread.

BROWN BREAD.

TAKE two quarts of corn meal, one quart of rye or wheat flour, and mix with one quart of sour milk or buttermilk, adding one large spoonful of saleratus, two small cupsful of molasses, a little salt and enough of water or sweet milk to make a thick batter. Bake in a deep dish three hours in a hot oven, letting it cool gradually another hour; or, as some prefer, it may be steamed until quite done, and then placed just long enough in the oven to give it a desirable firmness.

DYSPEPSIA BREAD.

THREE quarts of Graham flour, one quart of soft water, warm but not hot, one gill of fresh yeast, one teaspoonful of saleratus. If molasses is used, heap the teaspoon.

THIRDED BREAD.

ONE pint each of wheat flour, rye and Indian meal, half a teacupful of yeast; mix with warm water into a stiff dough; set to rise about eight hours, knead, make into loaves and bake in a hot oven.

RYE AND INDIAN BREAD.

Two parts of sifted corn meal, one part of rye flour, one teaspoonful of salt, one teaspoonful of saleratus, one tablespoonful of molasses; mix to a stiff dough with one part of water and two parts of milk. Bake slowly five hours.

MILK BREAD OR ROLLS.

WEIGH one pound of flour; put it in a tray; make a hole in the centre; put in yeast, one egg, two ounces of butter, quarter of a teaspoonful of salt, one teaspoonful of sugar; have half a pint of warm milk; put in a little; mix all well together; then add by degrees the flour and also the milk (it may not take the half pint of milk, but that depends on the flour); stir all well; work it for a few minutes until it is a stiff dough; take a little

15 *

flour, and rub off the paste which sticks to the tray; sift a little flour on the tray; put the dough in again; work it well; make into loaves, and set in a warm place till quite light; then egg over with a brush and bake in a *quick* oven. Rolls may be made in the same way by cutting the dough into pieces of suitable size.

FRENCH BREAD.

Two quarts of flour; scald one pint of it; butter, two ounces; mix with cold water two-thirds of a cup of yeast. When mixed, knead fifteen minutes, using as little additional flour as possible. Rise twelve hours; cut and work with a knife ten minutes before baking.

GERMAN BREAD.

One pint of milk well boiled, one teacupful of sugar, two tablespoonsful of nice lard or butter, two-thirds of a teacupful of baker's yeast. Make a rising with the milk and yeast; when light, mix in the sugar and shortening, with flour enough to make as soft a dough as can be handled. Flour the paste-board well, roll out about one-half inch thick; put this quantity into two large pans; make about a dozen indentures with the finger on the top; put a small piece of butter in each, and sift over the whole one tablespoonful of sugar mixed with one teaspoonful of cinnamon. Let this stand for a second rising; when perfectly light, bake in a quick oven fifteen or twenty minutes.

PLAIN CRISP BISCUITS.

Two pounds of flour, two eggs, one ounce of butter, a little salt, milk sufficient to make it into a stiff dough; beat the eggs, and mix them with the flour, butter and salt; pour in enough milk to form a stiff dough; knead till quite smooth; roll very thin; cut into round cakes and prick them with a fork. Bake them till very crisp in a slow oven.

DELICIOUS CORN BREAD.

Two cupsful of yellow corn meal, two cupsful of flour, one cupful of sugar, one egg, milk enough to make a moderately stiff batter, a piece of butter the size of an egg, one teaspoonful of soda, two tea-spoonsful of cream of tartar, one teaspoonful of salt.

ITALIAN BREAD.

ONE pound of butter, one pound of powdered loaf sugar, one pound and two ounces of flour, eight eggs, half a pound of citron and lemon peel. Mix as pound cake. If the mixture begins to curdle, which it is very likely to do, from the quantity of eggs, add a little flour. When the eggs are all used and it is light, stir in the rest of the flour. Bake in long, narrow tins papered and buttered. First put in a layer of the mixture, and cover it with the peeling cut in thin slices. Proceed in this way until three parts full, and bake in a *moderate* oven.

GRAFTON MILK BISCUITS.

BOIL and grate two white potatoes; add two teaspoonsful of brown sugar; pour boiling water over these, enough to soften them. When tepid, add one small teacup of yeast; when light, warm three ounces of butter in one pint of milk, a little salt, and flour enough to make a stiff sponge; when risen, work it on the board; put it back in the tray to rise again; when risen, roll into cakes, and let them stand half an hour. Bake in a *quick* oven. These biscuits are perfect.

FINE BREAKFAST ROLLS.

Two pounds of flour, quarter of a pound of butter, three medium potatoes boiled and mashed, one gill of yeast, one saltspoonful of salt; rub flour, butter and potatoes together till they are smooth, and add the salt and yeast, and milk enough to make soft dough; set to rise, and in the morning make into rolls and place them on buttered tins; in a few minutes they will be ready to bake in a *quick* oven.

FRIED CAKES.

Two cups of sugar, two cups of sweet milk, half a cup of butter, two eggs, two teaspoonsful of cream of tartar, one teaspoonful of soda, a pinch of salt, spice. Add flour in sufficient quantity to roll in shape, and fry in hot lard.

HARD TEA BISCUITS.

Two pounds of flour, a quarter of a pound of butter, a saltspoonful of salt, three gills of milk; cut up the butter, and rub it in the flour; then add the salt and milk; knead the dough for half an hour; make it into cakes about as large round

M

as a small teacup and half an inch thick. Prick
them with a fork; bake them in a *moderate* oven
until they are a light brown.

FRENCH ROLLS.

Two pounds of flour, two ounces of butter, two
eggs, one teacupful of yeast, one saltspoonful of
salt; rub the butter and flour together; whisk the
eggs and add them with the salt and yeast, and
sufficient milk to make dough; knead well, and
replace in pan to rise; when light, knead again
lightly; make into rolls about a quarter of an inch
thick; place on slightly-buttered tins, cover with
a clean towel, and set in a warm elevated place to
rise; when very light, bake in a *quick* oven.

POTATO ROLLS.

One pound of boiled and mashed potatoes, two
ounces of butter, one teaspoonful of salt, one teacupful of yeast, two pounds of flour, milk to make
a soft dough; boil and mash the potatoes, while
warm, with the butter, a little salt and milk sufficient to make them as soft as a batter; when cool,
add the flour and mix into a light dough; if neces-

sary, more milk may be added; knead well, return it to the pan in which it was mixed, and let it rise; when light, knead it over again, then make it into small cakes, place them on slightly buttered tins and put them in a warm place to rise; when light, bake in a *quick* oven; when done, wash the tops lightly with a little water, and cover them with a clean towel, to make them soft.

EGG RUSKS.

MELT three ounces of butter in a pint of milk; beat six eggs with a quarter of a pound of sugar; mix these with flour enough to make a batter; add one gill of yeast, half a teaspoonful of salt; when light, add flour enough to make it stiff enough to mould. Make them into small cakes, and let them stand a short time to rise before baking.

UNEXCELLED MILK ROLLS.

MIX one pint of milk with six ounces of butter, half a teacup of pulverized sugar, one teaspoonful of salt, one and a half teacups of yeast, and flour enough to make a sponge; let it stand till perfectly light; knead it into a loaf, return to the tray, and rise again; then roll out the dough, cut it into small cakes and stand half an hour. Bake in a *quick* oven fifteen minutes. Leave them in the pans till wanted for tea, to prevent the undercrust hardening. Yeast for these must be made the day preceding: potato yeast is best.

VINEGAR BISCUITS.

TAKE two quarts of flour, one large tablespoonful of lard or butter, one tablespoonful and a half of vinegar and one teaspoonful of soda; put the soda in the vinegar and stir it well; stir in the flour; beat two eggs very light and add to it; make a dough stiff enough to roll out, and cut with a biscuit-cutter two inches thick and bake in a *quick* oven.

BATTER CAKES.—VERY FINE.

ONE quart of unbolted flour, half a pint of Indian meal, one gill of yeast; mix the flour and meal, pour on enough warm water to make batter rather thicker than that for buckwheat cakes; add the yeast and a little salt; when light, bake on griddle not too hot.

BUTTERMILK BISCUITS.

MAKE smooth batter of one quart of buttermilk and flour; add two large spoonsful of white Indian meal, two eggs well beaten, salt, one teaspoonful of soda dissolved in milk; add flour to make soft dough; make into biscuits, and bake not too quickly.

SOUFFLE BISCUITS.

RUB four ounces of butter into a quart of flour; make it into a paste with milk; knead it well, roll it as thin as paper, and bake to look white.

SODA BISCUITS.

THREE pints of flour, three teaspoonsful of dry cream of tartar, butter the size of a walnut, one teaspoonful of soda dissolved in milk. Make a soft dough with milk, divide into small cakes and bake immediately fifteen minutes.

CRUMPETS.

Two pounds of flour, one gill of yeast, milk and water to make a stiff batter. Let it rise six hours. Bake in muffin-rings or on a griddle.

16

PLAIN MUFFINS.

ONE quart of flour, half a teacupful of yeast, salt to taste, warm water to make a thick batter; beat well with a spoon; rise eight hours; fill muffin-rings half full; bake fifteen or twenty minutes.

RICE MUFFINS.

BOIL soft and dry half a cup of rice; stir in three teaspoonsful of sugar, piece of butter the size of an egg and a little salt, one pint of sweet milk, one cup of yeast, two quarts of flour. Let it rise all night. If sour in the morning, add a little soda dissolved in milk, and bake in muffin-rings.

MILK MUFFINS.

THREE cups of flour, one pint of milk, two eggs well whisked, a little salt. Bake three-quarters of an hour.

EGG MUFFINS.

To one quart of milk add four eggs well beaten, a lump of butter size of an egg and flour enough to make a stiff batter. Stir in half a pint of yeast; let them stand till perfectly light and bake in tin rings on a griddle.

SWEET MUFFINS.

ONE half cup of yeast, two tablespoonsful of sugar, one egg, one pint and one-eighth of flour, one cup of milk.

RYE DROP CAKES.

To one pint of sour buttermilk add two eggs, a small teaspoonful of soda, a little salt and rye meal sufficient to make a batter that will spread a little, but not run. Drop in muffin-rings with a spoon. For baking they will require twice the time of common griddle-cakes. They are also nice baked in cups about fifteen minutes.

WAFFLES.

FOUR eggs, one quart of milk, quarter of a pound of butter, salt, flour to make a thin batter. Butter your waffle-irons well, and bake quickly.

WAFFLES WITH YEAST.

ONE quart of warm milk, one ounce of butter, three eggs, one gill of yeast, tablespoonful of salt, and flour enough to make a stiff batter. Let it rise all night.

RICE WAFFLES.

BOIL two gills of rice very soft; mix with it three gills of flour, a little salt, two ounces of melted butter, two eggs well beaten and as much milk as will make a thick batter; beat it till very light, and bake in waffle-irons.

CORN MEAL WAFFLES.

Two eggs, yolks well beaten, one tablespoonful of butter, one tablespoonful of flour, one teaspoonful of salt, one pint of sweet milk, one pint of meal twice sifted, half a teaspoonful of soda; add last the whites of the eggs well beaten.

HOMINY WAFFLES.

TAKE two teacups of hot hominy, one tablespoonful of butter; when cold, add one teacup of wheat flour, salt, as much milk as will make a stiff batter and three eggs beaten well; mix, adding a mite of soda, same of cream of tartar. Bake in waffle-irons.

NEW YEAR'S CRACKERS.

MIX with some fine sifted flour a pinch of salt, and make it into a smooth paste with some thin cream. Roll out thin, prick them all over, bake gently and store them as soon as cold in a dry canister or cake-box to keep them crisp. They are very good.

VELVET CAKES.

ONE quart of flour, three eggs, a quart of milk and a gill of yeast; make into a batter; let it rise well and add a large spoonful of melted butter, and bake not too fast in muffin-rings.

YORKSHIRE BISCUITS.

Two pounds of flour, a quarter of a pound of butter, one pint of rich milk, half a pint of yeast, two eggs; beat the eggs very light and mix them with the other ingredients into a dough; let it rise, and then work it over and make it into cakes. Place them on tins to rise again. When light, bake them in a *quick* oven.

CORN BATTER CAKES.

ONE quart of milk, three eggs, salt, and as much sifted corn meal as will make a thin batter; beat well together with one tablespoonful of wheat flour; bake in small cakes, and serve hot.

16 *

SPONGE GRIDDLE CAKES.

TAKE one quart of mush; while warm, add one pint of buttermilk, one pint of sweet milk or water, one teaspoonful of soda; stir in flour until it is a batter; let it rise until morning, then bake on the griddle and serve while still hot.

BUCKWHEAT CAKES.

ONE quart of buckwheat meal, one pint of wheat flour or Indian meal, half a teacupful of yeast, salt to taste; mix the flour, buckwheat and salt with as much water moderately warm as will make it into a thin batter; beat it well, then add the yeast; when well mixed, set it in a warm place to rise; as soon as they are very light, grease the griddle and bake them a delicate brown. Butter them with good butter and serve hot.

FLANNEL CAKES.

ONE quart of milk, four eggs, one cup of yeast, one dessertspoonful of salt, flour enough for a thinnish batter; set to rise as above; bake like buckwheat cakes. Cakes half Indian and half wheat are very nice. Quite good cakes may be made without the eggs.

FLANNEL CAKES.

ONE pint of fine Indian meal, one pint of flour, one teaspoonful of salt, two gills of yeast; mix the wheat and Indian meal together with as much tepid water as will make it into a batter not quite as thin as for buckwheat cakes; then add the salt and yeast, and set them in a moderately warm place to rise; when light, bake them on a griddle; butter and send to table hot.

HOMINY CAKES.

MIX with cold hominy an equal quantity of white flour until perfectly smooth; add a teaspoonful of salt and thin off with buttermilk in part of which a teaspoonful of soda has been dissolved; when of the consistency of griddle cakes, add a dessertspoonful of melted butter, and bake as usual. They are delicious, and the absence of eggs will not be noticed.

MOLASSES DELIGHTS.

ONE quart of meal or flour, half a pint of soft-boiled hominy, one tablespoonful of butter, cup and a half or two cups of clear molasses, milk to make stiff batter, and bake on griddle.

CORN MEAL CAKES, IN TINS.

ONE quart of meal, one pint of boiling milk, a teaspoonful of salt, a teaspoonful of soda; set it to rise in a warm place; beat three eggs and put in a little cream of tartar. Bake in tins and cut in squares for the table.

INDIAN PONE.

MAKE one quart of thin mush; when this is nearly cold, take as much meal as will make it into a thick batter; add salt to taste; cover it close and let it remain over night; in the morning, butter your pans and bake it in a *moderate* oven. It may be made in small cakes and baked on tins. Must be eaten hot. A little butter in the making adds much to the palatableness. Many prefer coarse meal, but fine yellow makes the better pone.

SHORT CAKES.

ONE pound and a quarter of flour, half a pound of butter; cut up the butter in the flour; add a little salt, and mix the whole into a dough with cold water; roll into small cakes; bake them a light brown on both sides; cut them open and butter while hot.

CHEESE BISCUITS.

Two ounces of butter, two ounces of flour, two ounces of grated cheese, a little Cayenne and salt. To be made into a thin paste and rolled out very thin, then cut in pieces four inches long and one inch broad; bake a very light brown, and send to table as hot as possible.

GENUINE SCOTCH SHORT-BREAD.

Two pounds of fine flour, one pound of fresh sweet butter, half a pound of finest sifted sugar; thoroughly knead together without one drop of water; roll out to half an inch in thickness, and place it on paper in a shallow pan; bake very slowly until of proper crispness. Some like to insert in top surface a few caraway confections and small pieces of orange-peel. The cake, to be good, must be very brittle—*scotice*, "short."

MILK BREAKFAST BUNS.

PLACE on a table or slab one pound of flour, half a teaspoonful of salt, two teaspoonsful of sugar, three teaspoonsful of fresh yeast, two ounces of butter and one egg; have some new milk, pour in a gill; mix all together, adding more milk to form a nice dough; then put some flour in a cloth; put the dough in and lay it in a warm place; let it rise for about two hours, cut it in pieces the size of eggs, roll them even and mark the top with a sharp knife; egg over and bake quick; serve hot or cold.

FINE ARROWROOT BISCUITS.

RUB together three-quarters of a pound each of sugar and butter; add three well-beaten eggs, and then stir in two cupsful each of sifted arrowroot and flour; roll out thin, cut them into proper size; place into buttered tins, and bake in a slow oven.

PLAIN ARROWROOT BISCUITS.

Two cupsful each of sifted arrowroot and flour, one cupful of sugar, two tablespoonsful of butter and a little yeast; knead well, roll out and cut into biscuits; place them on tins, and let them stand to rise for half an hour or upward before baking.

CINNAMON BREAD.

MAKE two pounds of dough just as for wheat bread, and let it get very light; melt a quarter of a pound of butter in half a pint of milk and beat three eggs; incorporate the butter, milk and eggs with the dough, and add a saltspoonful of soda dissolved in tepid water; mix in a bowl a pint of clean brown sugar with sufficient sweet butter to make a stiff paste, and flavor this mixture with two large tablespoonsful of ground cinnamon. Make the dough into a round loaf; cut deep incisions over its surface; fill these with the cinnamon mixture and close the orifices; bake as other bread, and when done, glaze it with the white of an egg and powdered sugar. Should be eaten fresh.

GRAHAM CAKES.

ONE pint of Graham meal, one cup of wheat flour, three-fourths of a cup of yeast, salt. Mix at night a stiff batter; in the morning thin a little with warm water, adding a little soda. Bake on a griddle.

GRAHAM BISCUITS.

ONE quart of meal, one teaspoonful of lard, two spoonsful of molasses, two spoonsful of wheat flour, one-half cup of yeast, salt. Mix as for any bread; let it rise all night. Put in muffin-rings in the morning, and let them stand half an hour before baking.

ECONOMY GRIDDLE CAKES.

SOAK stale bread in water till quite soft; strain off the water; rub the bread through a colander; add milk to make a stiff batter, and bake on griddle. Two or three eggs to each quart of soaked bread improve the cakes materially.

ECONOMY BREAD CAKES.

POUR sufficient boiling water over stale bread to soften it; mash it through a colander, and add as much wheat flour as bread, and as much milk as will make it as thick as batter usually is, one teaspoonful of soda, two teaspoonsful of cream of tartar. Bake immediately in *quick* oven.

EXCELLENT BREAKFAST CAKES.

A LARGE teaspoonful of baking powder mixed dry, with about three-quarters of a pound of flour, a piece of lard the size of a large walnut, a little salt, as much cold milk as will moisten the above, which is to be mixed with a spoon or knife very lightly and very quickly; roll out to half an inch in thickness, cut into cakes with the top of a dredging-box, and put them immediately on a hot griddle or into a warm oven.

HOMINY CAKES.

A PINT of small hominy, a pint of white Indian meal sifted, a saltspoonful of salt, three large table-spoonsful of fresh butter, three eggs, or three table-spoonsful of strong yeast, a quart of milk; having washed the hominy and soaked all night, boil it soft, drain, and, while hot, mix it with meal, adding the salt and butter. Then mix gradually with the milk, and set it away to cool. Beat the eggs very light, and add them gradually to the mixture. The whole should make a thick batter. Bake on a griddle.

GERMAN PUFFS.

SEVEN spoonsful of flour, three eggs, one quart of milk, a little salt; beat the flour and eggs together, then add the milk. Bake fifteen minutes in cups.

MARYLAND BISCUITS.

THREE pints of sifted flour, one tablespoonful of good lard, one pint of cold water, salt to the taste; make into a stiff dough; work it till it cracks or blisters, then break (do not cut) and make into biscuits; stick the top of them with a fork.

17

CORN BREAD.

ONE pint of white corn meal; stir into it one teaspoonful of dry saleratus and half a teaspoonful of salt; then add two eggs, one pint of sour milk and three tablespoonsful of sour cream; beat about five minutes, and bake in pans half an inch deep. If you have no cream, use a tablespoonful of butter.

RYE BATTERS.

ONE-HALF a cupful each of flour and molasses, two cupsful each of rye and sour milk, sufficient soda and salt.

WHEAT FLOUR CRACKERS.

ONE quart of flour, four ounces of butter or lard, half a teaspoonful of soda, the same of salt, sweet milk; rub the butter thoroughly into the flour and salt; dissolve the soda in the milk, and enough more to take up the flour, which should be made into a very stiff dough; the more the dough is pounded or kneaded, the better the crackers; roll out to the desired thickness—half an inch—and bake quickly.

HOW TO MAKE CAKES.

GENERAL REMARKS.

CAKE is indeed one of the luxuries of our table, yet it might almost claim a place among the necessaries, so universally does it demand at least an occasional use even among those of less than moderate means. Cake, when home-made, costs scarcely one-half the store-price; hence, the importance of the housekeeper's being thoroughly conversant with this branch of Domestic Economy. We can but give the outline, the theory: practice alone can ensure success; the most careful, painstaking housewife may meet with discouraging results in her first attempts, even though she may think she is following most exactly the details of the recipe; total failure at the first, resulting in heavy, soggy or doughy cake, should not discourage her, but should rather spur her to renewed efforts, with full determination to succeed. "If you don't succeed at first, try, try again." In cake making or baking, more than in any other line of culinary work, much indeed depends on the quality of the materials used, but far more on care and skill in manipulation. Attention to quantity of each ingredient is very necessary, if not absolutely indispensable, and to be sure of exactness it is necessary to have a clear conception of relative weights and measures. It is well to ascertain how much certain cups and bowls hold, and use them always for measuring ingredients.

Before proceeding to give recipes some general instructions applicable to most styles of cake will be found useful. Where yeast is used, special care must be exercised to have it sweet and free from bitterness. One very important fact is often overlooked—it is this: the ingredients, such as flour, butter, sugar, eggs, etc., should usually all be of a uniform temperature, rather *warmer* than their average natural heat. Eggs will beat better near a fire; they should be beaten very long, whites and yolks separately; a wooden bowl and wooden beater are preferable to others. Butter should be moderately soft, but not melted in the least. If only slightly melted, heavy, greasy cake is the sure result. Sugar should be rolled or sifted in a warm room before used. Flour or meal should also be invariably sifted. Currants should be thoroughly washed the day before they are wanted, and spread thin on tin near the fire to dry; if damp, they will make cake heavy; before putting them in the cake, dust them well with flour and shake them. Raisins should be stoned and chopped small. Lemon-peel, almonds, etc., should be beaten in a mortar with a few drops of wine or water to a smooth paste. All the ingredients should be properly prepared before commencing to mix any of them. Lemon-juice, vinegar or saleratus, when used, should be the last added. The moulds or pans (when paper is not used) should be well buttered; if the cake sticks, dip the pan for an instant in cold water, taking care that none gets to the cake itself. The heat of the oven should be carefully regulated; it should be just hot enough to raise the cake gently and gradually, without too soon hardening or crisping the top, but this is a point that can be learned only from experience. To determine when the cake is done, run into it a broom-straw; if a particle adheres to it, the cake is not done.

Cake should never be kept in wooden drawers or boxes, but in covered earthen pans or crocks, or tin boxes.

17 *

GINGERSNAPS.

ONE pint of molasses, half a pint of butter, ginger to taste, a teaspoonful of saleratus, flour enough to make a stiff dough, salt to taste; set the molasses on the fire; as soon as it becomes thin put in the butter and ginger; let it come to a boil; let it cool, and add the flour and saleratus; knead it smooth and stiff, roll thin, cut in size to suit, and bake in a *quick* oven. A very good snap may be made by substituting good sweet lard for butter, same quantity.

SUGAR GINGERSNAPS.

SAME as first of preceding, except substitute for the molasses ten ounces of white (not loaf) sugar, dissolved in one pint of sweet milk (or water).

IMPERIAL GINGERBREAD.

SIX ounces of butter rubbed into twelve ounces of flour; half a pint of molasses and a pint of cream, mixed carefully, and mix in a quarter pound of white sugar, two tablespoonsful of ginger and essence of lemon to suit; stir the whole well together into a stiff paste, adding a little flour, if necessary; cut into shapes or spread in a buttered pan, and bake in a *moderate* oven.

GINGERNUTS.

HALF a pound each of flour, butter and brown sugar, three tablespoonsful of ginger and molasses to make a stiff paste; roll thin, cut in shapes, sizes to suit, and bake in a *slow* oven.

HONEY GINGERNUTS.

HONEY and brown sugar each half a pound; put with a little grated lemon or orange-peel into a saucepan, and simmer well together; add quarter of a pound of butter, one ounce (or more to taste) ginger and flour to make a stiff dough; roll thin, cut in shapes size to suit, and bake in a *slow* oven.

SUGAR GINGERBREAD.

ONE pound of sugar, one pound of flour, five eggs; beat the sugar and eggs to a cream, and add ginger, rose-water and the flour, also teaspoonful of dissolved saleratus and salt to taste. Bake in loaf or divide into cakes.

COCOANUT GINGERBREAD.

TEN ounces of fine flour, six ounces of rice flour, rind of a lemon grated, one ounce of ginger; mix these well and pour on them a pound of treacle nearly boiling and five ounces of fresh butter and five ounces of sugar melted together in a sauce-pan; beat the mixture, which will be almost a batter, with a wooden spoon, till it is quite smooth; when it is quite cold, add five ounces of grated cocoanut; when this is thoroughly blended with the mass, lay the paste in small pieces upon a buttered tin, and bake in a *very slow* oven. The same recipe will answer for other kinds, by sub-stituting lemon, orange, citron, or other flavors, to taste, for cocoanut.

SUGAR GINGERBREAD, No. 2.

Two cupsful of butter, four cupsful of white (not loaf) sugar, one cupful of milk, two teaspoons-ful of saleratus, one egg, ginger to taste, and flour to make dough to roll out. Bake in a *moderate* oven.

GINGERBREAD.

A HEAPING teacupful of sifted flour; rub into it about a tablespoonful of butter; add one teacupful of molasses, ginger and salt to taste, and milk (or water) enough to make a thick batter; mix thor-oughly, and add a teaspoonful of saleratus dis-solved in milk; bake immediately in a *moderate* oven.

SOFT GINGERBREAD.

ONE cupful of molasses, one teaspoonful of salt in a cupful of cold water, nearly a tablespoonful or butter, one teaspoonful of ginger (other spices, if desired), flour to make a stiff batter, and add one teaspoonful of soda; bake in a *moderate* oven.

LEMON GINGERBREAD.

SQUEEZE out the juice of two or three lemons into half a pint of brandy; grate the peel, and mix with one pound of flour in a good-sized bowl; depress the flour in centre and pour in a pint of sugar-house molasses, a pint of melted butter and the brandy; add quarter of an ounce of cayenne pepper and ginger to taste, and mix thoroughly; bake in a *moderate* oven.

HARD GINGERBREAD.

ONE cupful of butter, two cupsful of white sugar, one-half cupful of sweet milk, one egg, ginger to taste, a little rose-water, flour to make dough, and a teaspoonful of saleratus; knead well and roll out; cut in long cakes, crease, and bake in a *slow* oven.

HARD GINGERBREAD, No. 2.

Two pounds of flour, half a pound of butter, one pint of molasses, quarter of a pound of sugar, one ounce of ginger, half a teaspoonful of soda, one teaspoonful of cream of tartar.

MOUNTAIN GINGERBREAD.

Six cups of flour, two cups of butter, two cups of sugar, two cups of molasses, four eggs, one tea-cup of ginger, one teaspoonful of soda, two tea-spoonsful of tartaric acid. This is a batter, and if baked in a Turk's head or bread-pan, keeps a long time, and is very nice.

NEW ORLEANS GINGERBREAD.

Half a pound of butter, quarter of a pound of brown sugar, one tablespoonful of ginger, one tea-spoonful of cinnamon, six eggs, three gills of mo-lasses, one gill of milk, one orange grated, half a pound of flour, half a pound of fine Indian meal, one tablespoonful of saleratus; beat the butter, sugar, spice and orange together until light; mix the wheat and Indian meal together, and beat in one-fourth; whisk the eggs until thick, and add half at a time; then stir the molasses and milk together, and add gradually; then the remaining wheat and Indian meal, one-half at a time; after beating all well together, stir in the saleratus, which mix well through, but not sufficiently to destroy the lightness produced; butter and line your pan with white paper, put in the batter, smooth over the top with a knife, and bake in a *moderate* oven.

WHITE GINGERBREAD.

Two and one-half pounds of flour, twenty ounces of sugar, eight ounces of butter, one tablespoonful of ginger, half a teaspoonful of cinnamon, the yolks of two eggs, half a pint of milk; rub the first five ingredients well together and add the others; knead till smooth; roll into thin sheets and cut to suit; butter tin slightly; do not let cakes touch each other; bake in a rather *quick* oven.

OUR LITTLE ONES.

Two pounds and a half of flour, half a pound of butter, two tablespoonsful of ginger, one and a half tablespoonsful of saleratus; rub the flour, butter and ginger together, then add the saleratus, with sufficient molasses to make a dough; knead well; after remaining a short time in a cool place, roll it into thin sheets, cut with a round cutter, place them on slightly buttered tins, then wash them over with thin molasses and water, and bake in a *moderate* oven. This is specially recommended as wholesome for children.

SELF-DIGESTERS.

Two pounds and a half of unbolted flour, half a pound of butter, one tablespoonful of ginger, one teaspoonful of allspice and cloves mixed, one tablespoonful of saleratus; mix all the ingredients with as much molasses as will make a stiff dough; knead it well, then roll in thin sheets and cut with a round cutter; place them on buttered tins, then wash them over with thin molasses and water, and bake in a *moderate* oven.

DOUGHNUTS.

Two teacupsful of sugar, three eggs, one and a half teacupsful of buttermilk or sour milk, two teaspoonsful of saleratus, one teaspoonful of salt, six tablespoonsful of melted lard, flour enough to roll out nicely; boil or fry in lard.

GINGER BISCUITS.

RUB half a pound of sweet butter into two pounds of fine flour; add half a pound of sifted sugar and three ounces of pounded ginger; beat up the yolks of three eggs; mix, and add milk to make a stiff paste; knead thoroughly, and roll out as thin as possible; cut into round biscuits; bake in a *slow* oven until crisp and of a pale-brown color.

GINGER COOKIES.

ONE cupful each of butter, sugar and molasses, one tablespoonful each of ginger and cinnamon, and two teaspoonsful of saleratus dissolved in three tablespoonsful of hot water. Bake quickly.

DOUGHNUTS, No. 2.

THREE pounds of flour, one pound of butter, one and a half pounds of sugar; shave the butter into the flour; beat six eggs very light and put them in; add a small cupful of yeast, one pint of milk, some cinnamon, mace and nutmeg; make up into light dough and let it rise; when very light, roll out, cut into small pieces and boil in lard.

18

GERMAN DOUGHNUTS.

ONE pint of milk, half a pound of flour, four eggs, salt to taste; boil the milk and pour it over the flour; beat it very smooth, and when it is cool, have ready the eggs well beaten; pour them into the milk and flour; add the salt and as much more flour as will make the whole into a soft dough; flour your board, turn the dough out upon it, roll it in pieces as thick as your finger, and turn them into the form of a ring; cook in plenty of boiling lard, and dust with sugar when cool.

LIGHT DOUGHNUTS.

ONE and a half pints of milk warmed, three-quarters of a pound of sugar, half a pound of butter and one nutmeg; make a sponge of these over-night with flour, putting in one teacupful of good yeast; fry in lard.

HASTY DOUGHNUTS.

ONE teaspoonful of soda, two teaspoonsful of cream of tartar, two cups of sugar, one pint of milk, half a nutmeg, flour enough to make a soft dough; boil or fry in lard.

PLAIN CRULLERS.

CUPFUL of sugar, full teaspoon of butter, three eggs and flour to make a stiff dough; knead, roll, cut into pieces to suit, and fry in lard.

CRULLERS.

THREE pounds of flour, ten eggs, eighteen ounces of white sugar, twelve ounces of butter, one teaspoonful each of cinnamon and nutmeg, one teacupful of rose-water, two tablespoonsful of saleratus; rub the butter, sugar and flour well together, and add the spices, rose-water and saleratus, and the eggs beaten very light; knead the dough thoroughly, and roll out to about half an inch thick; cut into strips, twist these in various forms, and fry in hot lard till they are light brown; sift sugar over them.

CREAM PANCAKES.

Two eggs beaten with half a pint of cream; add a small teacupful of sugar; make them as thin as possible; fry in lard, and dust well with grated sugar. They may be sprinkled with wine, fruit-syrup or grated nutmeg.

FRENCH STRAWS.

EIGHT eggs, ten ounces of sugar and half a teaspoonful of cinnamon and nutmeg mixed, flour to form a dough; beat the eggs very thick and add the sugar, spices and flour; knead well, and roll to about half an inch thick; cut in strips, give each a twist and boil them in lard to a rich yellow; sift sugar on when cool.

SOFT CRULLERS.

SIFT three-quarters of a pound of flour, and powder half a pound of loaf sugar; heat a pint of water in a round-bottomed saucepan, and when quite warm, mix the flour with it gradually; set half a pound of fresh butter over the fire in a small vessel, and when it begins to melt, stir it gradually into the flour and water; then add by degrees the powdered sugar and half a nutmeg grated; take the saucepan off the fire and beat the contents with a wooden spaddle till thoroughly mixed; then beat six eggs very light and stir them gradually into the mixture; beat the whole very hard till it becomes a thick batter; flour a pasteboard very well, and lay out the batter upon it in rings; have ready, on the fire, a pot of boiling lard of the very best quality; put in the crullers, removing them from the board by carefully taking them up, one at a time, on a broad-bladed knife; boil but a few at a time; they must be of a fine brown; lift them out on a perforated skimmer, draining the lard from them back into the pot; lay them on a large dish, and sift powdered white sugar over them.

PEARLS.

FIVE cups of flour, two cups of sugar, one cup of butter, one egg, one teaspoonful of pearlash, half a teacup of milk; bake not too quick.

EXCELLENT BREAD CAKES.

Two teacupsful of risen dough, half a teacupful each of butter and white sugar, two eggs and raisins to suit; mix, and add half a teaspoonful of soda and a teaspoonful of cream of tartar; rise a while after putting it in bread-pan or Turk's head.

COOKIES.

Two cupsful of sugar, three eggs, one cupful each of butter and fresh cream, one teaspoonful of soda, and flavor to taste; mix soft.

FRENCH LOAF.

FIVE eggs, half a pound each of flour and sugar, six ounces of butter; beat until light, and add half a pound of raisins stoned and dusted with flour; bake in a *quick* oven.

CREAM CAKES.

ONE cupful of cream, one cupful of sugar, two cupsful of flour, two eggs, one teaspoonful of saleratus; flavor to taste.

DIXIE BUNS.

RUB eight ounces of sugar and six ounces of butter into two pounds of flour; add one pint of warmed milk and one gill of baker's yeast; let the dough be quite soft; let it rise four hours in a warm place, then mould it and let it rise till morning; make into cakes; bake about twenty minutes.

POOR MAN'S CAKES.

Two cupsful of flour, one cupful each of sweet cream and sugar, one egg, one teaspoonful of soda and two teaspoonsful of dry cream of tartar. Bake carefully, and a very nice cake will result.

FRENCH LOAF, No. 2.

ONE pound each of flour, white sugar and raisins, half a pound of butter, cupful of new milk, five eggs and spice to taste; rub together the flour, sugar and butter till smooth; then add the milk, eggs well-beaten and spice, and finally the raisins, first stoned, cleaned, dusted with flour; work till smooth, and bake in a *moderate* oven.

OLD DOMINION BUNS.

HALF a pound each of butter and white sugar, four eggs, twelve ounces of flour, nutmeg to taste, half a teaspoonful of soda and one of cream of tartar; add currants, if desired.

PHILADELPHIA BUNS.

ONE pint of milk, one cupful of butter, three cupsful of sugar, one or two eggs, one pint of yeast, and flour enough to work into a soft dough at night; early in the morning add not quite half a teaspoonful of soda and two teaspoonsful of ammonia; now put in a little more flour, mould it well and return it to rise; when light, make into cakes, and let them stand half an hour or till light enough, then bake.

ONE, TWO, THREE, FOUR.

ONE cupful of butter, two cupsful of sugar, three cupsful of flour, four eggs; rub well together and add sweet milk or cream, nutmeg to taste, one teaspoonful of soda and two teaspoonsful of cream of tartar; bake carefully in a *quick* oven.

ALBANY CAKES.

CREAM sufficient, one pound of sugar and half a pound of butter, three eggs well beaten, one teaspoonful each of soda and cream of tartar; add one and a half pounds of sifted flour; this is a dough; bake in a *moderate* oven.

GOOD PLUM CAKES.

ONE and a half pounds of butter beat to a cream, three-quarters of a pound of sugar finely powdered; these must be beaten together until white and smooth; take six eggs, the yolks and whites to be beaten separately; when the whites are beaten to a stiff froth and ready to put to the cake, mix in the yolks, then add them to the butter; beat it enough to mix them; add to it one pound of flour and one pound of currants; do not

beat it much after you put in the flour; let it
stand in a cold place for two hours; bake it about
one hour and a half.

GRAFTON CAKE.—VERY FINE.

One pint of flour, half a pint of sugar, one
tablespoonful of butter, two teaspoonsful of cream
of tartar, one teaspoonful of soda, one egg; make
a batter of milk mixed until quite thin. This
is the best cake for the materials used.

COTTAGE CAKE.

One cupful of butter, three cupsful of sugar,
two cupsful of sweet milk, one quart of flour
mixed with four teaspoonsful of cream of tartar,
two teaspoonsful of soda dissolved in the milk,
two eggs, one pound of raisins, half a pound of
citron. Makes a large cake.

INDIAN PUFFS.

Into one quart of boiling milk stir eight tablespoonsful of meal and four tablespoonsful of brown
sugar; boil five minutes, stirring constantly; when
cool, add six well-beaten eggs; bake in buttered
cups half an hour.

ALMOND CAKES.

RUB two ounces of butter into five ounces of flour; beat one egg with two and a half ounces of powdered loaf sugar; mix ingredients, and add two and a half more of powdered loaf sugar, one ounce of blanched sweet almonds and a little almond flavor; break into small pieces, roll in your hand, sprinkle with pulverized sugar, and bake lightly.

F. F. V. CAKES.

HALF a pound of flour, six ounces of sugar, four ounces of butter, two eggs, one wineglassful of new milk and one small teaspoonful of ammonia; beat the butter, add the eggs, then the flour, dissolve the ammonia in the milk; currants and candied peel to taste; bake in loaf or cakes.

CREAM CAKE.

ONE cupful of butter, three cupsful of sugar, four cupsful of flour, one cupful of sweet cream, five eggs, one teaspoonful of saleratus, two teaspoonsful of cream of tartar; rub together the first three, beat the eggs and mix the ingredients; bake lightly.

PERKINS' CAKE.

ONE quart of flour, two cupsful each of sugar and milk, a piece of butter, two eggs, two teaspoonsful of cream of tartar, one teaspoonful of soda; mix, and bake carefully in a *quick* oven.

CUSTARD CAKES.

Two cupsful of sugar, two-thirds of a cupful of butter, one cupful of milk, one teaspoonful of soda, one and a half teaspoonsful of cream of tartar, two and a half cupsful of flour, three eggs. To make the custard for the cake, take one cupful of milk, one tablespoonful of corn-starch dissolved in it, and brought to a boiling heat so as to be thick like starch, the yolk of one egg dropped in to color it; flavor with lemon; let it cool. Bake your cake in round pie-tin; enough batter in a tin so that when they are baked two of them put together will make one cake; make the custard first, let it cool, then put the cakes together when they are warm; put plenty of custard between them.

CREAM PUFFS.

SIX ounces of flour, four ounces of butter, five eggs, one large cupful of cold water; let the water and butter come to a boil, throw in the flour all at once and let it boil till the flour is well cooked; let it cool, and add the eggs one at a time without beating; drop tablespoonsful on a buttered tin and bake light brown or golden color. Make the cream for the inside thus: one large cupful of sweet milk, half a cupful of sugar, quarter of a cupful of flour (or a little corn-starch is preferred by many), one egg beaten; stir over the fire till it thickens, and flavor to suit taste.

CORN-STARCH CAKES.

ONE cupful each of butter, sweet milk and corn-starch, two cupsful each of sugar and flour, whites of five eggs beaten to a stiff froth, two teaspoonsful of cream of tartar and one teaspoonful of saleratus; flavor to taste; bake lightly.

JOSEPHINE CAKES.

Two tablespoonsful of sugar, one nutmeg grated, a little lemon-peel, three tablespoonsful of butter, two tablespoonsful of cream, two cupsful of milk, four cupsful of flour, four eggs, one teaspoonful of soda, two teaspoonsful of cream of tartar; bake half an hour; eat hot, with fresh butter.

PLAIN CITRON CAKE.

Six ounces each of butter, sugar and flour, four eggs well beaten, a little citron, one teaspoonful of cream of tartar, half a teaspoonful of soda; beat together thoroughly about half an hour; bake in patty-pans.

SUGAR CAKE.

Three pounds of flour, one pound of butter, one teaspoonful of pearlash dissolved in half a pint of water; put in the water a pound and a half of sugar; rub the flour and butter together, roll thin, and bake in a *quick* oven.

PLAIN CUP CAKE.

Two cupsful of butter well-creamed, two cupsful of sugar, one teaspoonful of soda dissolved in sour milk, flour enough to work well; cut into shapes to suit, and bake lightly.

S. C. A. CAKE.

Three-quarters of a pound of butter, one pound of sugar, eight eggs, one pound of flour, the juice and grated rind of a lemon, one pound of seedless raisins; separate the yolks and whites

19

of the eggs, beat them to a froth, mix them with
the butter and sugar, previously stirred together
to a cream; add the flour and lemon; just before
putting it into the pans for baking, stir in the
raisins.

SCOTCH CAKES.

THREE-QUARTERS of a pound of flour, three
ounces of butter, three ounces of lump sugar, sal
ammonia about the size of a hazel-nut; warm the
butter in a little milk, and mix the whole into a
stiff paste; cut into small rounds, and bake in a
cool oven

SILVER CAKE,

WHICH may be colored as the marble cake, and
which is delicious and very pretty, less troublesome and less expensive, may be made as follows:
the whites of seven eggs, three cupsful of powdered
white sugar, one cupful of butter, four cupsful of flour,
one cupful of sour cream (if cream is sweet, use a
teaspoonful of cream of tartar), one-half teaspoonful of soda; beat the eggs separately, and add the
flour, eggs and cream alternately, until they are
all well mixed; if you wish to color it, take a

small portion of the batter and color it with cochineál, and put it between two layers of white batter; cut slips of citron and rub flour on them, and stick them in the cake after it is in the mould.

SPICE CAKE.

THIS can be made with advantage at same time as the above: the yolks of seven eggs, two cupsful of brown sugar, one cupful of molasses, one cupful of butter, one large coffeecupful of sour cream, one teaspoonful of soda (just even full), and five cupsful of flour, one teaspoonful of ground cloves, two teaspoonsful of cinnamon, two teaspoonsful of ginger, one nutmeg and a small pinch of Cayenne pepper; beat eggs, sugar and butter to a light batter before putting in the molasses; then add the molasses, flour and cream; beat it well together, and bake in a *moderate* oven; if fruit is used, take two cupsful of raisins, flour them well and put them in last.

MARBLE CAKE.

ONE pound each of sugar, flour and butter, the whites of sixteen eggs, quarter of a pound of bleached and split almonds, half of a citron sliced and sufficient cochineal (which should be procured at confectioner's, as that prepared by druggists is not so suitable) ; cream together the butter and flour ; beat together very light the egg-whites and sugar ; put all together and beat thoroughly ; color one-third of the batter any shade you like; put well-greased tissue-paper around the mould, then put in half of the white batter, a layer of citron and almonds, the colored batter, another layer of citron and almonds, and the remainder of white batter; bake in a *moderate* oven.

GEORGIA MARBLE.

THE *white:* Whites of seven eggs, one cupful of butter, two cupsful of sugar, three cupsful of flour, half a cupful of sweet milk, half a teaspoonful of soda and one teaspoonful of cream of tartar. The *dark:* Yolks of seven eggs, one cupful of molasses, two cupsful of brown sugar, one cupful of sweet milk, five cupsful of flour, one of butter, spice to taste, one teaspoonful of soda, two of cream of tartar ; make the *white* and the *dark* separately; then make two cakes thus: put in your moulds, first one spoonful of the *dark*, then one of the *white,* and so alternately; bake very carefully.

COCOANUT CAKE.

ONE nut grated fine, one pound each of flour and sugar, one teacupful of milk, eight eggs; spice to taste; bake carefully in a *moderate* oven.

SALLY WHITE CAKE.

ONE pound of butter, one pound of white sugar, one pound of flour, twelve eggs, one pound of citron cut fine, one cocoanut grated, one pound of almonds (weighed in the shell) blanched and pounded, one teaspoonful of cinnamon, one wineglassful of wine, and the same quantity of brandy; mix the citron with the flour, and make as pound cake.

SALLY LUNNS.

ONE pint of flour, one teaspoonful of yeast, two eggs, a piece of butter the size of an egg, two tablespoonsful of sugar; mix with milk to a thick batter.

HICKORY-NUT CAKE.—VERY FINE.

ONE pound of flour, one pound of sugar, three-quarters of a pound of butter, six eggs, two tea-spoonsful of cream of tartar, one teaspoonful of soda, half a cupful of sweet milk; beat the cake

19 *

thoroughly, and then stir in a small measure of hickory-nuts, first, of course, taking them from the shell; bake in a steady but not *quick* oven.

CULPEPPER CAKE.

ONE cupful of sugar, one cupful of sour cream, two of sifted flour, two eggs, one teaspoonful of cream of tartar, half a teaspoonful of soda, half a teaspoonful of salt; flavor with essence of almond. It is quickly made, and delicious when eaten fresh.

SOUTHERN FAVORITE.

TAKE four ounces of butter, eight ounces of sifted sugar, four ounces of flour, four ounces of ground rice and five eggs; put the butter to melt into a small saucepan, the flour, rice and sugar in a basin, to which add one whole egg and the yolks of the remaining four, reserving the whites to be whisked; mix well with a spoon for two or three minutes, then beat the whites to a strong froth, and proceed to mix them with the butter; add a small quantity of the whites at first until it becomes smoothly united; the remainder of the whites should then be added, and gently though thoroughly mixed; bake in a papered tin, in a moderately heated oven; four or six ounces of currants may be mixed with the batter previous to adding the whites, if desired.

DUTCH PUPPET.

ONE pint of milk, three eggs, one cupful of butter, flour enough to make a spoon stand in it, and yeast enough to make it rise.

SNOW-DRIFT CAKE.

THREE cupsful of flour, two cupsful of sugar, one-half a cupful of butter, one cupful of sweet milk, the whites of five eggs beaten to a stiff froth, one teaspoonful of cream of tartar, one-half a teaspoonful of soda; sift the flour, and do not pack it when measuring it.

RAISIN CAKE.

TAKE two cupsful of butter, two cupsful of sour milk, two cupsful of molasses, four cupsful of sugar, half a dozen eggs, twelve cupsful of flour, two teaspoonsful of soda, two cupsful of raisins, and spice to your taste.

WALNUT CAKES.

ONE pound of sugar, six eggs, three teaspoonsful of yeast powder, half a pound of butter, flour to make a dough, and one cupful of walnut kernels; bake in a *moderate* oven.

FAIRFAX CAKES.

THREE cupsful each of sugar and water, one cupful of butter, five cupsful of flour, four eggs, one teaspoonful of soda and two teaspoonsful of cream of tartar; bake in a *quick* oven.

DEPARTMENT LUNCH CAKES.

Two quarts of flour, four eggs, one pound of sugar, one large spoonful of lard, one gill of sweet milk, one teaspoonful of soda, two teaspoonsful of cream of tartar; work well; cut with a cake-cutter, and bake in a *quick* oven.

BLACK CAKE.

TAKE two pounds of currants, two pounds of raisins, one pound of citron, one pound of butter, one pound of sugar, one nutmeg, twelve eggs, one large tablespoonful of cinnamon, one tablespoonful of allspice, one tablespoonful of cloves, one-half tablespoonful of mace, one (ordinary size) cup half full of Madeira wine, one teacupful of brandy and one teaspoonful of rose-water; put the spices in the liquors; prepare the butter and sugar together; add twelve eggs well beaten together; then the fruit and liquors alternately; chop the fruit, and put flour enough to make it dry, and to prevent its sinking in the cake; let it bake about three hours and a half or four hours in a *moderate* oven. Have greased paper around the sides, as well as at the bottom of the pan in which you bake, and let the cake remain in the pan or mould until the next morning after it is made, and cover the pan with a heavy cloth.

SNOW CAKE.—DELICIOUS.

ONE pound of arrowroot, quarter of a pound of pounded white sugar, half a pound of butter, the whites of six eggs, flavoring to taste of essence of almonds, or vanilla, or lemon; beat the butter to a cream; stir in the sugar and arrowroot gradually, at the same time beating the mixture; whisk the whites of the eggs to a stiff froth; add them to the other ingredients, and beat well for

P

twenty minutes; put in whichever of the above flavorings may be preferred; pour the cake into a buttered mould or tin, and bake it in a *moderate* oven from one to one and a half hours. *This is a genuine Scotch recipe.*

OXFORD CAKE.

ONE pound of flour, a dessertspoonful of bread-powder, one egg and half a pint of cream, half a teaspoonful of suet, two teaspoonsful of loaf sugar powdered; rub the dry ingredients well together, then briskly mix in first the cream and then the egg; bake quickly on buttered tins. If yeast be preferred, the milk should be a little warmed and strained through the yeast as for bread; add the egg last; let the dough stand to rise; then bake half an hour in a *quick* oven.

CORN-STARCH DAINTIES.

THE whites of twelve eggs, three cupsful each of flour and sugar, one cupful each of corn-starch, milk and butter, one teaspoonful of soda and two teaspoonsful of cream of tartar; flavor to taste, and bake in a pan in a *moderate* oven. Ice or not to taste.

CHINESE CAKES.

BEAT the yolks of six eggs well, and to each yolk add a tablespoonful of sugar and one tablespoonful of flour and any flavoring preferred; drop them on a hot pan well greased, and bake in a *quick* oven; make them small. They look pretty with other kind of cake, and are very nice.

WHITE CAKE.

CUPFUL of butter, two cupsful of sugar, three (heaped) cupsful of flour, one cupful of sweet milk, whites of six eggs, one teaspoonful of yeast powder; make a loaf, which bake about an hour.

In connection with this it will be found advantageous to make

SPONGE CAKE.

ONE of the very nicest of cakes (when well made), and one of the most difficult to make just right; the absence of butter makes it the more difficult to avoid the leathery toughness so often met with in what is popularly miscalled Sponge Cake. The first of the following recipes is preferable if you can get the knack of following it successfully; the second will be available if you cannot make the first suit you:

1. Sift half a pound of flour (arrowroot is still better) in a shallow pan; beat twelve eggs till very thick, light and smooth; you need not separate the yolks and whites if you know the true way of adding the flour; beat a pound of powdered loaf sugar gradually (a little at a time) into the beaten eggs, and add the juice and grated rinds of one or two large lemons or oranges; lastly, stir in the flour or arrowroot; it is highly important that this be done slowly and lightly, not stirring to the bottom of the pan; have ready buttered either a turban mould or small tins; put the mixture in, grate powdered sugar profusely over the surface to give it a gloss like a very thin crust, and set it immediately into a brisk oven. The small cakes are called Naples biscuits, and require no icing. A turban cake may be iced plain, without ornament. A very light sponge cake, when sliced, will cut down rough and coarse-grained, and it is desirable to have it so. Be especially careful in the baking.

2. Same as above, except you separate the whites and yolks of the eggs, beating the whites to a stiff froth; beat the sugar and lemon with the yolks, add the whites and then the flour or arrowroot.

LADY FINGERS

ARE mixed in the same manner and of the same ingredients as the best sponge cake. When the mixture is finished, form the cakes by shaping the batter with a teaspoon upon sheets of soft white paper slightly damped, forming them like double ovals joined in the centre. Sift powdered sugar over them, and bake them in a *quick* oven till slightly brown; when cool, take them off the papers; they are sometimes iced.

ALMOND SPONGE CAKE.

THE addition of almonds makes this cake very superior to the usual sponge cake. Sift half a pound of fine flour or arrowroot; blanch in scalding water two ounces of sweet and two ounces of bitter almonds, renewing the hot water when expedient; when the skins are all off, wash the almonds in cold water (mixing the sweet and bitter), and wipe them dry; pound them to a fine smooth paste (one at a time), adding, as you proceed, rose-water, to prevent their oiling; set them in a cool place; beat twelve eggs till very smooth and thick, and then beat into them gradually a pound of powdered loaf sugar in turn

20

with the pounded almonds; lastly, add the flour, stirring it round slowly and lightly on the surface of the mixture, as in common sponge cake; have ready buttered a *deep* square pan; put the mixture carefully into it, set into the oven, and bake till thoroughly done and risen very high; when cool, cover it with plain white icing flavored with rose-water, or with almond icing. With sweet almonds always use a small portion of bitter; without them, *sweet* almonds have little or no taste, though they add to the richness of the cake.

SPONGE CAKE.

WE add two other methods, said by a competent lady to produce very fine cake:

1. Six eggs, same weight of sugar, half weight of flour, half a lemon squeezed in, the whole of the lemon-skin grated; beat the yellow to a froth, then add the sugar; when well beaten, add the white (which must be very light), then put in the juice and grating, last flour, a teaspoonful of salt.

2. Five eggs, half a pound of sugar, six ounces of flour, leaving out two tablespoonsful; beat the whites of the eggs to a froth; add the sugar and unbeaten yolks alternately, leaving out one yolk; add flour last.

MERINGUE CAKE.

Make a light sponge cake (of twelve eggs, one pound of sugar, one lemon and three-quarters of a pound of flour), and divide the batter into three parts, and bake in three separate pans; put a thick layer of marmalade or preserves on the top of the cake; take the whites of nine eggs and two pounds of best refined powdered white sugar, and beat the eggs very light; add the sugar, and beat both until they can stand alone; add a little extract of lemon or vanilla to flavor it; put this on the marmalade cake; place it in an oven just warm enough to dry it (so as to harden it in about ten minutes), and let it be a very light brown.

ROLL CAKE.

Make a sponge cake in the usual way and divide (half) the batter, and bake it in a broad square pan; trim the edges when done, and put on the fruit, and roll it up while it is hot (as you would a roll-dumpling), and have your dish inverted and well greased with butter to keep the cake from sticking. These cakes should not be iced, but prettily ornamented. The marmalade of green apples is the nicest fruit used, as it retains its color and flavor so well.

LITTLE PLUMS.

HALF a pound of sugar and a quarter pound of butter beaten to a smooth cream; add three well-beaten eggs, one pound of flour, four ounces each of seedless raisins and currants, half a teaspoonful of baking soda dissolved in water, and milk to make a stiff paste; dredge flour on tins, drop the paste on in small drops, and bake in a *quick* oven.

CAROLINA PLUM CAKE.

MIX two quarts of flour with a pound of sifted sugar, three pounds of currants, half a pound of raisins, stoned and chopped, quarter of an ounce of mace and cloves, a grated nutmeg, the peel of a lemon cut fine; melt two pounds of butter in a pint and a quarter of cream, but not hot; the whites and yolks of twelve eggs beaten apart, and half a pint of good yeast; beat them together a full hour; put in plenty of citron and lemon; then butter your hoop or pans, and bake.

GOOD PLUM CAKE.

AN equal weight of butter and flour, quarter of a pound of cut peels and citrons, double the weight of butter in currants, the grating of three lemons and half a nutmeg, half an ounce of pudding spice, one glass of brandy, and the same quantity of eggs as the weight in butter; beat your butter as for pound cake; put in a few chopped sweet almonds; paper and butter a hoop, bottom and sides; then put in your mixtures; bake in a *slow* oven; take off the hoop when done, but not the paper.

FINE ALMOND CAKE.

BLANCH, dry and pound to a paste half a pound of fresh sweet almonds, with two ounces of bitter; mix with them a few drops of cold water to prevent oiling; add ten fresh eggs beaten light as possible; throw in gradually a pound of dry sifted sugar and half a pound of softened (not hot) butter; beat all together slowly and thoroughly, and add the grated rind of two sound fresh lemons; bake an hour and a half in a steady oven, and ice or not to taste.

CURRANT JUMBLES.

ONE pound each of flour and powdered loaf sugar, half a pound each of butter and currants, eight eggs, brandy to taste; bake on tins.

WHITE MOUNTAIN CAKE.

ONE pound of flour, one pound of sugar, half a pound of butter, six eggs, one cupful of milk, one small teaspoonful of saleratus dissolved in the milk; bake like jelly cake, four in number; frost the first cake on top, lay on another and frost in like manner, and in like manner the other two; when all are done, even the edges with a knife and frost the sides, and the " White Mountain " is finished.

FROSTING FOR THE WHITE MOUNTAIN CAKE. —Whites of four eggs made thick with sifted refined sugar; beat the eggs to a standing froth and add the sugar and juice of one lemon; do not put the cake by the fire to harden the frosting. The White Mountain cake is very nice indeed, particularly for weddings or parties.

CHARLESTON CAKE.

ONE cupful of butter, one cupful of sweet milk, two cupsful of coffee sugar, three eggs, one teaspoonful of soda, one and a half teaspoonsful of cream of tartar, flour to make as stiff as cup cake. This will make two loaves of cake, or one loaf of cake and put the remainder in two round tin plates, and you will have enough for a nice Washington pie, with a little jelly of any kind put between them.

JUMBLES.

SIX eggs, half a pound of sugar, two cupsful of butter, one pint of sweet milk, flour to make stiff dough and a little saleratus; roll, and cut with a cake-cutter, sift sugar over, and bake in a *quick* oven.

COCOANUT JUMBLES.

GRATE one large cocoanut; rub half a pound of butter with half a pound of sugar, one pound of sifted flour, and wet it with three eggs, beaten, and a little rose-water; add by degrees the nut, so as to make a stiff dough; bake in a *quick* oven from five to ten minutes.

CONFEDERATE BRANDY JUMBLES.

ONE pound of flour rubbed with a quarter of a pound of butter, one pound of sugar beaten with four eggs; flavor with rose-water, brandy and spice; bake on tins.

RICE JUMBLES.

HALF a pound of sugar beaten in four eggs, quarter of a pound of butter and half a pound of ground rice; flavor to taste; bake on tins. A little grated nutmeg will improve this.

GERMAN ALMOND PUFFS.

QUARTER of a pound of almonds beaten very fine, with rose-water, six eggs well eaten, leaving out two of the whites, two spoonsful of flour, two ounces of butter, a little nutmeg and six ounces of sugar, all well mixed with a pint of cream; bake in buttered patty-pans; serve up with wine sauce.

BACHELOR'S CAKE.

ONE pound of flour, half a pound of sugar, quarter of a pound of butter or lard, four wine-glasses of milk, half a pound of Sultana raisins, quarter of a pound of currants, the same of candied peel, quarter of a nutmeg, two teaspoonsful of ground ginger, one teaspoonful of cinnamon and one teaspoonful of carbonate of soda; mix well together, and bake slowly for an hour and a half.

ANCIENT MAIDEN'S CAKE.

QUARTER of a pound each of fresh sweet butter and pulverized loaf sugar; cream these together; a few drops of extract of lemon, of vanilla, of rose, of peach or other flavor to taste, the whites of five eggs beaten as light as possible, and lastly quarter of a pound of flour gently stirred in; bake in scalloped pans; if the A. M.'s matrimonial prospects are good, frost or ice with icing of proper flavor, otherwise serve plain.

INTRODUCTION CAKE.

TWELVE eggs, one pound of sugar, three-quarters of a pound of flour, three tablespoonsful of water; separate the eggs, beat the yolks, sugar and water together until very thick and light; then whisk the whites until stiff and dry, which stir in lightly with the flour, half of each at a time; butter and line your pan with white paper, put in the batter, and bake in a *moderate* oven.

ACQUAINTANCESHIP CAKES.

Two and a half pounds of unbolted flour, half a pound of butter, one quarter of a pound of sugar, one tablespoonful of saleratus; rub the butter, flour and other ingredients together and mix with as much molasses as will make a dough; knead well, make it into round cakes, and pat them flat with the hand; wash them over with thin molasses and water, and bake in a *moderate* oven.

QUIZ CAKE.

THREE eggs, half a cupful of butter, one cupful each of sugar and sweet milk, two cupsful of flour, one teaspoonful of soda, two teaspoonsful of cream of tartar, and spice to taste.

SWEET DROPS.

ONE quart of milk, two eggs, three ounces of butter, one teacupful (or more to taste) of rye meal, flour or arrowroot, to make batter, one teaspoonful of soda, two teaspoonsful of cream of tartar; drop on buttered tins, and bake briskly till slightly colored.

FLIRTATION CAKES.

THREE cupsful each of sugar and butter, five eggs, one cupful of milk, five cupsful of flour, to taste, raisins, currants, spice, salt; bake in small scalloped tins; grate cocoanut over them, and sift fine sugar on them.

LOVE CAKES.

ONE pound of pulverized sugar, the whites of five eggs, half a pound of sweet almonds, one ounce of bitter almonds; mix the almonds, blanch and pound them quite fine; beat the eggs very dry, and add the sugar gradually, a teaspoonful at a time, until all is added; then stir in the almonds lightly, put parts on white paper with a teaspoon, about an inch apart, and bake in a *slow* oven. Be very careful in the baking; they should not darken.

KISSES.

WHITES of four eggs beaten very light; mix with the froth enough fine sifted sugar to make it very stiff; drop on paper in drops half the size you want the cakes, and bake in a *very slow* oven; take them off of the paper and put together two-and-two; this recipe will yield a fair-sized cake-basketful. It adds much to their beauty when served up to tint half of them pale pink, and unite white and pink.

RIVAL CAKE.

Two cupsful of sugar, four eggs, one cupful of melted butter, two and a half cupsful of milk and flour to make a stiff batter, two teaspoonsful of cream of tartar and one teaspoonful of soda; bake half to three-quarters of an hour.

JEALOUSY PUFFS.

Two cupsful of sugar, one cupful each of butter and sweet cream, three cupsful of flour, three eggs, one teaspoonful of soda, two teaspoonsful of cream of tartar, and flavor to taste; bake quickly.

LOVE CAKES, No. 2.

THREE eggs, five ounces each of sugar and flour, rose-water; spice or flavor to taste; drop on papered tin, and sift sugar on them; bake lightly and in a *slow* oven.

ENGAGEMENT CAKE.

ONE pound each of sweet butter and sugar, eight eggs, eight ounces of flour, small cupful of sweet cream, one teaspoonful of saleratus, and flavor with rose-water and nutmeg, or to taste.

WEDDING CAKE.

FOUR pounds of flour, three pounds of butter, three pounds of sugar, four pounds of currants, two pounds of raisins, twenty eggs, half a pint of brandy or lemon brandy, one ounce of mace, three nutmegs. A little molasses makes it dark-colored, which is desirable. Half a pound of citron improves it, but it is not necessary. To be baked two hours and a half or three hours. An excellent recipe.

VERY RICH WEDDING CAKE.

TAKE four pounds of fine flour, four pounds of fresh butter; sift two pounds of powdered sugar, and grate to it quarter of an ounce of nutmeg; break eight eggs (yolks and whites separately) for each pound of flour; wash and pick four pounds of currants, and dry them before the fire; crush the butter between the hands until it is reduced to a cream, then beat it up with the sugar for fifteen minutes; beat the whites of the eggs to a stiff froth, and mix with butter and sugar; beat the yolks half an hour, and mix them in; put in the flour and nutmeg, and beat it up; pour in a pint of brandy, and add a quantity to taste of citron cut in strips; pour it into the baking-tin, and when it has risen and browned, cover with paper, lest it should burn. Great care must be taken in baking this cake to have the oven of the proper heat.

THE LITTLE FOLKS' JOYS.

ONE cupful of white sugar, one cupful of rich sour cream, one egg, two cupsful of flour, half a teaspoonful of soda, and flavor to taste; bake about half an hour; nicest eaten fresh and warm.

SILVER CAKE.

Two teacupsful of white sugar, three-fourths of a cupful of butter, one cupful of sweet milk, four cupsful of flour, whites of six eggs beaten to a stiff froth, one teaspoonful of soda, two teaspoonsful of cream of tartar; flavor with vanilla, rose, nutmeg or lemon; rub sugar and butter to a cream, and add the other ingredients; bake in a *quick* oven; may be iced.

DRIED APPLE CAKE.

TAKE two cupsful of dried apples, stew just enough to cut easily; chop about as fine as raisins, and boil them in two cupsful of molasses till preserved through; drain off the molasses for the cake; then add two eggs, one cupful of butter, one cupful of sour milk, two teaspoonsful of soda, four cupsful of flour, spices of all kinds; add the apple the last thing.

GOLD CAKE.

Two teacupsful of white sugar, three-fourths of cupful of butter stirred to a cream, two cupsful of flour, yolks of six (or eight) eggs, half a teaspoonful of soda dissolved in half a cupful of milk, one teaspoonful of cream of tartar; bake in a *moderate* oven; may be iced.

DRIED APPLE CAKE, No. 2.

Two and a half cupsful of dried apples stewed until soft; add a cupful of sugar, and stew for a few minutes; chop the mixture fine, and add half a cupful of cold strong coffee, a cupful of sugar, two eggs, half a cupful of butter, one teaspoonful of soda, and nutmeg, cinnamon, etc., to taste.

YANKEE FRUIT CAKE.—UNRIVALED.

THREE-QUARTERS of a pound of butter, three-quarters of a pound of sugar, three-quarters of a pound of flour, eight eggs, one gill of cream, one teaspoonful of cinnamon and nutmeg mixed, half a gill of brandy, one pound of currants (washed, dried and picked), one pound of raisins (seeded and chopped); beat the butter, sugar and spice until very light, then stir in the cream and one-fourth of the flour; whisk the eggs until thick, which add by degrees, then the remainder of the flour, half at a time; lastly, the fruit; beat all well together; butter and line your pan with white paper, and bake in a *moderate* oven.

GREEN APPLE CAKES.—FINE.

ONE pound of flour, half a pound of sugar, two eggs, a little salt and one yeast powder; grate six large apples and rub them well into the other ingredients; add milk sufficient to make a dough, cut into thin cakes, and bake quickly.

FRUIT CAKE.

FIVE cupsful of flour, two cupsful of sugar, two cupsful of butter, one cupful of liquid (about equal quantities of brandy, milk and molasses), four eggs, two pounds of raisins, citron, currants if you choose, one teaspoonful of saleratus, spice to taste, cloves, cinnamon or nutmeg.

FARMER'S FRUIT LOAF.

SOAK three cupsful of dried apples over-night in cold water enough to swell them; chop them in the morning, and put them on the fire with three cups of molasses; stew until almost soft; add a cupful of nice raisins (seedless, if possible), and stew a few moments; when cold, add three cupsful of flour, one cupful of butter, three eggs and a teaspoonful of soda; bake in a steady oven. This will make two good-sized pansful of splendid cake; the apples will cook like citron, and taste deliciously. Raisins may be omitted; also spices to taste may be added. This is not a dear, but a delicious, cake.

FRUIT LOAF.

TAKE one pound of flour, nine eggs, one pound of butter, one cupful of molasses, one pound of brown sugar, three pounds of currants, one pound of citron, three pounds of raisins, half a pound of flour rubbed in with the fruit, mace and nutmeg.

POUND CAKE.

ONE pound each of sugar and butter, ten eggs, one nutmeg grated, twenty ounces of flour, one wineglassful of rose-water; cream the butter and sugar; beat it some, and add by degrees the ingredients named; first, the yolks well beaten, nutmeg, rose-water, whites, lastly flour; make

21 *

this now very smooth, put in half a teaspoonful of soda and one teaspoonful of cream of tartar, the latter dry; bake in a "Turk's turban," to secure lightness. Baking is a nice point; the oven must be warm, and getting warmer, not hot to be cooled; if the latter, the cake is sure to be heavy—browning rapidly prevents the inner part rising.

CONFEDERATE FRUIT CAKE.

Two cupsful each of flour and molasses, one pint of dried fruit parboiled and fine chopped, one tablespoonful of lard and a small teaspoonful of soda dissolved in half a wineglassful of vinegar.

CITRON POUND CAKE.

ONE full pound each of butter and loaf sugar, one scant pound of flour, ten eggs (eleven, if small), one large spoonful each of rose-water and brandy, one nutmeg grated, one pound of citron; wash the citron in warm water, dry it on a towel, cut in thin pieces, then chop it very fine; put all the ingredients together as in "Pound cake;" add the fruit last; beat well; then butter and line your pan with white paper, put in the batter, spread it smooth with a knife and bake in a *moderate* oven.

A VERY FINE POUND CAKE.

ONE pound and a quarter of butter, one pound of sugar, one pound of flour, ten eggs, one nutmeg grated, one glassful of brandy and wine mixed; beat the butter and sugar light; then by degrees add the wine, brandy, nutmeg and one-fourth of the flour; whisk the eggs until very thick, which stir in the butter and sugar gradually, then add the remaining flour, one-third at a time; beat all well together; line your pan with white paper, put in the batter, smoothe the top with a knife and bake in a *moderate* oven about two hours and a half.

SPICE POUND CAKE.

HALF a pound of butter, half a pound of sugar, six eggs, one pound of flour, one tablespoonful of cinnamon, two tablespoonsful of ginger, four tea-cupsful of molasses, one tablespoonful of saleratus; stir the butter and sugar to a cream; beat the eggs very light and add to it, after which put in the spice, molasses and flour in rotation, stirring the mixture all the time; beat the whole well before adding the saleratus and but little afterward; paper the pans before you put in the mixture, and bake in a very *moderate* oven.

QUEEN CAKE.

ONE pound each of butter and sugar, fourteen ounces of flour, ten eggs, one nutmeg grated, two tablespoonsful each of wine and brandy; beat the butter and sugar until very light, to which add the wine and spice, with one-fourth of the flour; whisk the eggs until thick, and add half at a time with the remainder of the flour; after beating all well together, let the batter remain a short time in a cool place; then fill your pans rather more than half full, and bake in a *quick* oven. The brandy may be omitted. Ice when cool.

ORANGE CAKE.

MAKE a mixture precisely as for queen cake, only omit the wine and brandy, and substitute the grated yellow rind and the juice of four large ripe oranges, stirred into the batter in turn with the egg and flour; flavor the icing with orange juice.

LEMON CAKE

Is also made as above, substituting for the oranges the grated rind and juice of three lemons. To give a full taste, less lemon is required than orange.

A PLAIN JELLY CAKE.

ONE cupful each of sugar and flour, three eggs, half a teaspoonful of soda; bake, and while warm spread jelly between layers.

A RICH JELLY CAKE

MAY be made with little trouble by baking some of your batter when you make pound cake in cakes on a griddle, and while warm spreading jelly between layers of these.

ALMOND CUSTARD CAKE.

FOUR eggs beaten separately, four tablespoonsful of white sugar, twelve ounces of sweet and four ounces of bitter almonds blanched and cut fine, a pint of sour cream, flavor to taste; put in the egg-whites last; mix as thick as sponge-cake batter; put layers of jelly between as in jelly cake.

BRUNSWICK JELLY CAKES.

STIR together half a pound of powdered white sugar and half a pound of fresh butter till perfectly light; beat the yolks of three eggs till very thick and smooth; sift three-quarters of a pound

of flour and pour it into the beaten eggs with the
butter and sugar; add a teaspoonful of mixed
spice (nutmeg, mace and cinnamon) and half a
glass of rose-water; stir the whole well, and lay
it on your paste-board, which must first be sprinkled with flour; if you find it so moist as to be
unmanageable, throw in a little more flour; spread
the dough into a sheet about half an inch thick,
and cut it out in round cakes with the edge of a
tumbler; lay them in buttered pans and bake
about five or six minutes; when cold, spread over
the surface of each cake a liquor of fruit-jelly or
marmalade; then beat the whites of three or four
eggs till it stands alone; beat into the froth, by
degrees, a sufficiency of powdered loaf sugar to
make it as thick as icing; flavor with a few drops
of strong essence of lemon, and with a spoon heap
it up on each cake, making it high in the centre;
put the cakes into a coal oven, and as soon as the
tops are colored of a pale brown, take them out.
These cakes are delicious.

LEMON PUFFS.

TAKE a pound of finely-powdered loaf sugar
and mix it with the juice of two lemons; beat

the white of an egg to a complete froth; then add it to the lemon and sugar and beat the whole for half an hour; then well beat three more eggs and grate the outside rind very fine from the peel of the two lemons you have used the juice of; add this and the eggs to the previous mixture, and well mix the whole; sprinkle some finely-powdered sugar on a sheet of writing-paper and drop the mixture upon it; a *moderate* oven will bake them in a few minutes.

COCOANUT POUND CAKE.

THREE cupsful of flour, one cupful of butter, two cupsful of sugar, one cupful of milk, whites of six eggs, half a teaspoonful of soda and one teaspoonful of cream of tartar; when these are thoroughly mixed, grate in about two-thirds of a small cocoanut; bake briskly.

RICE POUND CAKE.

ONE pound each of butter and powdered loaf sugar, twelve ounces of flour, eight ounces of rice flour, twelve eggs; mix as for Italian Bread (page 176). The following ingredients may be added, to taste: two pounds of currants, twelve ounces of lemon or orange peel, one grated nutmeg and a little pounded mace; bake in a papered hoop, not too fast.

SODA JELLY CAKE.

ONE cupful of rich sweet cream, two cupsful of sugar, two eggs, half a teaspoonful of soda, one teaspoonful of cream of tartar sifted in the flour; make as stiff as batter cakes and bake immediately; spread jelly in layers.

JELLY ROLL.

To three well-beaten eggs add one cupful of powdered sugar and one cupful of flour; stir well, and add one teaspoonful of cream of tartar, half a teaspoonful of saleratus dissolved in three tea-spoonsful of water; bake in two pie-pans; spread as evenly as possible; have ready a towel, and as soon as done, turn the cake on it, bottom side up, then spread evenly with jelly, roll up quickly and wrap closely in the towel.

GERMAN CITRON-ALMOND CAKES.

BEAT up four eggs; beat into them half a pound of butter melted until it becomes liquid, one pint and a half of warm milk and one teacupful of yeast; stir in as much flour as will make the mixture stiff, then tie it loosely in a cloth, put it into a pail of water and leave it there until it rises to the top; take the dough out of the cloth, mix with it three-quarters of a pound of sugar, the same of raisins, chopped lemon-peel, citron and almonds, and divide it into cakes two inches across; bake on tins.

SIX-MONTHS' CAKE.

FOUR eggs, five cupsful of flour, two cupsful of sugar, one cupful of molasses, one and a half cupsful of butter, one cupful of sweet milk, one pound of seeded raisins, one teaspoonful of saleratus, one teaspoonful each of cloves, cinnamon and allspice. This cake keeps well six months.

LOGSDON CAKE.

TAKE a quantity of light dough the size of a small bowl; add two eggs, one cupful of sugar, half a pint of milk, butter and lard the size of a walnut, one teaspoonful of soda or baking powder; mix well together and flavor with essence of lemon; bake one hour. This cake is cheap and delicious. Try it.

22

SORGHUM CAKE.

THREE cupsful of flour, one cupful each of butter (or lard) and sorghum, four eggs, half a teaspoonful of soda, spice to taste.

IMITATION POUND CAKE.

ONE pound each of flour and sugar, half a pound of butter, six eggs, two teaspoonsful of cream of tartar sifted in the flour, one teaspoonful of soda dissolved in half a teacupful of cream or buttermilk; season and flavor to taste. This is scarcely inferior to pound cake, except that it does not keep so well.

BUTTERMILK CAKE.

ONE cupful of butter, two cupsful of buttermilk, three cupsful of sugar, five cupsful of flour, four eggs, soda enough to sweeten the buttermilk.

BLUEBERRY CAKE.

ONE pint of rich milk, one cupful of sugar, one quart of berries, half a cupful of butter, three eggs, two tablespoonsful of molasses, two teaspoonsful each of cream of tartar and saleratus.

PLAIN LOAF CAKE.

THREE cupsful of yeast, three and a half cups-ful of sugar, two cupsful of butter, one cupful of sour milk, four eggs; stir the butter, sugar and eggs together, and add two teaspoonsful of soda, nutmeg, cinnamon and raisins.

HUME CUP CAKE.

THREE eggs, five cupsful of flour, three cupsful of sugar, one cupful of sour milk, one cupful of butter, one teaspoonful of saleratus; flavor to taste.

CUP CAKE.

HALF a cupful of butter and four cupsful of sugar creamed together, five well-beaten eggs, one teaspoonful of soda dissolved in one cupful of cream (or milk), six cupsful of flour, nutmeg, one teaspoonful of dry cream of tartar.

NO-EGG CAKE.

ONE cupful of sugar, one cupful of butter, nutmeg, one cupful of milk, two ounces of cur-rants (or not), one teaspoonful of dry cream of tartar, half a teaspoonful of soda dissolved in milk, flour enough to make a batter.

TIP-TOP CAKE.

Two cupsful of butter, one cupful of sugar, one cupful of sweet milk, four cupsful of flour, six eggs.

THE SAME, IMPROVED.

Two cupsful of sugar, one cupful of butter, one cupful of milk, six eggs, a little lemon and cinnamon, and flour enough to make it of the consistency of pound cake.

SCOTCH SNAPS.

One pound of brown sugar, one pound of flour, half a pound of butter, two eggs, cinnamon; roll very thin and cut into shapes to suit, to bake.

NEW HAVEN COMMENCEMENT CAKE.

ONE pound each of sugar and flour, five eggs, twelve ounces of butter, one cupful of yeast, three nutmegs, two teaspoonsful of cinnamon; rise overnight; in the morning add one teaspoonful of soda, and chopped raisins and citron to taste; let it stand an hour, and bake; a little raspberry vinegar or melted currant jelly may be added with advantage; ice or not to taste.

LOAF DUTCH CAKE.

ONE cupful of light bread dough, one egg, sugar and salt to taste, half a teaspoonful of soda, half a pound of raisins, and, if desired, a little butter and nutmeg; work very smooth, let it rise about half an hour, and bake as bread.

PRINCE GEORGE CAKE.

Two eggs, two cupsful of sugar, half a cupful of butter, one cupful of sweet milk, three cupsful of flour, one teaspoonful of cream of tartar, half a teaspoonful of soda and one teaspoonful of essence of lemon.

ALMOND MACAROONS.

HALF a pound of sweet almonds, half a pound of fine white sugar, the whites of two eggs; blanch the almonds and pound them to a paste; add to them the sugar and the eggs after they have been beaten to a froth; work the whole well together with the back of a spoon; then roll the preparation in your hands in balls about the size of a nutmeg; lay them on a sheet of paper at least an inch apart; bake in a cool oven a light brown.

22 *

ORANGE-FLOWER MACAROONS.

Two pounds of powdered loaf sugar, whites of seven eggs, two ounces of orange blossoms; treat and bake as preceding.

SHREWSBURY CAKES.

TAKE quarter of a pound of butter well worked; mix it with one pound of brown sugar, one egg well beaten, as much flour as will make it stiff; roll it, then cut with a tin mould, and bake the cakes in a *slow* oven.

AUGUSTA CREAM CAKE.

ONE cupful of white sugar, two-thirds of a cupful of sweet milk, one and two-thirds cupsful of flour, one egg, one tablespoonful of melted butter, one teaspoonful of soda, two teaspoonsful of cream of tartar; bake in three cake tins.

PRINCESS CAKES.

HALF a pound each of butter and sugar, one pound of rice flour, six eggs, one gill of sweet wine, one teaspoonful of caraway seed, one teaspoonful of soda, quarter of a pound of raisins; add water to form a batter, drop into buttered pans, and bake until done.

ICE CREAM CAKES.

HALF a cupful each of milk and butter, one cupful of sugar, two cupsful of flour, three eggs beaten, whites and yolks separately, one teaspoonful of cream of tartar, half a teaspoonful of soda, and flavor with vanilla.

TIPSY CAKE.

CUT a small cake in slices; put them into a basin and pour some wine and a little rum over; let soak for a few hours; put into a dish and serve with some custard. It may be decorated with a few blanched almonds or whipped cream and fruit. These may be made with small sponge cake by soaking them in some wine in which currant jelly has been dissolved; take twelve of them stale, soak well, put in a dish, cover with jam or jelly, and thus make four layers, decorating the top with cut preserved fruit; dish with custard or whipped cream.

NORFOLK CAKES.

ONE cupful of butter, two cupsful of brown sugar, one cupful of sour milk or cream, three and a half cupsful of flour, four eggs, one teaspoonful of saleratus, raisins, spice and one glassful of brandy; bake in small seal-shells.

COFFEE CAKES.

FIVE cupsful of flour, one cupful of butter, one cupful of coffee prepared as for the table, one cupful of molasses, one cupful of sugar, one cupful of raisins, one teaspoonful of soda; spice with cloves and cinnamon.

IMPROVED JUMBLES.

ONE pound each of butter and sugar, one and a half pounds of flour; put by a little of the sugar to roll them in; beat three eggs well, add a little nutmeg; this must be made into a soft dough; do not roll it on the pasteboard, but break off pieces of dough the size of a walnut and make into rings; lay them on tins to bake an inch apart, as it rises and spreads; bake in a *moderate* oven. These jumbles are very delicate, will keep a long time, and are a decided improvement on the old sorts.

NO-EGG CREAM CAKES.

FOUR cupsful of flour, three cupsful of sugar, one cupful of butter, two cupsful of sour cream, three teaspoonsful of saleratus dissolved in a little cold water, half a grated nutmeg and a teaspoonful of essence of lemon.

CIDER CAKE.

ONE teacupful of butter, three teacupsful of sugar, two teacupsful of flour, one teaspoonful of soda in two tablespoonsful of water, one grated nutmeg and half a teacupful of milk; mix, and add one teacupful of cider and four more teacupsful of flour.

VERY CHOICE WAFERS.

ONE pint of cream, half a pound of flour, half a pound of sugar; stir the cream into the flour by degrees until perfectly smooth; then beat in the sugar and as many bitter almonds pounded to a paste as will flavor it; if too thick, add a little more cream; the batter must be very thin; heat your irons and grease them with butter; bake them a light brown, and roll them as soon as they are taken out of the irons.

JEFFERSON CAKES.

FOUR eggs, one cupful of butter, two cupsful of sugar, one cupful of sweet milk, five cupsful of flour, two teaspoonsful of cream of tartar, one tea-spoonful of soda; bake in cups, and ice in fancy figures.

WAFERS.

QUARTER of a pound of sugar, quarter of a pound of butter, half a pound of flour, the white of one egg, half a teacupful of milk, saltspoonful of cinnamon; put the butter in the milk and warm it until the butter is melted; mix the sugar and flour together, add the white of an egg and cinnamon, then the butter and milk by degrees; make the wafer-tongs hot over a clear fire, rub the inside well with butter, then put in a spoonful of batter; close the tongs, put them over the fire, turn frequently, and when done, roll quickly.

PIONEER CAKE.

THREE cupsful of sugar, one cupful of butter, six cupsful of flour, six eggs, two teaspoonsful of cream of tartar, one teaspoonful of soda, one pound of dried cherries and spice to taste.

SPANISH BUNS.

Two pounds of flour, one pound of butter, one pound of sugar, one gill of yeast, two tablespoonsful of rose-water, one tablespoonful of wine, four eggs, one teaspoonful of cinnamon and nutmeg mixed; rub the butter, sugar and flour together, then add the sponge and other ingredients; beat all well together with milk sufficient to make a batter that will just drop from the spoon; mix them in the afternoon, and when the weather is cold, set them in a moderately warm place to rise; next morning stir them lightly; put in shallow tin pans, smooth them over with a knife, cover and set in a warm place to rise; bake in a *moderate* oven; ice them, or when cool, sift sugar over them; cut into squares with a sharp knife.

STAR CAKE.

ONE cupful and a half of sugar, one cupful of butter, two and a half cupsful of flour, half a pound of raisins, half a cupful of milk, three eggs and one teaspoonful of soda; bake in a scolloped pan, and when done, arrange white and pink candy on the top in shape of stars (or other shapes to taste).

FEDERAL CAKES.

Two pounds of flour, one pound of sugar, half a pound of butter, the yolks of two eggs, one and a half tablespoonsful of saleratus, half a pint of milk; rub the butter, sugar and flour together, then add all the other ingredients; knead the whole into a smooth dough; roll it out into thin sheets, cut the cakes in the form of a diamond, and bake them on greased tins in a *quick* oven.

WASHINGTON CAKE.

ONE pound of butter, one pound of sugar, one pound and a quarter of flour, ten eggs, one gill of cream, one wineglassful of wine, one pound of raisins (seeded and chopped), one pound of currants (washed, dried and picked), one teaspoonful of cinnamon and cloves mixed, the grating of one nutmeg; beat the butter and sugar light, to which add the cream, with one-fourth of the flour; whisk the eggs until thick, and stir in by degrees; after mixing well, add the remainder of the flour, spice and wine alternately; beat all well together, then stir in the fruit; butter and paper your pan, put in the batter, spread it over smooth and bake in a *moderate* oven.

VANILLA CAKES.

THREE-QUARTERS of a pound of pulverized sugar, the whites of six eggs, one-fourth of a vanilla bean pounded very fine; whisk the whites until stiff and dry; add the sugar gradually, one teaspoonful at a time, after which stir in the vanilla; then with a teaspoon place on paper in cakes the size of a macaroon, and a quarter of an inch apart each way; place the paper on tins, and bake in a *moderate* oven. They require to be very delicately baked, and must not be removed from the paper until perfectly cold.

MERVELLS.

ONE cupful of butter, one cupful of sugar, three eggs, half a wineglassful of milk, one teaspoonful of saleratus, half a teaspoonful of cinnamon, enough flour to make a dough; beat the butter and sugar to a cream; whisk the eggs, and add them to it, also the milk, saleratus and cinnamon; put in as much flour as will make a dough; roll it into thin sheets; cut into narrow slips; twist and drop them in boiling lard; when sufficiently cooked, take them out, and when cool, sift sugar over them.

23

SEED CAKES.

Two pounds of flour, one pound of sugar, fourteen ounces of butter, one tablespoonful of caraway seed, half a pint of milk, two tablespoonsful of saleratus; rub the butter, sugar and flour together, then add all the other ingredients; knead all well together into a smooth dough; roll it out quite thin, cut with a round cutter, place them on tins, and bake in a *moderate* oven. The quantity of milk in this as in all other hard cakes appears small, but after kneading it a little while will be found quite sufficient; to add more would spoil them.

LADY CAKE.

ONE pound and a quarter of butter, one pound and a quarter of sugar, one pound and a half of flour, the whites of twenty eggs, half a gill of rose-water, one ounce of bitter almonds; beat the butter and sugar until very light, blanch and pound the almonds to a paste, to which add the rose-water; stir this into the butter and sugar; beat it well, then whisk the whites stiff and dry, add them by degrees alternately with the flour, until all is well beaten together; bake in shallow pans or in deep ones, like pound cake, in a *moderate* oven.

APEES (A. P.'S).

ONE pound and a half of flour, one pound of sugar, one pound of butter, one gill of milk; rub the butter, sugar and flour together; add the milk; stir the mixture with a knife or spoon into a dough; turn it out, and work it until it becomes perfectly smooth; roll it into thin sheets, cut with a small cutter, place on tins, and bake them in a cool oven. It will take a few minutes to knead all the ingredients into a dough, but, as the quantity of milk is quite sufficient, it would spoil them to add more.

VERY RICH CITRON CAKE.

ONE pound each of butter, sugar, flour and citron, ten eggs, one scant wineglassful of brandy diluted with rose-water, one grated nutmeg; beat the butter, sugar and nutmeg until very light; stir in the brandy and one-fourth of the flour; whisk the eggs thoroughly and add alternately with the remaining flour, one-third at a time; cut the citron thin and into very small pieces and stir into the mixture; beat all well together; bake in a *moderate* oven. If desired this may be iced with lemon-flavored icing.

MERINGUES.

ONE pound of sugar, half a pound of butter, one pound of flour, the yolks of six eggs, one nutmeg, half a wineglassful of rose-water; beat the butter and sugar to a cream; whisk the eggs until they become thick; then put the butter, sugar and eggs into the flour; lastly, add the nutmeg and rose-water; mix the dough well, flour your board, and roll it half an inch thick; cut it into cakes and put them into a shallow pan; do not let them touch; bake five minutes in a *quick* oven; when cool, lay on each a lump of currant jelly; then take the whites of six eggs and whisk them until they become perfectly dry and stiff; add to them gradually one pound of powdered sugar, so as to make an icing; with a spoon heap on each lump of jelly as much of this icing as will cover it; place the cakes in a cool oven until the icing becomes firm and of a pale-brown color.

COLUMBIA CAKE.

Two cupsful of sugar, two cupsful of flour, six eggs, juice and rind of two lemons, two saltspoonsful of cream of tartar; four saltspoonsful of soda dissolved in two large spoonsful of warm water, to be put in at the last; bake in two loaves.

BURGESS CAKES.

HALF a pound of butter, half a pound of sugar, one pound of flour, three eggs, one tablespoonful of brandy, one teaspoonful of cinnamon and nutmeg mixed, half a pound of currants; beat the butter, sugar, spice and brandy until light; whisk the eggs thick and add alternately with the flour; then stir in the currants; with a teaspoon put them on tins slightly buttered; they should be rather larger than macaroon; bake in a *moderate* oven.

ROCK CAKES.

THREE-QUARTERS of a pound of sweet almonds, blanched and cut into small pieces, one pound of pulverized sugar, the whites of five eggs; beat the whites until very dry, then add the sugar very gradually, a teaspoonful at a time; when done, stir in the almonds, place the mixture on white paper with a teaspoon, in conical shapes; put the paper on tins, and bake in a cool oven until they can be removed from the paper without breaking.

SWISS CAKES.

ONE pound each of butter and sugar, one pound and three-quarters of flour, nine eggs, two table-

23 *

spoonsful of rose-water; beat the butter, sugar
and rose-water until very light; add one-fourth
of the flour; whisk the eggs until very thick and
stir in gradually, mixing all well; add the remainder of the flour, one-third at a time; beat all
well together; bake in a *moderate* oven; when
cool, ice, and before the icing is dry mark it into
squares, and again diagonally, with a knife.

THE GALETTE.

This is a favorite in France; it may be made
rich or plain by varying the allowance of butter,
and by using or omitting egg-yolks. One pound
of flour and twelve ounces of butter rubbed well
together, salt to taste, the yolks of two or three
eggs, a small cupful of sweet rich cream, an ounce
of sifted sugar, if desired; when thoroughly though
lightly worked together, roll into a complete round,
not quite an inch thick, score in small diamonds,
brush over with egg-yolk, and bake about an hour
in a tolerably brisk oven.

JOLLIES.

Four eggs, half a pound of sugar, four ounces
each of butter and flour; flavor with lemon or

orange-peel grated, or with mace and cinnamon to taste; bake in small buttered patty-pans about fifteen minutes.

ROCHERS.—EXCEEDINGLY FINE.

SEVEN ounces of sweet and one of bitter almonds, six ounces of candied orange-peel, one ounce of citron or green ginger, two ounces of flour, twelve ounces of sugar, half a teaspoonful each of mace and cinnamon, whites of three large eggs; blanch, dry and chop very fine the almonds; mix with the orange-rind and citron (or ginger), and add the other ingredients, beating the egg-whites as stiff as possible and putting them in last; roll the mixture into balls about a scant inch in diameter, and bake on paper about twenty minutes; they should be quite crisp, but not highly colored.

ICING.

THIS elegant finish is not difficult to apply; it is made by beating the whites of eggs to the stiffest froth and sifting into this, little by little, fine powdered loaf sugar until it is quite thick; flavor with essence of vanilla, or to taste; lay it on with a broad case-knife, and smooth with another knife dipped in water; set the iced cake in a cool oven, with the door open, or on the hearth under the oven, to dry.

If you wish to ornament with figures or flowers, make up rather more icing, keep about one-third out until that on the cake is dried, then with a clean glass syringe apply it in such forms as you desire, and dry as before; what you keep out to ornament with may be tinted pink with cochineal syrup, blue with indigo, yellow with saffron, green with spinach syrup, and brown with chocolate, purple with cochineal syrup and indigo. This tinting is troublesome, but adds much to the beauty of the cake, though not to the quality.

The icing may be handsomely ornamented, too, by putting on, when partially dry, rich-colored, ripe fruit, such as strawberries, red currants, etc., or small confections (assorted colors). Sweet-scented leaves as well as rose-petals are sometimes used.

If you desire to give the icing a frosted appearance all over or in spots, sprinkle it, when it is almost dry, very lightly, in very minute sprays, with rose-water; or, if you prefer to give it a highly polished, glossy appearance all over or in spots, dilute a little icing and put on very gently when the first coat is quite dry.

CHOCOLATE ICING.

ONE cupful of milk, quarter of a pound of the best prepared chocolate, one cupful of powdered sugar, one teaspoonful of vanilla; scald the milk and chocolate, then add the sugar, etc.; pour the mixture on the well-beaten white of an egg; this will ice a large cake or pudding. Other kinds may be made by substituting lemon, orange, nutmeg or any flavor desired.

ALMOND ICING.

ONE pound of sweet almonds, with enough bitter to give flavor, and one pound of loaf sugar; beat them until well mixed and very fine; put in a pan with the whites of ten eggs that have been previously well beaten; beat well together with a wooden spoon, and lay smoothly on the cake, about an inch thick, half an hour before it is baked.

FROSTING.

FOR the white of one egg take nine heaping teaspoonsful of white sugar and one teaspoonful of corn-starch; beat the eggs to a stiff froth, so that the plate can be turned upside down without the egg falling off; stir in the sugar and the starch slowly with a wooden spoon, ten or fifteen minutes constantly; then sift over it fine sugar and grated cocoanut or other fruit, if desired, or grated nut-kernels; or a few assorted colors of small confections add to beauty as well as taste. To frost a common-sized cake one and one-half eggs will suffice.

WHIPPED CREAM.

A DELIGHTFUL dressing for some sorts of cake is made thus: One pint of rich cream, enough fine pulverized loaf sugar to thicken; stir it well; set it on fire till it warms through; flavor to taste, and color if desired; let it cool and spread on the cake.

SAUCE FOR CAKE.

ONE cupful of sweet milk, one egg, one tea-spoonful of starch, one tablespoonful of flour, two tablespoonsful of sugar.

How to Make Pastry.

GENERAL REMARKS.

Scarce anything can be more unwholesome and deleterious than the tough, rancid or heavy compounds so frequently served up under the tempting appellations of pies and pudding, and yet a little care in the selection of ingredients and in their manipulation will secure pastry that will prove not only palatable but nutritious. One fact must always be borne in mind—that inferior ingredients cannot be made into superior compounds, though the finest ingredients may be ruined by careless or ignorant handling. In the making of pies, the preparation of the fruit, etc., is but a small part of the work; the manufacture of light, sweet and moderately brittle paste or crust is the grand desideratum. Hence, the importance of attention to the recipes for making paste; even the already proficient pie and pudding maker will find it no disadvantage to study them, and compare the processes given with those she has hitherto used.

Before giving specific recipes, it will not be amiss to make some suggestions of general application:

1st. The best place to roll paste on is a marble slab, and the best shape for the rolling-pin is straight, equally thick at ends and centre; avoid hard or heavy rolling or kneading.

2d. Be careful to have all the materials *cool*— the butter and lard hard.

3d. Put the several ingredients together quickly and handle as little as possible; slow mixing and contact with the hands or fingers have a tendency to make tough crust.

4th. Except in puff paste, lard and butter in about equal proportions make the best crust; that made of butter alone is almost sure to be tough, and of lard alone, though tender, is white and insipid. Beef drippings or the drippings of fresh pork in lieu of butter and lard make a very light and palatable crust, lighter and more tender than that made with butter alone, much nicer tasted than that made with lard alone, and nearly or quite equal to that made with butter and lard combined; never use mutton drippings in crust.

5th. Always roll *from* you; twice will answer for rolling out the paste, but each additional time, if rolled lightly, adds to its richness and lightness.

6th. Use very little salt and very little water; the latter, unless you want tough crust, pour in gradually, but a few drops at a time.

7th. Use plenty of flour on paste-board, to keep the paste from sticking.

8th. Pastry, except "raised" crust, should not stand a minute after prepared before it is placed in the oven.

9th. Special care is requisite with the oven; the heat should have a body to it, and the fire be looked to lest it desert you; the oven should be quite brisk, but not sufficiently so to scorch the paste before it has had time to rise; if too slack, the paste will not rise at all, but look white and clammy, while the best paste has a tinge of yellow; if permitted to scorch or brown, it becomes rancid.

10th. The filling should be perfectly cool when put in, or it will make the bottom crust sodden.

11th. Always carefully sift your flour before using it.

12th. In making juicy pies cut a slit in the top to let the steam escape; invert a very small cup on the centre of the pie: the extra juice will be drawn under the cup.

13th. For the best puff pastes, always wash your butter; unless very salt, it need not be washed for plainer pastes; to make the butter hard in warm weather, wash it in iced water; then place it between the folds of a towel and put it on a large piece of ice; after remaining an hour, turn it over, that it may become equally hard all through.

14th. Use a cool knife in working paste.

15th. Work the crust for one pie at a time.

16th. In winter, as soon as the paste is made, put it on a dish, cover with a cloth, and set it in a cold place until perfectly hard; by letting it remain two or three hours, it will puff much more than if baked soon after mixing. Be careful not to let it freeze. In summer, place it between the folds of a clean napkin and put it on a large flat piece of ice, which first cover with a thick cloth to prevent the paste from getting the least damp; turn over when it gets cold, so as to get it cold throughout.

17th. Always bake pies and puddings in tin plates; the paste bakes more thoroughly.

18th. To make pastry that will be entirely

wholesome, mix one ounce of carbonate of soda with seven drachms of tartaric acid. Put into a glass jar, with a closely-fitting lid, after having incorporated it fully. It is then fit for use, and pie-crust should not be made without it; use a teaspoonful to every two pounds of flour.

Almost every sort of pastry is better eaten fresh; if not eaten when just out of the oven, it should be warmed before served; it is more palatable, as well as more wholesome, warm; a very rich crust, especially that of mince pies, will keep good two or three weeks.

PLAIN FAMILY PASTE.

Two pounds of flour, half a pound each of butter and lard; work well, but lightly. Or, as some will prefer, take twelve ounces of butter and four of lard; this makes a very agreeable crust. The amount of shortening may be doubled, if desired, or drippings (see 5th, under General Remarks) may be substituted for butter and lard.

RAISED CRUST FOR PIES.

ONE pound of flour, three ounces of butter, tablespoonful of good lively yeast, milk to form a dough; rub the butter in the flour, add the milk and yeast, and set it aside to rise; when light, roll it out thin, and line your plates; put in the fruit, roll out the cover, place it over and set the pies in a *quick* oven. This is very nice for those who cannot eat rich paste.

A GOOD PASTE FOR DUMPLINGS.

To one pound of flour add a little salt and as much boiling water as will make it into a stiff dough; flour your pie-board, turn the dough out and work it lightly, then take a piece, roll it thin, and it is ready for the fruit. Dumplings covered with paste made in this way should always be boiled in cloths or nets, and will be found much more digestible than when made in the usual manner.

A PLAIN CRUST.

ONE bowlful of lard, one bowlful (scant) of water, three bowlsful of flour; mix all well together, and roll out, using "patent flour" (if convenient). In the preparation of puddings baked in crust, the under part of the crust can be made by this method, and half a pound of richer paste used as an edge.

POTATO PASTE.

BOIL three moderate-sized potatoes till very soft; peel and mash them fine and smooth; put into a deep pan and mix well with a quart of flour and half a pint of lard, or with half a pint of beef dripping or the dripping of fresh roast pork. Having mixed the mashed potatoes, dripping and flour into a lump, roll it out into a thick sheet; sprinkle it with flour, and spread over it evenly a thin layer of dripping or lard; fold it again, and set it in a cool place till wanted. It is good for meat pies and for boiled meat pudding, or any sort of dumplings.

GOOD, NOT RICH, PASTES.

VERY good crust for every-day family pies may be made by wetting up the flour with sour milk or cream sweetened with saleratus; a little butter may be used, if desired, although the crust will be more light without it. Light wheat dough, with a little butter worked in, makes healthful upper crust for pies. Very plain paste may be made by using a quarter of a pound of lard to every pound of flour. This, to be sure, will not be rich, but with a bit of dissolved sal-volatile and a skillful hand will

24 *

produce quite as palatable and more healthful an article than that which is so often made of oily or rancid butter.

PUFF PASTE.

THREE-QUARTERS of a pound of butter to three-quarters of a pound of flour; divide the butter into five or six equal parts; cut up two of these parts into the sifted flour in very thin slices; pour in a very little water at once, and stir with a knife; when it is stiff turn it out upon the board, roll it gently with the pin, dust on flour, roll it up; repeat this till you have mixed in the remaining pieces of butter; then roll it up, and it is ready for use; if these directions are carefully followed, and it is not spoiled in baking, it will rise to a nice thickness and appear in flakes and leaves, according to the number of times it is rolled out.

FINE PUFF PASTE.

THREE-QUARTERS of a pound of butter with a pound or quart of flour; dissolve a lump of sal-volatile (easily obtained at the druggist's) in a little cold water; divide the butter into four parts; rub one part into the flour, wet it up with a little cold water, adding the salts; next dredge the board

thick with flour, put upon it a second portion of
the butter in very thin slices, dredge again thick
with flour, roll it out once and lay it aside; thus
proceed with the two remaining portions of butter.
Turn out upon the board the paste or dough which
was previously mixed, roll it out gently, lay upon
it one of the butter sheets, dredge on a little flour,
roll it up; roll it out again, lay upon it another
butter sheet and proceed as before till all the butter is incorporated. This, if well baked, will ensure a beautiful puff paste, and is very easily made
after one trial, although the printed instructions
may look complicated.

PASTE SHELLS.

TAKE sufficient rich puff paste prepared as in
the two preceding recipes, roll very thin, cut to
shape, and bake in a brisk oven in tin pans.
Baked carefully, free from damp fruit, the paste
rises better. When cool, fill the shells with stewed
fruit, with jelly or preserves, with rich cream
whipped to a stiff froth, with ripe raspberries or
strawberries, or with sliced peaches. This makes
an exceedingly delicious light dessert for dinner,
and is equally palatable at supper. Raspberries,

strawberries or sliced peaches, smothered with whipped cream, on these shells, cannot be excelled.

EGG-PASTE SHELLS FOR TARTS.

Rub quarter of a pound of butter into a pound of flour; add two tablespoonsful of powdered loaf sugar and the well-beaten yolks of two eggs; work well with a wooden spoon, and roll out very thin; rub it over with the well-beaten white of an egg, and put instantly into a *quick* oven. This paste may be baked as shells or with fruit as tarts; in the latter case, sift fine sugar over the fruit before baking.

SUET PASTE.

Rub half a pound of fresh beef-suet chopped very fine, but not melted, three-fourths of a pound of flour and a teaspoonful of salt well together; put in just enough water to make a stiff paste, work well and roll twice at least. This paste is excellent for fruit puddings and dumplings that are boiled; if well made, it will be light and flaky, and the suet imperceptible. It is also excellent for meat-pies, baked or boiled.

DRIED FRUIT PIES.

WASH the fruit and soak it over-night; next morning stew it until nearly done, and sweeten to taste. The crust, both upper and under, should be rolled thin; a thick crust to a fruit pie is undesirable; the top crust should be cut large enough to *hem* over the under one; put in the fruit cold, with plenty of juice; prick the top crust about the centre and *hem* the edges well together to keep in the juice: to "hem," the top crust must be folded over and under the edge of the bottom crust, lying between it and the pie dish; then dress the edge around with your thumb, and the pie is effectually "sealed." Place at once in a moderately hot oven, and bake quickly.

GREEN APPLE PIE.

WE will give two methods, ourselves preferring the first, though the second is unexceptionable:

1. Pare and core tart apples (sweet apples never make good sauce or pies); stew them gently to a stiff smooth sauce, which flavor to taste and pass through a sieve or colander; set it aside till quite cold; bake a shell and put in your cold sauce (don't be stingy with your sauce), and cover with whipped

cream or top-crust shells, or leave it uncovered, sifting plenty of sugar and grating nutmeg over it.

2. Pare, core and quarter tart apples, stew slightly, sweetening and flavoring to taste; strain off as dry as possible and do not mash your apples. For crust, baking, etc., see directions for "Dried Fruit Pies."

JELLY AND PRESERVED FRUIT PIES.

PRESERVED fruit and jellies require no baking; hence, always bake a shell (see page 283) and put in the sweetmeats afterward; you can cover with whipped cream (see page 274), or bake a top-crust shell; the former is preferable for delicacy.

RHUBARB PIE.

SKIN the stalks, cut them into small pieces, wash and put them in a pipkin to stew with no more water than what adheres to them; when done, mash them fine and put in a small piece of butter; when cool, sweeten to taste; if liked, add a little lemon-peel, cinnamon or nutmeg; line your plate with thin crust, put in the filling, cover with crust, and bake in a *quick* oven; sift sugar over it when served.

PEACH PIE.

BAKE rich shells about two-thirds done; if your peaches are fully ripe, cut them into halves or quarters, put in the shell, sweeten and flavor to taste, cover or not as you choose, and finish baking in a *quick* oven; if the peaches are ripe but not soft, it will improve the flavor to sugar them down some hours before you wish to use them; if not ripe, they should be stewed. You can make a delightful pie or tart by omitting top-crust and substituting for it a thick covering of whipped cream (see page 274).

STRAWBERRY OR RASPBERRY PIE

MUST be made just as directed above for ripe peaches, except that berries must not be cut.

REAL CHEESECAKE.

FOUR ounces of rich (not strong or old) cheese cut into small pieces and beaten (a little at a time) to the consistency of butter; add equal weight of sweet fresh butter, mixing the two thoroughly; add gradually five eggs beaten stiff and smooth; line pan on bottom and sides with paste (puff is best), fill with the mixture, grate nutmeg over the surface, and bake not too fast. If you wish it sweet, put in white sugar before you mix in the eggs; also add spices to taste.

BRANDY-WINE CHEESECAKE.

HALF a pound each of butter and sugar, eight eggs, one pint of milk, quarter of a pound of currants, four ounces of bread, one tablespoonful each of brandy, wine and rose-water, one small nutmeg grated, half a teaspoonful of cinnamon; put the milk on to boil; beat up four eggs and stir into it; when it is a thick curd, take it off, and when cool, mash it very fine; crumb the bread and mix with the curd; beat the butter and sugar to a cream; add the curd and bread to it; then whisk the other four eggs thick and light, and pour them into the mixture; then add gradually the brandy, wine, rose-water and spice, and lastly the currants; line square tin pan, put in the filling, and bake in a *quick* oven.

EGG-COCOANUT CHEESECAKE.

TWELVE hard-boiled eggs rubbed through a sieve (while hot), half a pound of butter, half a pound of pounded loaf sugar, half a pound of currants and a little nutmeg; brandy may be added, which flavors them nicely, or, if preferred, a little essence of lemon or almond.

RICE CHEESECAKE.

QUARTER of a pound of butter, two ounces of ground rice, boiled and beaten; mix well with sifted sugar to taste; when quite cool, add the rind and juice of one lemon and two eggs well beaten; this will keep a month in a cool place.

LEMON CHEESECAKE.

THREE ounces of butter, half a pound of loaf sugar, three eggs, leaving out the whites of two, the grated rind and juice of one large lemon; boil it till the sugar is dissolved and it becomes the consistency of honey; line the pan with egg-paste (page 284), put in the above mixture, and bake in a *quick* oven.

CREAM CHEESECAKE.—VERY DELICIOUS.

ONE pint of sweet cream, the whites (well beaten) of three eggs; flavor in either of the following two ways: 1. One dozen or so of bitter

25

almonds pounded and boiled in just enough milk; or, 2. The juice and grated outside rind of a large lemon or orange well mixed with four ounces of powdered loaf sugar; mix the flavoring through the cream and egg-whites, line your pan with egg-paste (page 284) or rich puff paste, put in the mixture, sift fine sugar over, and bake in a *quick* oven.

CUSTARD PIE.

Boil three pints of milk and let it cool; add three well-beaten eggs, two tablespoonsful of sugar and a little salt; flavor with vanilla or rose; line your pie-plate with paste, put in the custard, and bake till it is nearly firm. It is an excellent plan to set your lined plate in the oven till it begins to bake before putting in the custard: this prevents the crust from getting soft and soggy.

CUSTARD PIE, No. 2.

One quart of milk, one tablespoonful of flour, one ounce of butter, six ounces of sugar, six eggs, rose, orange or other flavor to taste; set the milk on the fire; as soon as it boils put in the flour mixed in cold milk to the consistency of cream, and stir well and let it boil a few minutes; then remove from the fire, and stir in the butter and sugar; when cool, whisk the eggs perfectly light and stir them and the flavoring in. As to baking, see preceding recipe.

FLORENDINES.

ONE quart of milk, three tablespoonsful of rice flour, half a pound of sugar, four ounces of butter, six eggs, two tablespoonsful of rose-water, salt, nutmeg and cinnamon to taste; set the milk on the fire, and soon as it comes to a boil stir in the rice flour mixed with a little cold milk to the consistency of cream; let it simmer a few minutes, take it off the fire and stir in the butter and salt; when cool, gradually stir in the eggs whisked thick; then add the other ingredients, and mix thoroughly; line your plates with puff or egg-paste (page 284), fill with the custard, and bake in a *quick* oven.

PUMPKIN PIE.

BOIL the pumpkin in a very little water, and strain it through a sieve; add to the pulp thus obtained milk, salt, cinnamon or ginger, sugar and as many eggs as you wish; when no egg, or only one, is used, pulverized cracker forms a good substitute; line a deep pie-plate with plain paste, fill with the pumpkin, and bake. The proportions of the different ingredients vary so much to suit various tastes that we do not attempt here to designate them.

A JERSEY GIRL'S RECIPE.—UNRIVALED.

Cut the pumpkin in half, remove the seeds, put the halves in a dripping-pan, skin side down, bake in a *slow* oven until you can readily scrape all the pulp out of the rind with a spoon (if it is brown as a nicely-baked loaf of bread, so much the better); mash fine, and while hot add (the quantities here are to each quart of pumpkin) four ounces of butter; when cold, sweeten to taste and add one pint of cream or milk, the yolks of three eggs (if milk is used, use four eggs) well beaten, cinnamon and nutmeg to taste, one wineglassful of wine or brandy and the whites of the eggs beaten to a stiff froth; stir well before adding the egg-whites and very lightly afterward; line deep pie-plates with egg-paste (page 284), or plainer paste if you prefer it; put in plenty of the mixture, and bake in a *quick* oven.

A cover or top-crust made similar to icing and put on before baking, or whipped cream dressing (page 274), adds to the appearance and to the quality of this and the almond, citron, cocoanut, lemon, etc., custard pies.

THE DOWN-EAST RECIPE.

THREE pounds of pumpkin, six ounces of butter, six eggs, two tablespoonsful of wine, one table-spoonful of brandy, sugar, salt and spice to taste; cut the pumpkin in slices, pare it, take out the seeds and soft parts, cut it into small pieces and stew it in very little water until it becomes tender; then press it in a colander until quite dry, turn it out in a pan, put in the butter and a little salt, mash it very fine; when cool, whisk the eggs until thick, and stir in; then add sugar with the brandy, wine and spice; line your plates with paste, put in plenty of filling, and bake in a *quick* oven; when done, grate nutmeg and sift sugar over it.

CARROT PIE.

A VERY good substitute for pumpkin pie may be made by using carrots instead of pumpkin in the preceding recipe.

25 *

SWEET POTATO PIE.

BOIL sweet potatoes till you can mash them; then skin, mash, and strain the water out of them; add to each half pound one quart of milk, three spoonsful of melted butter, four well-beaten eggs, and sugar and spice to taste.

WHITE POTATO PIE.

PRECISELY the same way, except you substitute white for sweet potatoes.

ALMOND CUSTARD PIE.

HALF a pound each of butter and sugar, five eggs, one tablespoonful each of brandy, wine and rose-water, half a pound of sweet and two ounces bitter almonds blanched, dried and pounded to a paste; beat the butter and sugar until light; whisk the eggs until thick, and add by degrees; then stir in the almonds, with the wine, brandy and rose-water, half of each at a time; let it remain a short time in a cool place; line your plates with puff or egg paste, not forgetting to roll it much thinner in the centre than at the edge; fill with the custard, and bake in a *quick* oven; when done and cool, sift white sugar over it. The brandy and wine may be omitted.

CREAM PIE WITHOUT CREAM.

Two eggs, half a cupful of sugar, three table-spoonsful of flour, one pint of sweet milk; bring the milk to a boil, mix the sugar, flour and eggs well beaten, and put them in the boiling milk; when it begins to thicken, flavor with lemon or to taste, and let it get cold; bake a shell and fill it with the custard.

IMITATION COCOANUT CUSTARD PIE.

Same as cocoanut custard pie, substituting grated raw sweet potato for the nut.

MARMALADE CUSTARD PIES.

Bake rich puff or egg-paste shells, and fill with custard made as follows: beat the yolks of six eggs till thick and firm; stir in twelve ounces of marmalade or jelly (or stewed fruit is almost equally good); boil about ten minutes, stirring well all the time; take it off and put it in a stone-ware dish; when quite cold, fill with it the shells, and serve with powdered loaf sugar and rich cream, or cover with icing made of the whites of the eggs and sufficient sugar, and set it in the oven and let it brown very slightly. The quantity of marmalade or jelly may be increased or decreased according to the fruit and to taste.

LEMON CUSTARD PIE, No. 2.

GRATE one-half outside of a lemon and squeeze out the juice, yolks of two eggs, two tablespoonsful heaped of sugar, half a cup of water, one teaspoonful of butter; stir well, and bake in a deep dish lined with crust; beat the whites of the eggs to a stiff froth; stir in two tablespoonsful of pulverized sugar and spread over the top of the pie as soon as it is baked; set in the oven till the top is nicely browned.

BANANA CUSTARD PIE.

SAME, except you take full-ripe bananas mashed to a paste; flavor with rose.

FRUIT CUSTARD PIE,

OF almost any flavor, can be readily made by substituting the fruit desired for those in the recipes above. In all custard pies it will be found advantageous to use a shell partially baked before putting in the custard.

PINE-APPLE CUSTARD PIE.

SAME as almond custard pie, except you use stewed pine apple instead of almonds; flavor with lemon or orange.

CITRON CUSTARD PIE.

SAME as almond, except that you substitute half a pound of citron chopped fine for the almonds.

COCOANUT CUSTARD PIE.

SAME as almond, except that you use half a pound of grated nut instead of the almonds, and omit the yolks of the eggs.

LEMON CUSTARD PIE.

HALF a pound each of butter and sugar, two ounces of stale sponge cake rubbed fine, five eggs, one tablespoonful each of brandy and rose-water, the juice and the grated yellow rind of one large lemon; beat the butter and sugar very light and add the sponge cake; stir in gradually the eggs whisked thick, and lastly stir in, half at a time, the lemon, brandy and rose-water; mix thoroughly without much beating; line plates with puff or egg-paste, fill with the custard, and bake in a *quick* oven. (See remark at end of pumpkin pie recipe, page 291.)

ORANGE CUSTARD PIE.

SAME as preceding, substituting the juice and grated peel of an orange for the lemon.

PINE-APPLE TART.

TAKE a fine large ripe pine-apple; remove the leaves and quarter it without paring, standing up each quarter in a deep plate, and grating it down till you come to the rind; strew plenty of powdered sugar over the grated fruit; cover it, and let it rest for an hour; then put it into a porcelain kettle, and steam it in its own syrup till perfectly soft; have ready some empty shells of puff-paste; bake in patty-pans or in soup-plates; when they are cool, fill them full with the grated pine-apple; add more sugar, and lay round the rim a border of puff-paste.

GOOSEBERRY PIE.

STEW your gooseberries with plenty of white sugar, and use plain puff-paste for crust.

APPLE-PUMPKIN TART.

Boil separately equal quantities of tart apples and pumpkin, and mash them well together; add a few currants, and sugar and nutmeg to taste; bake with a light crust top and bottom. The pumpkin must be strained as dry as possible.

CRANBERRY TART.

Stew your cranberries well, and sweeten to taste while stewing; mash them smooth (some prefer them not mashed); line your plates with thin puff-paste, fill, lay strips of rich puff-paste across the top, and bake in a *moderate* oven. (See articles on "Shells" for the best method of making cranberry pies and tarts.)

QUINCE TART.

Wash well, pare and core some fine ripe quinces, having cut out all the blemishes; put the cores and parings into a small saucepan and stew them in a little water till all broken to pieces; then strain and save the quince-water; having quartered the quinces, or sliced them in round slices, transfer them to a porcelain stew-pan, and pour over them the water in which they were boiled;

when quite soft all through, sweeten to taste; line deep plates with rich puff-paste, and bake; then when both the shells and the fruit are cold, fill the shells to the top; serve with powdered loaf sugar and rich cream, or dress with whipped cream (page 274).

PEACH PIE, No. 2.

FREESTONE peaches make the best pies, and the more juicy, the better. Peel and quarter your peaches; stew in their own juice, putting in no water or as little as possible, and with white sugar sweeten to taste while stewing; a flavor that most persons consider delightful is imparted to them by putting in some fresh green peach leaves, or some peach-stone kernels blanched, the leaves or kernels to be picked out immediately when done stewing; have ready baked shells, fill to top with the peaches (the latter cold, the shells not quite cold), cover and treat as directed in articles on shells (page 283). If the peaches are very ripe and juicy, they need not be stewed, but pare, quarter, sweeten with plenty of white sugar and set them aside till the sugar is well dissolved through the fruit, and they are then ready for the shells.

RED CURRANT PIE

Is made in the same way as gooseberry, and is deservedly very popular when well made and baked just right.

FRUIT TARTS

MAY be made in substantially the same way of almost any fruit that is not so sweet as to cook insipid.

MOLASSES PIE

MAKE a plain paste, allowing one quart of flour to quarter of a pound of fresh butter and quarter of a pound of lard; cut up the butter into the pan of flour, and rub it into a dough with half a tumbler of cold water; roll out the paste into a sheet, and with a broad knife spread all over it one-half of the lard; sprinkle it with flour, fold it and roll it out again; spread on the remainder of the lard, dredge it slightly, fold it again and then divide it into two sheets; line with one sheet a pie-dish and fill it with West India molasses mixed with butter and flavored with ginger and cinnamon, or lemon or orange; put on the other sheet of paste; crimp or notch the edges; bake it of a pale brown, and send it to table fresh, but not hot.

26

CHERRY PIE.

THIS is one of the most delightful of pies if made correctly. Those who have not time or are too lazy to remove the stones should never attempt to make cherry pies. Having removed the stones, put in sugar to taste, and stew the cherries slowly till they are quite done if you use shells, or till nearly done if you use paste; a few of the pits added in stewing increase the richness of the flavor, or if you do not like this, use almond or vanilla flavoring.

PLUM PIE.

THIS must be made same as preceding, except flavor with orange or lemon peel.

MINCE PIE.

FOR crust use rich puff-paste, and roll not quite so thin as for fruit pies, though on the other hand it must not be thick; don't stint your filling: a thin mince pie is a mean affair; mince pie should never be served cold, especially if it contain suet; many prefer it warmed up, rather than fresh from the baking. Any one of the following recipes will give good mincemeat:

1. Four pounds of tongue or tender beef, three pounds of suet, eight pounds of chopped tart apples, three pounds each of currants (washed, dried and picked) and seeded raisins (Sultana raisins are preferable), six pounds of white sugar, or brown if preferred, two pounds of citron chopped fine, the grating of one orange, one ounce of cinnamon, quarter of an ounce each of cloves, mace and allspice, four nutmegs grated, one quart of Madeira wine, one pint of brandy; boil the meat in salt water until tender; when cold, chop it very fine; after removing every particle of membrane from the suet and chopping it fine, mix it through the meat, with salt just sufficient to remove the fresh taste; to this add the apples, after which, the sugar, fruit, spice and other ingredients; mix all well together and cover close; if too dry (before using), the quantity required may be moistened with a little sweet cider. This cannot be excelled.

2. TEMPERANCE.—An unexceptionable mincemeat may be made as above without the wine or brandy by substituting good cider. Cream of tartar is said to make a good substitute.

3. PLAIN.—Boil till tender about three pounds of lean stewing beef; chop very fine one pound of

suet (cold roast beef, if quite fat, will answer the purpose without the addition of suet) ; pare, core and chop enough apples to weigh at least as much as the meat; stone and chop three pounds of raisins; mix these together well, and add one pound of brown sugar and half a pint of molasses, one tablespoonful of cloves, one tablespoonful of cinnamon, one nutmeg grated, one teaspoonful of ginger and one teaspoonful of black pepper, a little salt, one tablespoonful of extract of lemon or vanilla, or the rind and juice of two or three lemons; moisten with sweet cider, or a little sharp vinegar instead. This will make very good pies, but will not keep long.

4. RICH.—Boil till tender a beef tongue weighing about four or five pounds (this should lie in salt water a day or two before boiling) ; when cold, mince it very fine, after removing the skin and all unnecessary fat which surrounds it; chop two pounds of suet very fine, also at least six pounds of the best tart apples; prepare four pounds of raisins and the same of currants; mix all these together, and add the juice and rind of four fresh lemons, four grated nutmegs, two teaspoonsful of cloves and a few blades of mace, one pound and a half of white sugar and one pound of citron cut in

slips; one pound of sweet almonds blanched and pounded in a gill of rose-water is a fine addition; mix all these, and moisten with three pints of port wine or brandy; then closely pack and tightly cover. It will keep excellently all winter.

5. DELICATE.—Boil calf's feet very tender with a little salt, and when cold, chop the meat fine; put in a small proportion of suet, and apples, spices, currants, light wine or cider and sugar; citron, green ginger or sweet almonds will be a decided improvement. This is delicious, but will not keep well.

6. COUNTRY PIG. — Boil very tender pigs' tongues and hearts, and when cold, chop fine; then measure and mix as follows: One bowlful of minced meat, two bowlsful of apples chopped fine, one bowlful of cider (boiled); one and a half cupsful of molasses, one cupful of sugar, two dessertspoonsful of cloves, two dessertspoonsful of cinnamon, two dessertspoonsful of allspice, a little nutmeg, a double handful of raisins and a few currants or a little citron or green ginger.

7. EGG INSTEAD OF MEAT.—To enough tart apples to weigh about twelve ounces when pared, cored and chopped fine, add six large eggs beaten thick and half a pint of cream; spice, sugar,

26 *   U

raisins and currants, wine or cider, as for mince-meat. This makes exceedingly delicious pies, but it will not keep.

8. No-MEAT.—Take one pound of currants, one pound of apples chopped fine, one pound of moist sugar, one pound of suet well chopped, one pound of raisins stoned and chopped, the rind and juice of two lemons, nutmeg, one teaspoonful each of cinnamon, clove and ginger, and one glassful of wine. To keep this you must pack it well, air-tight, and set in a cool place.

LENT PIE.

ONE pint and a half of new unskimmed milk, three ounces of rice flour, three ounces of butter, four ounces of sugar, six eggs, four to six ounces of currants; boil fifteen minutes the rice flour in the milk; take off the fire and stir in the butter and sugar; then add the eggs well beaten; season and flavor to taste; line large patty-pans or large saucers with thin plain or puff-paste, and when the mixture is quite cold, fill them about three-fourths full, sprinkle the currants over the tops, and bake fifteen or twenty minutes in a *moderate* oven. A plainer kind may be made as follows:

One quart of milk, five ounces of rice flour, one ounce and a half to three ounces of butter, four ounces of sugar, four large eggs and three ounces of currants; season and flavor to taste.

NEW LEMON PIE.

Two grated lemons, two eggs, one pint of New Orleans molasses, two and one-half tablespoonsful of corn-starch mixed in a little water; mix all together, and boil for a few minutes in one quart of water; bake with two crusts. This recipe makes about eight pies.

RICH CREAM PIE.

Six eggs, two cupsful each of sugar and flour, two teaspoonsful of cream of tartar, one teaspoonful of soda dissolved in two teaspoonsful of cold milk; rub the cream of tartar in the flour; stir the eggs, sugar and flour a minute, and add the soda when it is ready to bake; this makes three pies; split them when cold, and put in the following cream: One pint of milk, one cupful of sugar, one-half a cupful of flour, two eggs; beat eggs, sugar and flour together and pour into the boiling milk; flavor with lemon or vanilla.

CHERRY AND CURRANT TART.

STEM and stone your cherries; take an equal weight of very ripe red currants, press them through a sieve, add the juice to your cherries with the crumb of two sponge cakes, quarter of a pound of sugar and one wineglassful of brandy; put it into a tart-dish lined with a rim of paste, cover it with a top crust, and bake it for an hour.

TOMATO MINCE PIE.

To one peck of green tomatoes add seven pounds of sugar; chop fine, and stew two hours; when nearly cold, add five lemons chopped fine; put in a cool, dry place, to be used at convenience; when you bake, use thin puff under-crust, with or without upper-crust.

POTATO PIE.

ONE pound of potatoes, white or sweet, mashed and worked smooth, half a pound of sugar, four eggs, juice and grated rind of two large lemons or two small oranges, one cupful of rich milk, quarter of a pound of melted butter; bake with an under-crust only, or with both under-crust and whipped cream cover.

HOW TO MAKE PUDDINGS.

GENERAL REMARKS.

AMONG the luxuries of the dinner-table there is not one that is more universally appreciated by every taste than a *good* pudding, and there is no department of the culinary art that demands closer care and clearer judgment than the making, baking or boiling and serving of puddings; while all kinds, from the rich Plum to the plain Hasty Pudding, depend as much on the cook as upon the materials used: the boiled puddings are especially difficult to get done just right; a very slight mistake or seemingly trifling neglect will too often convert what should be delicious and nutritious into a distasteful, heavy, injurious substance. The General Remarks under the heads of Cakes and Pastry mostly apply to the several classes of Puddings, and there remains little to say as to selection of best quality of ingredients and the exercise of great care in their manipulation and cooking.

Boiled custard puddings must not be boiled over a hot fire rapidly, but *simmered steadily;* if boiled too vigorously, the surface will be honeycombed instead of smooth and velvety; a well-buttered piece of writing paper should be laid between the custard and the cloth if boiled in a basin, or between the custard and the lid if boiled in a mould; the mould or basin should also be well buttered and filled full; after it is taken from the fire it should stand in the basin or mould full five minutes before it is emptied out, or it will break or spread.

Boiled batter puddings are usually lighter and better boiled in a cloth with plenty of room to swell; the water should be ready boiling, and the pudding put in instantly as soon as well beaten up and tied in the cloth; the cloth should be steeped in hot water and well floured before it receives the pudding.

Unless you want it to become heavy, you must hurry your pudding to table as soon as it is done; batter puddings and those made with paste are especially liable to settle if they are allowed to cool in the slightest degree before they are dished

up, and while in the water if you allow the boiling to stop for an instant, the pudding is almost
sure to become heavy and uneatable.

All sweet puddings require a *little* salt, to prevent insipidity, and to draw out the flavor of the
several ingredients, but a grain too much will
spoil any pudding.

In puddings where wine, brandy, cider, lemon-
juice or any acid is used, it should be stirred in last,
and gradually, or it is apt to curdle the milk or eggs.

The pudding-cloth should be very carefully
kept; if not quite clean and perfectly dry, or if
kept in a damp place, it very soon gets musty or
nasty, and will spoil any pudding boiled in it; as
soon as the pudding is taken from it, it should be
thrown into ley-water or water in which soda (two
ounces to the gallon) has been dissolved, to soak;
then washed thoroughly, to get every particle of
grease and batter off, and carefully rinsed and
dried quickly, in the open air if possible. It is
better to make the pudding-cloth of stout muslin
that will not too readily admit the water to the
pudding.

Under the head of Pastry we have given recipes
for making paste for such fruit and other puddings
as are made with paste, and here, before giving

specific recipes, we present a paragraph of general directions how to mix

BATTER FOR PUDDINGS.

PUT the flour and salt into a bowl, and stir them together; whisk the eggs thoroughly, strain them through a fine hair-sieve, and add them very gradually to the flour, for if too much liquid be poured to it at once it will be full of lumps, and it is easy, with care, to keep the batter perfectly smooth; beat it well and lightly with the back of a strong wooden spoon, and after the eggs are added, thin it with milk to a proper consistency; the whites of the eggs beaten separately to a solid froth, and stirred gently into the mixture the instant before it is tied up for boiling, or before it is put into the oven to be baked, will render it remarkably light. When fruit is added to the batter, it must be made thicker than when it is served plain, or the fruit will sink to the bottom of the pudding. Batter should never stick to the knife when it is sent to the table; it will do this both when a less than a sufficient number of eggs is mixed with it and when it is not enough cooked; about four eggs to the half pound of flour will make it firm enough to cut smoothly.

PEAR, PEACH OR APPLE PUDDING.

PARE some nice ripe pears (to weigh about three-fourths of a pound); put them in a sauce-pan with a few cloves, some lemon or orange peel, and stew about a quarter of an hour in two cupsful of white wine; put them in your pudding-dish, and having made the following custard, one pint of cream, four eggs, sugar to taste; beat eggs and sugar well, grate some nutmeg, add the cream by degrees, stirring all the time,—pour this over the pears, and bake in a *quick* oven. Apples or peaches served likewise will be found tip-top.

BREAD-TOP CUSTARD PUDDING.

ONE quart of new milk, three eggs, half a pound of sugar, a little salt; pour these into your pudding-dish, mix well, slice thin some bread, butter it, and lay the slices over the top of your pudding; bake about one hour.

RICE PUDDING.—VERY NICE.

BOIL one cupful of rice slowly; cool, add one cupful of milk, one small teaspoonful of soda if the milk be sour, one spoonful of lard or butter, two eggs, a little corn-starch; stir thoroughly; bake in a *slow* oven.

27

QUINCE, APPLE OR GOOSEBERRY PUDDING.

PARE and core three large quinces, and boil them till soft, but not till they break; drain off the water, and mash the quinces with the back of a wooden spoon; stir into them quarter of a pound of sugar and the juice of an orange or small lemon, and set them away to cool; when quite cold, mix with them about two ounces of butter and seven eggs (which have been well beaten), and bake the mixture in puff-paste; before they go to table, grate white sugar over the top, or they may be covered with icing or whipped cream and brandy. Apple puddings may be made in the same manner, and also puddings of stewed gooseberries.

APPLE AND SAGO PUDDING.—NO EGGS.

WASH one teacupful of large sago, and let it stand one hour or more in one pint of cold water; butter a suitable dish, and put a layer of sliced tart apples, sweetened and flavored, on the bottom; strain the sago nearly dry, and spread it over the apples; put another layer of apples, sift plenty of sugar, and grate nutmeg over the top, and bake in a *moderate* oven. It may be eaten hot with wine or brandy dip, or cold with sweetened cream.

RICE PUDDING.—NO EGGS.

Wash and pick two tablespoonsful of rice, put it in a deep pie-dish and with it a like quantity of sugar; pour in a pint of sweet milk; float on the top a few shavings of butter or a small quantity of nice minced beef suet; bake very slowly for at least two hours.

COTTAGE PUDDING.

One heaping pint of flour, half a cupful of sugar, one egg, one cupful of milk, one teaspoonful of soda dissolved in the milk, two teaspoonsful of cream of tartar rubbed dry in the flour; bake in a *moderate* oven; serve with wine or brandy sauce.

QUEEN PUDDING.

Two cupsful of sugar, one cupful of butter, one cupful of sweet milk, four cupsful of flour, six eggs, one wineglassful of wine; bake in pudding-dish.

CREAM PUDDING.—STEAMED.

One cupful of sour cream, three cupsful of flour, one egg, a little salt, one teaspoonful of soda; steam half an hour.

AUGUSTA PUDDING.

NINE tablespoonsful of flour, ten eggs and one quart of milk; boil the milk; pour it over the flour; let it stand till it is cool, and then put in the eggs, which have been beaten separately and very light; bake it in a tin mould or dish, and in a *quick* oven; serve with cream sauce.

INDIAN APPLE PUDDING.—NO EGGS.

HEAT one quart of milk to boiling, then stir in slowly one teaspoonful of Indian meal; mix with this about six good apples pared and sliced, and add two tablespoonsful of sugar, one tablespoonful of butter, and a little allspice and nutmeg; pour the whole into a deep dish, and bake until done, or about two hours.

ARROWROOT PUDDING.

BOIL one quart of milk, and stir into it four heaping tablespoonsful of arrowroot dissolved in a little milk, mixed with four well-beaten eggs and two tablespoonsful of white sugar; boil three minutes; eat with cream and sugar. This pudding is improved by flavoring with lemon, and pouring into wet moulds.

INDIAN PUDDING.—NO EGGS.

Mix three pints of Indian meal, one pint of wheat flour, two pints of sweet milk, one pint of sour milk, one cupful of molasses, one tablespoonful of salt, and one teaspoonful of saleratus; bake three hours.

NUTMEG PUDDING.

Pound two fine large or three small nutmegs; melt three pounds of butter, and stir into it half a pound of loaf sugar, a little wine, the yolks of five eggs well beaten and the nutmeg; bake on a puff-paste.

POTATO AND CHEESE PUDDING.

Twelve ounces of boiled, skinned and mashed potatoes, one ounce of cheese grated fine, one ounce of suet, one gill of milk; mix it all together; if not proper consistency, add a little water, and bake it in an earthen pan.

SWEET OR IRISH POTATO PUDDING.

Five large potatoes, boil, peel, mash; add four eggs, one cupful of milk; boil four hours, or steam same length of time. (This recipe is for sweet potatoes, but Irish potatoes, with sugar to taste, are nearly as good.) To be eaten with lemon sauce, made as follows : Drawn butter, well sugared, sugar boiled in, and the juice and grated rind of one lemon added; a little wine also, if convenient.

CREAM PUDDING.

BEAT six eggs well, and stir them into one pint of flour, one pint of milk, a little salt, the grated rind of a lemon and three spoonsful of sugar; just before baking, stir in one pint of cream, and bake in a buttered dish.

STEAMED PUDDING.

ONE cupful each of suet chopped fine, seedless raisins, molasses and sweet milk, one teaspoonful of soda, one of cream of tartar, two cupsful of flour, saltspoonful of salt; steam two hours. To be eaten with vinegar sauce.

SPICED MOLASSES PUDDING.

SIFT into a pan one quart of yellow Indian meal; simmer over the fire one quart of milk, one pint of West India molasses stirred in while the milk is boiling; put the milk and molasses into a large pan, and mix gradually into them the corn meal while they are quite warm; add one large tablespoonful of ground ginger and one heaped teaspoonful of powdered cinnamon; beat the whole mixture long and hard, for on that will chiefly depend the lightness of the pudding; if batter is too thin, add gradually a little more corn meal, if too thick, a little more milk and molasses; then pour the pudding mixture into the pudding-cloth; tie it up, making the string very secure, but leave between the batter and the tying place, for the pudding to swell in boiling, at least one-third; keep it steadily boiling for about three hours; turn the pudding; if the water boils away too much, replenish it with boiling water.

FARINA PUDDING.

BOIL one quart of milk, stir in slowly three tablespoonsful of farina, let it boil a few minutes; beat two eggs and four tablespoonsful of sugar with one pint of milk, and mix thoroughly with the farina; when it has cooled so as to be little more than lukewarm, put in pans, and bake in a *moderate* oven.   Eat with cream sauce.

SODA PUDDING.

TAKE one teacupful of sugar, two teacupsfuls of sweet milk, five tablespoonsful of melted butter, two eggs, four teacupsful of flour, one teaspoonful of soda, two teaspoonsful of cream, two teaspoonsful of cream of tartar; serve with plain sauce No. 1 (page 346).

RICH JAM-CUSTARD PUDDING.

LINE a deep dish with puff-paste, having first buttered it well; put on this a layer of jam, then a layer of custard, then jam, then custard, until the dish is nearly full, putting a layer of custard on top; slice some minced peel, and cut it in diamonds and arrange on top; bake twenty minutes in a *quick* oven; beat up the whites of the eggs that were used for the custard into a stiff froth, with a little powdered sugar; pile it on the pudding as high as possible, and serve.

DELMONICO PUDDING.

ONE quart of sweet milk; set it on the fire, and just before it begins to boil, put in the yolks of five eggs beaten thick with five tablespoonsful of powdered sugar; then mix four tablespoonsful of

corn-starch with a little cold milk, work it smooth
and pour on it the boiling custard; mix and boil;
when done, pour it into a buttered dish, and let it
cool while you make an icing of the whites of the
eggs and sufficient pulverized sugar; when the
custard is cold, put on the icing, and bake light
brown in a *moderate* oven; serve cold with rich
cream and nutmeg sauce.

APPLE-BUTTER PUDDING.

Six eggs, whites and yolks beaten separately,
one teacupful each of butter, sugar and apple-
butter beaten with the yolks; stir in the beaten
whites with one pint of cream; bake in light
plain or puff crust.

LIGHT FRUIT PUDDING.

Two and a half cupsful of light bread dough,
one cupful of sugar, three-fourths of a cupful of
butter, two eggs, half a teaspoonful of soda, one
glassful of wine or brandy, cinnamon, cloves and
nutmeg, half a pound of currants, the same of
seedless raisins, quarter of a pound of finely
chopped citron; bake carefully, so as not to have
the crust hard; serve with wine sauce.

TRANSPARENT PUDDING.

BEAT eight eggs very light; add half a pound of pounded sugar, the same of fresh butter melted, and half a grated nutmeg; set it on the fire and keep stirring till it is rather thick; line a dish with puff-paste; pour in the mixture, and bake it half an hour in a *moderate* oven; sift sugar over it, and serve up hot.

APPLE ROLL PUDDING.

MAKE your paste with one pound of flour, quarter of a pound of butter, or two ounces each of lard and butter, and water to form not a very stiff paste; peel and slice some tart apples; roll paste thin; spread sliced apples on it; dredge on a little flour and roll it very tight; cut the ends even, wrap in a thick cloth and boil one hour, and serve with butter and sugar.

ROYAL PUDDING.

IT will be found best to prepare the ingredients the day before, and cover closely. Grate a stale loaf of bread, boil one quart of milk and turn boiling hot over the grated bread; cover and let steep an hour; in the mean time pick, soak and dry half a pound of currants, half a pound of raisins, quarter of a pound of citron cut in large slips, two nutmegs, one tablespoonful of mace and cinnamon; crush half a pound of loaf sugar with half a pound of butter; when the bread is ready, mix with it the butter, sugar, spice and citron, adding a glassful of white wine; beat eight eggs very light, and when the mixture is quite cold, stir them gradually in; then add by degrees the raisins and currants dredged with flour; stir the whole very hard; put it into a buttered dish; bake two hours; send to the table warm. Eat with wine sauce, or wine and sugar.

TAPIOCA PUDDING.—GOOD AND CHEAP.

PUT one teacupful of tapioca and one teaspoonful of salt into one pint and a half of water, and let it stand several hours where it will be quite warm, but not cook; peel six tart apples, take out the cores, fill them with sugar, in which is grated a little nutmeg and lemon peel, and put them in a pudding-dish; over these pour the tapioca, first mixing with it one teaspoonful of melted butter and a little cold milk; bake one hour; eat with sauce.

RICE FLOUR PUDDING.

ONE pint and a half of milk, three ounces and a half of ground rice, three ounces of moist sugar, one ounce and a half of butter, four eggs and some grated lemon peel; bake slowly for half an hour, or longer if not quite firm.

RICE MERINGUE PUDDING.

To one quart of milk put one cupful of rice, and simmer slowly until it is thick and the rice perfectly tender; then stir in a tablespoonful of butter, three tablespoonsful of sugar and the yolks of three eggs while it is hot, with salt to taste; grate in the peel of a lemon and pour it in a shallow pudding-dish lined with rich paste, and bake a light brown. To the whites of the three eggs beaten stiff add six tablespoonsful of powdered sugar and the juice of a lemon; cover the top of the pudding, and put it back in the oven five minutes.

VERY RICH RICE MERINGUE PUDDING.

BOIL half a cupful of rice in one quart of milk for three hours, or till quite thick; sweeten and flavor to taste, and let it cool; beat with it the yolks of four eggs and scant cupful of butter; put the mixture into your pudding-dish; then, when cold, spread over some jam or jelly, and having beaten the whites of four eggs very light, add to the froth fine sugar to thicken like icing, flavor with almonds, and spread over the mixture; bake light brown; eat with sweet cream.

QUEEN OF PUDDINGS.

ONE pint of nice bread crumbs to one quart of milk, one cupful of sugar (half in the pudding and half saved for the top), the yolks of four eggs beaten, a piece of butter the size of an egg; flavor to taste; bake till done, but not watery; whip the whites of the eggs stiff, and beat in the half cupful of sugar saved; spread over the pudding a layer of jelly or any sweetmeat you may prefer; pour the whites of the eggs over this, replace in the oven, and bake lightly.

PEACH GOVERNOR.—PERFECTLY DELICIOUS.

LINE a deep dish with rich thick crust; pare and cut into halves or quarters some juicy, rather tart peaches; put in sugar, spices and flavoring to taste; stew it slightly, and put it in the lined dish;

28

cover with thick crust of rich puff-paste, and bake well; when done, break up the top crust into small pieces and stir it into the fruit; serve hot or cold; very palatable without sauce, but more so with plain rich cream or cream sauce, or with rich brandy, wine or vinegar dip.

OTHER GOVERNORS,

MADE according to above recipe, substituting apples, quinces, gooseberries, blackberries or other juicy, tart fruit for the peaches, are almost as delicious as the peach governor; pine-apples, too, make a governor that cannot be excelled.

SNOW-APPLE PUDDING.

ROAST nicely and well-done some of the finest large apples you can find, and to each half a pound of the pulp, after the skins and cores are removed, take an equal weight of finely powdered loaf sugar and the whites of two eggs; first beat the egg-whites to a stiff froth, then add, part at a time, the sugar and the apple-pulp; beat all together to a snow, till it stands perfectly stiff; with the egg-yolks make a sweet custard and put it in the bottom of a buttered dish, and pile the snow on, and bake slowly a little. Savoy cakes or sweetmeats in with the custard add to the eatableness of this delightful pudding.

BREAD-AND-BUTTER PUDDING.—FINE.

BUTTER thin slices of bread and place in a deep dish; between every layer sprinkle well cleansed currants and chipped citron; beat three eggs well, stir with them one pint and a half of milk and a pinch of salt; pour over the bread, and bake slowly, with a cover on, three-quarters of an hour; then take the cover off and brown; eat with wine or lemon sauce.

CANARY PUDDING.

THREE eggs and their weight in sugar and butter; melt the latter without oiling; add the sugar and the rind of one small lemon, very finely minced, and then gradually dredge in as much flour as is equal to two of the eggs; stir the mixture thoroughly; whisk and beat well the eggs, and add them last; again mix well together all the ingredients, and boil for two hours in a buttered mould or basin; serve with sweet or wine sauce.

ENGLISH ROLL PUDDING.

ROLL out half an inch thick a paste made of suet chopped fine, flour, water and a little salt; spread over it preserves of any small kind—damsons, currants, berries or the like; dust a little flour over it, roll up, wet and pinch the ends tight, and tie in a cloth wet with cold water and well floured; boil or steam one or two hours, according to size, and eat hot with rich sauce.

SPOTTSYLVANIA PUDDING.

MAKE a butter crust or a suet one, using for a moderate-sized pudding from three-quarters to one pound of flour, with the other ingredients in proportion; butter a basin; line it with some of the paste; pare, core and cut into slices enough apples to fill the basin; add sugar to taste, flavor with lemon peel and juice, and cover with crust; pinch the edges together, flour the cloth, place it over the pudding, tie it securely, and put it into plenty of fast-boiling water; let it boil from one and a half to two and a half hours, according to its size; send to table promptly. Care must be taken to keep completely covered with water and boiling steadily all the time.

BIRD'S NEST PUDDING.

Mix two large tablespoonsful of flour (or one and a half tablespoonsful of corn-starch) with a pint of milk, a little salt and two well-beaten eggs; have ready six tart apples peeled, cored and filled with sugar, strips of citron and spice to taste; set the apples in a buttered earthen pudding-dish; pour over them the batter, and bake three-quarters of an hour; eat with sweet sauce flavored with lemon.

SAGO PUDDING.

Wash one cupful of sago; put it in your pudding-dish and pour on one quart of boiling water, stirring all the time; put in a little salt and one cupful of sugar; let it stand before baking several hours; bake slowly one hour; eat with sweet butter sauce.

BROWN BREAD PUDDING.

Half a pound of stale brown bread grated, the same quantity of currants and shred suet, a little nutmeg and sugar to taste; add four eggs, one spoonful of brandy and two spoonsful of cream; boil in a basin or cloth three hours.

28 *

FRUIT RICE PUDDING.

ONE large teacupful of rice, a little water to cook it partially; dry, line an earthen basin with part of it; fill nearly full with pared, cored and quartered apples, or any fruit you choose; cover with the balance of your rice; tie a cloth tightly over the top, and steam one hour. To be eaten with sweet sauce. Do not butter your dish.

RED CURRANT PUDDING.

A GOVERNOR (see page 326) made of red currants is very nice, but probably the best way to treat this fruit is as follows: Press the currants through a sieve to free it from pips; to each pint of the pulp put two ounces of crumbed bread and four ounces of sugar; bake with a rim of puff-paste; serve with cream. White currants may be used instead of red.

BREAD MERINGUE PUDDING.

ONE pint of stale bread crumbed, one quart of milk, the yolks of four eggs beaten lightly, one small cupful of white sugar, the grated rind of a small lemon and a piece of butter the size of an egg; mix all well together, and bake; when cool, spread it well with acid preserves or jelly; beat the whites of the eggs stiff with five tablespoonsful of sifted sugar and the juice of one lemon; spread it over the top, and put it into the oven to brown quickly; to be eaten with cream.

LEMON-POTATO PUDDING.

THREE ounces of potatoes (weighed after boiling and paring), the peel of two large lemons, two ounces of white sugar, two ounces of butter; boil the lemon peel until tender, and beat it with the sugar; boil the potatoes and peel them; mix all together with a little milk and two eggs; bake slightly; best with acid sauce.

SOUFFLE PUDDING.

PUT six ounces of corn-starch into a stewpan, with eight ounces of pounded loaf sugar; mix smoothly together, and add four ounces of fresh butter and a few drops of vanilla flavoring; stir briskly over the fire until it boils, and then work in vigorously yolks of six eggs, and then the whites whisked to a stiff froth; they are to be slightly incorporated with the batter; bake in a buttered dish; serve with or without sauce.

COTTAGE PUDDING.

ONE pound and a quarter of flour, fourteen ounces of suet, one pound and a quarter of stoned raisins, four ounces of currants, five ounces of sugar, quarter of a pound of potatoes smoothly mashed, half a nutmeg, quarter of a teaspoonful of ginger, the same of salt and of cloves in powder; mix the ingredients thoroughly; add four well-beaten eggs with quarter of a pint of milk; tie the pudding in a well-floured cloth, and boil it four hours; serve with sweet or lemon dip.

THUN PUDDING.

CHOP very small two ounces of almonds and some lemon peel; put them in a saucepan with one pint of milk and sugar to taste; when this begins to boil, stir in slowly one large cupful of ground rice, and let it boil ten minutes, stirring the whole time; pour in a mould, and when cold, turn out; put two ounces of white sugar in a pan, with a little water; stir until melted and become a light golden brown; add one pint of milk; bring this to a boil, then strain it, and add the yolks of four eggs; put the latter mixture on the fire and stir until it thickens; when cold, pour it round the pudding.

MACAROON PUDDING.

FILL the bottom of your baking-dish with macaroons soaked well in white wine; then pour over them a rich custard, adding whatever sweetmeats you please; the dish may be lined with puff-paste. Care must be taken in baking, as it is peculiarly apt to burn.

CHESTER PUDDING.

Two ounces of butter, four ounces of white sugar, one and a half ounces of sweet and bitter almonds blanched and pounded, one lemon (the juice and the peel grated), the yolks of four eggs; put all this in a stewpan over the fire, and stir it till it nearly boils, then pour it into a pie-dish lined with light pastry, and bake it; the whites of the eggs to be beaten up into snow and put over the pudding just before it is taken out of the oven; strew a little pounded sugar over it.

CHOCOLATE CREAM PUDDING.

GRATE quarter of a pound of the best chocolate; pour on it one teacupful of boiling water; let it stand by the fire until thoroughly dissolved; beat eight eggs lightly, omitting the whites of two;

stir them by degrees into one quart of rich cream, alternately with the chocolate and three table-spoonsful of white sugar; put the mixture into a dish, and bake it ten minutes.

SUET PUDDING.

PUT into a bowl half a pound of chopped suet, one pound of flour, two eggs, one teaspoonful of salt, nearly half a pint of milk; beat all well to-gether, put into a bag; boil one hour and a half.

CARROT PUDDING

HALF a pound each of grated carrots and pota-toes, suet chopped fine and flour; spices, salt, raisins and citron to taste; steam five hours; eat with wine sauce.

PLUM PUDDING.—WITHOUT EGGS.

HALF a pound of grated bread crumbs, quarter of a pound of chopped suet, one tablespoonful of flour, half a pound of currants, two and a half ounces of sugar, one glassful of brandy, milk enough to make a stiff batter; boil in a cloth four hours, or bake it, adding quarter of a pound of raisins.

QUICK PUDDING.

Soak and split some crackers; lay the surface over with raisins and citron; put the halves together, tie them in a bag and boil fifteen minutes in milk and water; delicious with rich sauce.

ICE OR FROZEN PUDDING.

One pint of cream, half a pint of milk, the yolks of four eggs, one ounce of sweet almonds pounded and half a pound of sugar; put them in a stewpan on a gentle fire; stir the cream until the consistency of custard; take off the fire, and when cold, add two wineglassesful of brandy; put in the freezer, and when partially congealed, add one pound of preserved fruit, with a few currants; cut the fruit into small pieces and scatter with the currants well over the surface; when frozen sufficiently, serve like ice cream.

NONPAREIL PLUM PUDDING.

Half a pound of raisins stoned and chopped, half a pound of currants well cleaned and dried, quarter of a pound each of candied orange and lemon peel sliced thin, half a grated nutmeg, half a teaspoonful of cinnamon, half a teaspoonful of salt, the grated rind of two fresh lemons, the juice of one, one pound of fine bread crumbs, three-quarters of a pound of finely-shred fresh suet, half a pound of powdered sugar, two glasses each of brandy and wine, and seven eggs; first beat the eggs very stiff, yolks and whites separately; then add the spices, the salt and the peels; then the sugar, raisins and currants; next the crumbs and suet; last the lemon juice, brandy and wine; beat all together very smooth; pour into a pudding-cloth, bag or mould, and boil six hours; serve with wine, hard sauce or any that suits the taste of those who are to eat it.

METROPOLITAN PUDDING.

ONE of the best baked puddings that was ever served in the Metropolitan Hotel, New York: Five tablespoonsful of corn-starch to one quart of milk; dissolve the starch in part of the milk, heat the milk to nearly boiling; having salted it a little, add the dissolved starch to the milk; boil three minutes, stirring it briskly; allow it to cool, and thoroughly mix with it three eggs well beaten and three tablespoonsful of sugar; flavor to your taste, and bake half an hour.

TIMELESS PUDDING.

SCALD one quart of milk; take three table-spoonsful of cold milk, three tablespoonsful of flour and three eggs; rub well together, and pour the batter in while the milk is hot; bake half an hour; butter and sugar, flavored with nutmeg, beat to a cream, for dressing

OLD ENGLISH PLUM PUDDING.

To make what is termed a pound pudding, take of raisins well stoned, currants thoroughly washed, one pound each; chop one pound of suet very fine and mix with them; add quarter of a pound of flour or bread very finely crumbed, three ounces of sugar, one ounce and a half of grated lemon peel, a blade of mace, half a small nutmeg, half a dozen eggs well beaten; work it well together, put it into a cloth, tie it firmly (allowing room to swell), and boil not less than five hours; it should not be suffered to stop boiling till done.

PLAIN BATTER PUDDING.

ONE quart of milk, six eggs, nine tablespoons-ful of flour, a little salt and one teaspoonful of butter; bake half an hour or upward.

29

HONEST PLUM PUDDING.

TAKE one pound of bread, break it small and soak in one quart of milk; when soft, mash the bread, and mix with it three large spoonsful of flour previously mixed with a cup of milk; add half a pound of brown sugar, one wineglassful of wine, one wineglassful of brandy, one teaspoonful of salt, the same of pulverized mace and cinnamon, or a rind of a lemon grated. The whole should be well stirred together with quarter of a pound of chopped suet or melted butter; add ten eggs well beaten, one pound of Zante currants, and the same of seeded raisins; boil it in a bag made of thick cotton cloth, and before filling, it should be wrung out of hot water and floured inside; it must not be entirely filled with the pudding, as it will swell when boiling; place an old plate at the bottom of the pot in which you boil the pudding, to keep the bag from sticking to it and burning; let the water boil when you put the pudding in, and in a few minutes turn the bag over. There should be water enough to cover the pudding all the time it is boiling. When you wish to turn out the pudding, immerse the bag in cold water a minute, and it will easily slip out. This pudding will require three or four hours to boil thoroughly.

BEST CHRISTMAS PLUM PUDDING.

ONE pound of raisins, one pound of currants, one pound of bread crumbs, half a pound of suet chopped fine, eight eggs, one quart of milk, one teacupful of sugar, one nutmeg, quarter of a pound candied citron, quarter of a candied lemon cut in strips, salt and other spice to taste; boil slowly for four hours, and eat with rich sauce.

HARRISON PUDDING.

ONE cupful of molasses, one cupful of sweet milk, one cupful of suet, three cupsful of flour, two cupsful of fruit, one teaspoonful of soda and one teaspoonful of cinnamon; butter the dish, put in and steam two hours; serve with sweet sauce.

CONNECTICUT MAIZE PUDDING.

SUFFICIENT quantity of sweet milk for the pudding desired, salt to the taste, and stir in Indian meal till a little milk will rise on the top by standing; if too thick, it will be hard; fill a pudding-crock or dish, and tie a cloth tightly over it; put into boiling water sufficient to keep it covered, and boil steadily three hours; fruit may be added if desired; served with sweetened cream.

NOTTINGHAM PUDDING.

PEEL six good apples; take out the cores with
the point of a small knife, but be sure to leave the
apples whole; fill up where the core was taken
from with sugar and lemon-juice or spice; place
them in a pie-dish and pour over them a nice
light batter prepared as for batter pudding, and
bake them an hour in a *moderate* oven.

EXCELSIOR APPLE PUDDING.

BREAD crumbs, suet, apples, currants and brown
sugar half a pound of each, a dozen sweet almonds
chopped fine, one wineglassful of brandy, a little
cinnamon and spice to taste, the apples to be
pared, cored and chopped fine, the suet shred and
chopped; mix all well together, adding the whites
of eggs just before the brandy, which should be
the last ingredient put in; boil for three hours,
either in a pudding-bag or a mould well buttered.

DORA'S WHORTLEBERRY PUDDINGS.

1. ONE quart of sour milk or buttermilk, one
teaspoonful of soda, a little salt; make a thick
batter of wheat meal or Graham, and stir in one
pint of huckleberries. This makes a large pud-

ding, and should be steamed in a two-quart basin two hours; any sauce is good, but I prefer sweetened cream.

2. One pint of sweet milk scalding hot, a large pinch of salt; stir in flour till quite thick; let it cool while you beat up four eggs; stir in the eggs and one pint of huckleberries; steam nearly two hours, and serve with sweetened cream.

Either of these puddings is good with any fruit —apples, crab apples, berries or raisins.

CARROT-POTATO PUDDING.

One pound of flour, one pound of suet chopped fine, three-quarters of a pound of sugar, one pound each of carrots and potatoes well boiled and mashed together, half a pound of raisins, three-quarters of a pound of bread crumbs, spice, flavoring and peel optional; mix the whole together with a little water; it must not be too stiff, and certainly not too moist; rub a basin well with dripping, and boil for three hours.

CREAM TAPIOCA PUDDING.

Soak three tablespoonsful of tapioca in water three hours; put the same in one quart of boiling

29 *

milk; boil fifteen minutes; beat the yolks of four eggs in one cupful of sugar; stir them into the pudding five minutes before it is done; flavor with lemon or vanilla; beat the whites of four eggs to a stiff froth with three tablespoonsful of sugar; put this over the pudding, and bake five minutes; one spoonful or two of prepared cocoanut in with the yolks and sugar is very good; cocoanut can also be sprinkled over the top, on the whites, before putting in to brown.

JERSEY PUDDING.

BUTTER a deep pudding-dish; line the bottom with thin slices of very light bread well buttered; pare half a peck of juicy freestone peaches; put a layer of peaches, then a layer of sugar; then more peaches, sugar and bread alternately, until the dish is nearly full; lastly, fit a cover of bread and butter on the top; put a plate over it, and set it in the oven; when the juice begins to boil up, take off the plate; bake it until the peaches are perfectly tender; let it get cold, and it is delicious.

PEACH DUMPLINGS.

SUBSTITUTE peaches for apples in recipe on page 345, and you will have delightful dumplings.

THE BEST BREAD PUDDING.

TAKE the inside of a small loaf of baker's bread, put into a deep pan with two ounces of butter; pour over it one pint of boiling milk; after remaining a sufficient length of time to become completely saturated, with a spoon mash it until very smooth and fine; whisk six eggs until thick and light, which stir in gradually; then add one quart of milk; mix all well together, and sweeten to taste; pour the mixture into a pudding-dish, sift a little cinnamon over the top, and bake in a *quick* oven; when done and cold, have ready some fine ripe peaches, which pare, slice and sugar; just before sending the pudding to table, place as many on the top as the dish will conveniently hold, and sift over white sugar. This is second to none, especially with cream sauce.

CULPEPPER PUDDING.

SIX large pippin apples, six large tablespoonsful of sugar, quarter of a pound of butter, quarter of a pound of stale sponge cake crumbed, six eggs, one small nutmeg grated, the grating and juice of one large lemon; pare, core and quarter the apples, put them in an earthen pipkin in half a pint of water to stew; when soft, but not broken, drain and mash them smooth with the butter; when quite cold, add the sugar, sponge cake, nutmeg and lemon alternately; then whisk the eggs until very thick, which stir in gradually; mix all well together, then put it in a buttered dish, and bake in rather a *quick* oven three-quarters of an hour; when done, sift white sugar over; if liked, ornament with thin slices of citron.

PRESERVE DUMPLINGS.

PRESERVED peaches, plums, quinces, cherries or any other sweetmeat; make a light crust, and roll a small piece of moderate thickness, and fill with the fruit in quantity to make the size of a peach dumpling; tie each one in a dumpling cloth, drop them into hot water, and boil half an hour; when done, remove the cloth, send to table hot, and eat with cream.

PLUMPING CURRANTS FOR PUDDINGS.

BEFORE putting them into puddings currants should be plumped. This is done by putting boiling water on them; soak them well, and lay them on a sieve or cloth before the fire; pick them clean from the stones; this makes them look larger and improves the flavor, besides cleaning them.

APPLE DUMPLINGS.—BOILED.

PEEL and cut the apples into halves, scooping out the cores; take one pint and a half of flour, three-fourths of a cupful of sour milk and cream, one-fourth of a teaspoonful of soda; stir the soda into the milk until it foams; mix the dough stiff enough to roll easily; just before covering fill the places scooped out of the apple with sugar and half an almond; when ready, drop them into boiling water. Dumplings are much more delicate and healthy by not having grease in the pastry. Almost any moderately tart fruit can be used instead of apples.

BAKED DUMPLINGS.

USE raised or puff-paste instead of the boiled dumpling paste.

TEMPERANCE FOAM SAUCE.

BEAT up, as for hard sauce, white sugar with butter, until very light, in the proportion of half a cupful of butter to one cupful of sugar; flavor with essence of lemon or bitter almonds; fifteen minutes before serving, set the bowl in a pan of hot water and stir it till hot. It will rise in a white foam to the top of the bowl.

NUN BUTTER.

FOUR ounces of butter, six ounces of sugar, as much wine as the butter will take; beat the butter and sugar together, and gradually add the wine and a little nutmeg.

WINE SAUCE.

Two ounces of butter, two teaspoonsful of flour, half a pint of boiling water, one gill of Madeira wine, quarter of a pound of sugar, half a grated nutmeg; mix the flour and butter together, pour in the boiling water, let it boil a few minutes; then add the sugar and wine; just before going to table add the nutmeg; serve hot.

PLAIN SAUCES.

1. SUBSTITUTE vinegar or lemon juice for the wine in the recipe for Nun Butter.

2. Omit the wine from the wine sauce, and you will have a very nice sauce.

3. An excellent sauce may be found at close of recipe for Sweet or Irish Potato Pudding (page 317).

Light Desserts, Creams, Etc.

GENERAL REMARKS.

This head includes some of the most delicate and delicious dishes that can be gotten up for the table. Most of them are cheap and economical, while none are very costly, and all are not only palatable but wholesome; many are nice supper desserts. The only general direction that we need offer is—care: in no branch of culinary economy is this more essential than in the preparation of the little delicacies that add so much to the attractiveness of a well-kept table.

BAKED FRUIT.

Apple.— An apple may be spoiled in the baking—often is. Your dish must be scrupulously clean, and your baking must be done leisurely. You can reduce, burn an apple in a short time, but if you bake for several hours—

three to four, more or less, according to your fruit, some kinds baking more readily than others—you will have a soft, pulpy fruit, wrinkled and brown, and shining, whole, or perhaps with a slight vertical break, which break must occur, if it occur at all, toward the last of the baking; occurring early, it will intercept the baking at that place, as the exposed part is a powerful non-conductor or resister of heat. On the other hand, the peel is a good conductor, and, with a moderate fire, will bake and finish your fruit. It will do this without breaking the skin, though it may strain it at first (or at any stage) very tightly; yet a good strong skin will resist the strain sufficiently to keep it intact and preserve the juice, which must not be permitted to escape. Of course only sound apples, thoroughly free from vermin and rot, sound throughout, core and all, must be used. For if there is a worm or rot or any foreign odorous substance, this itself is cooked, and penetrates more or less the whole mass. When your apple is done, just done, take it out and at once cool it. This in order to have as little of the core affect the flavor of the fruit as possible. Cooked with the rest, it will do this, and the longer it is hot, the more the bitter principle of the seeds will be distributed. The better way (and the only one if your fruit is quite sour) is to lay the fruit open, smoking hot; take out the core, clean and sprinkle sugar over the mass; work a little with the spoon, so as to mix and fine the pulp well, then close as before; set away till cold, and serve with or without rich cream.

PEARS.—1. Take quarter of a peck of pears, wash and put them into a pan, with one pound of brown sugar and half a pint of water; bake in a *moderate* oven until the fruit becomes tender; when cool, and before sending to table, sift over white sugar.

2. Pare and put the fruit into a pan, and to quarter of a peck of pears, allow three half pints of steam syrup; let them bake slowly in a *moderate* oven until soft.

3. Pare and core the pears, without dividing; place them in a pan, and fill up the orifice with brown sugar; add a little water, and let them bake until perfectly tender.

APPLE FLOAT.

TAKE six large apples, pare, slice and stew them in as much water as will cover them; when well done, press them through a sieve and make

30

very sweet with crushed or loaf sugar; while cooling, beat the whites of four eggs to a stiff froth, and stir in the apples; flavor with lemon or vanilla; serve with sweet cream. Quite as good as peaches and cream.

DELICIOUS DISH OF APPLES.

TAKE two pounds of apples, pare and core them, slice them into a pan; add one pound of loaf sugar, the juice of three lemons and the grated rind of one; let these boil about two hours; turn it into a mould, and serve with thick custard or cream.

APPLE SOUFFLE.

STEW the apples with a little lemon peel; sweeten them, then lay them pretty high round the inside of a dish; make a custard of the yolks of two eggs, a little cinnamon, sugar and milk; let it thicken over a slow fire, but not boil; when ready, pour it in the inside of the apple; beat the whites of the eggs to a strong froth, and cover the whole; throw over it a good deal of pounded sugar, and brown it a fine brown.

POMMES AU RIZ.

PEEL a number of apples of a good sort, take out the cores, and let them simmer in a syrup of clarified sugar, with a little lemon peel; wash and pick some rice, and cook it in milk, moistening it therewith by little and little, so that the grains may remain whole; sweeten it to taste, and add a little salt and a taste of lemon peel; spread the rice upon a dish, mixing some apple preserve with it, and place the apples upon it, and fill up the vacancies between the apples with some of the rice; place the dish in the oven until the surface gets brown, and garnish with spoonsful of bright-colored preserve or jelly.

GREEN CORN DELIGHT.

TAKE a dozen ears of green corn (sweet is best), and, without boiling, grate or scrape off the grains; into this stir two tablespoonsful of flour, also a well-beaten egg, a little salt, a couple of spoonsful of sugar, and, lastly, about a gill of sweet milk and a small lump of butter; stir all together well, and bake in a well-buttered tin pan for one hour in a hot oven; eat with butter and sugar or sweetened cream.

FLOATING ISLAND OF APPLES.

BAKE or scald eight or nine large apples; when cold, pare them and pulp them through a sieve; beat up this pulp with sugar, and add to it the whites of four or five eggs previously beaten up with a small quantity of rose-water; mix this into the pulp a little at a time, and beat until quite light; heap it up on a dish, with a rich custard or jelly around it.

APPLE SNOW.

STEW some fine flavored sour apples tender, sweeten to taste, strain them through a fine wire sieve, and break into one pint of strained apples the white of an egg; whisk the apple and egg very briskly, till quite stiff, and it will be as white as snow; eaten with a nice boiled custard it makes a very desirable dessert.

QUINCE DELIGHT.

BAKE ripe quinces thoroughly; when cold, strip off the skins, place them in a glass dish, and sprinkle them with white sugar; serve with rich cream. This makes a beautiful dish; it is simple and inexpensive, also a general favorite.

APPLE CHARLOTTE.

TAKE any number of apples you may desire to use; peel them, cut them into quarters and take out the core; cut the quarters into slices, and let them cook over a brisk fire with butter, sugar and powdered cinnamon until they are *en marmalade;* cut thin slices of crumb of bread, dip them in butter, and with them line the sides and bottom of a tin shape; fill the middle of the shape with alternate layers of the apple and any preserve you may choose, and cover it with more thin slices of bread; then place the shape in an oven or before the fire until the outside is a fine brown, and turn it out upon a dish, and serve either hot or cold.

CHARLOTTE RUSSE.

TAKE one ounce of isinglass or of gelatine, and soften it by soaking it a while in cold water; then boil it slowly in one pint of cream sweetened with quarter of a pound of fine loaf sugar (adding a handful of fresh rose leaves, if convenient, tied in a thin muslin bag) till it is thoroughly dissolved and well mixed; take it off the fire, and set to cool, and beat together till very light and thick four whole eggs and yolks only of four others;

30 *

stir the beaten eggs gradually into the mixture of
cream, sugar and isinglass, and set it again over
the fire; stir it well, and see that it only simmers,
taking it off before it comes quite to a boil; then,
while it is warm, stir in sufficient extract of roses
to give it a high rose flavor and a fragrant smell;
have ready two moulds lined with lady cake or
almond sponge cake; fill them with the mixture
and set them on ice; before they go to table ice
the tops of the charlotte, flavoring the icing with
rose.

CHOCOLATE CHARLOTTE RUSSE.

HAVING soaked in cold water one ounce of isinglass or of gelatine, shave down three ounces of
the best chocolate, which must have no spice or
sugar in it, and mix it gradually into one pint of
cream, adding the soaked isinglass; set the cream,
chocolate and isinglass over the fire in a porcelain
kettle, and boil it slowly till the isinglass is dissolved thoroughly and the whole is well mixed;
then take it off the fire and let it cool; have ready
eight yolks of eggs and four whites beaten all together until very light, and stir them gradually
into the mixture in turn with half a pound of
powdered loaf sugar; simmer the whole over the

fire, but do not let it quite boil; then take it off, and whip it to a strong froth; line your moulds with sponge cake, and set them on ice. If you like a strong chocolate flavor, take four ounces of the cocoa.

A DISH OF SNOW.

TAKE a large cocoanut, break it in pieces, pare off the dark skin; throw the pieces into cold water, wipe them dry, and then grate them on a coarse grater; serve the grated nut in a small glass bowl or dish, to be eaten with ices, preserves, jellies or jams.

MOCK CHARLOTTE RUSSE.

ONE cupful of butter, two cupsful of sugar, four cupsful of flour, one cupful of sour milk, four eggs, one teaspoonful of soda; bake in layers as for jelly cake. For the inside: One pint of sweet milk, the yolks of two eggs, one heaping table-spoonful of corn-starch; sweeten to taste, and flavor; bring the milk to a boil; then add the corn-starch moistened with a little milk; stir it a few moments and remove from the fire; put the cakes together cold.

ITALIAN CHARLOTTE.

SOAK in equal portions of wine and water sweetened with loaf sugar some slices of sponge cake;
put them in a glass bowl; make a custard in proportion of eight eggs to one quart of milk and six
ounces of sugar; when cold, lay the custard over
the sponge cake; beat the whites of three eggs to
a froth; add by degrees three tablespoonsful of
powdered loaf sugar; flavor with lemon or vanilla,
and with a spoon lay it tastefully over the top.

CROQUETTES DE POMMES.

COOK the apple just as for the charlotte, but
instead of putting it into the jelly shape you roll
into balls or rather cakes, which you cover with
egg and bread crumbs, and fry of a rich brown.

FLOATING ISLANDS.

1. ONE quart of cream, whites of five eggs, half
a pound of powdered loaf sugar; whisk the eggs
to a froth, add the sugar, one teaspoonful at a
time, and flavor with vanilla; sweeten and flavor
the cream with wine to taste; pour it into a bowl
or dish, and place the island tastefully on top.

2. One quart of milk sweetened, the whites of

six eggs, wine to the taste, half a pound of pulverized sugar for the island, a little currant jelly; beat the eggs, and add the half pound of sugar by degrees, and as much currant jelly as will make it a fine pink; pour the milk in a glass bowl; with a tablespoon place the island on it in heaps, tastefully arranged.

SILVER LAKE CUSTARD.

TAKE two pounds of sponge cake (baked in a square pan); place it in a deep dish; then take three pints of cream or rich milk, one gill of Madeira wine and sweeten to taste, with which saturate the sponge cake completely; have ready an island made as above, No. 2, and with a tablespoon place it on the top of the cake, not allowing the spoonsful to touch; if in strawberry season, just before going to table place six or eight large strawberries on each spoonful; sift white sugar over, and eat with the remaining cream. This is very nice, and likewise ornamental.

BALLOONS.

ONE pint of milk, three eggs, one pint of flour; separate the eggs, beat the yolks until light, and mix with the milk, and stir into the flour gradually; beat it well with one saltspoonful of salt; then whisk the whites until stiff and dry, and stir through lightly, half at a time; butter small cups, fill them half full of the mixture, and bake in a *quick* oven; when done, turn them out of the cups, place them on a heated dish, and send to table hot; eat with wine sauce.

CUP CUSTARD.

EIGHT eggs, five ounces of sugar, one quart of new milk, sugar to taste; beat the eggs, add the sugar and milk with a little rose-water and the grating of an orange or lemon; fill your custard-cups, sift a little cinnamon over the top, set them in the oven in a shallow pan of hot water; as soon as the custard is thick, take them out or it will be spoiled with whey; let them be cold when sent to table; they are very nice with fresh fruit sugared and placed on the top of each—strawberries, peaches or raspberries, as preferred.

FRENCH CUSTARD.

ONE quart of milk, eight eggs, sugar and cinnamon to taste; separate the eggs, beat the yolks until thick, to which add the milk, a little vanilla, and sweeten to taste; put it into a pan or farina kettle, place it over a slow fire and stir it all the time until it becomes a custard; then pour it into a pudding-dish to get cold; whisk the whites until stiff and dry; have ready a pan of boiling water, on the top of which place the whites; cover and place them where the water will keep sufficiently hot to cause a steam to pass through and cook them; place in a dish (suitable for the table) a layer of custard and white alternately; on each layer of custard grate a little nutmeg with a teaspoonful of wine; reserve a layer of white for the cover, over which grate nutmeg; then send to table, and eat cold.

SYLLABUB.

1. ONE quart of rich milk (or cream), half a pint of wine, six ounces of loaf sugar; put the sugar and wine in a bowl, and the milk lukewarm in a separate vessel; when the sugar is dissolved in the wine, pour the milk in, holding it high; grate nutmeg over it.

2. Three pints of cream, half a pound of sugar, half a pint of wine; mix the ingredients together as directed in Syllabub No. 1.

CUP CUSTARD.—NOT COOKED.

ONE quart of new milk, one pint of cream, four ounces of powdered loaf sugar, three tablespoonsful of wine in which rennet has been soaked; mix the milk, cream and sugar, and stir in the wine; then pour into custard-cups, and set away till it becomes a curd; grate nutmeg on top, and eat with cream thoroughly cold.

COLD CUSTARD.

TAKE one-fourth of a calf's rennet, wash it well, cut it in pieces and put it into a decanter with one pint of Lisbon wine. In a day or two it will be fit for use. To one pint of milk add one teaspoonful of the wine; sweeten the milk and flavor it with vanilla, rose-water or lemon; warm it a little and add the wine, stirring it slightly; pour it immediately into cups or glasses, and in a few minutes it will become a custard. It makes a firmer curd to put in the wine, omitting the sugar. It may be eaten with sugar and cream.

NEW YEAR'S TRIFLE.

THIS is a very pretty dish. Stick small Savoy or sponge cakes full of candied citron spikes, and pour over it currant syrup or any fruit syrup preferred diluted with the juice of a lemon; when the moisture is absorbed, pour a rich cold boiled custard made from the yolks of eggs over the cake, and pile upon the top the white, beaten to a stiff froth, with powdered sugar, and garnish with bits of firm, red currant jelly.

RASPBERRY FOOL.

PUT your fruit for quarter of an hour into an oven; when tender, pulp it through a sieve, sugar it, add the crumbs of sufficient sponge cake to thicken it; put into a glass mould or into custard-cups, and lay some thick cream on the top; if for immediate use, the cream may be beaten up with the fruit. Other light berries and fruit may be treated same way.

BLANC MANGE.

BREAK one ounce of isinglass in very small pieces, and pour on it one pint of boiling water; next morning add one quart of milk; boil it till the isinglass is dissolved; strain it; put in two ounces of sweet almonds blanched and pounded; sweeten it, and put it in the mould; when stiff,

31

turn them into a deep dish, and put raspberry cream around them, or dress with syllabub nicely frothed; some moulds require coloring. (For coloring, see page 272.)

TAPIOCA BLANC MANGE.

HALF a pound of tapioca soaked an hour in one pint of milk, and boiled till tender; sweeten to taste, and put into a mould; when cold, turn it out, and serve with strawberry or raspberry jam round it and a little cream.

JAUNE MANGE.

1. DISSOLVE one ounce and a half of isinglass in one pint and a half of water; add to it one pint of white wine, the yolks of eight eggs and the juice of three lemons; boil the peels in the liquor, beat the eggs with the juice of the lemons, sweeten to your taste; boil it all together, strain it and put it into moulds.

2. Put one ounce of isinglass, taking out a pinch, into a basin; pour over it half a pint of boiling water; let it stand covered over before the fire all night; then put it over the fire, and make it hot; add to it four yolks of eggs well beaten,

half a pint of sherry wine, the juice and rind of one lemon, sweeten it to your taste; let it boil gently for quarter of an hour; this quantity will make one good-sized mould.

JACQUE MANGE.

To two ounces of isinglass add one pint of water; dissolve it over the fire, and add the rind of two large lemons grated; when it has boiled a little, put in one pint of white wine, then the yolks of eight eggs thoroughly beaten, the juice of two lemons and sugar to taste; the eggs, lemon-juice and sugar should be previously mixed together with a small quantity of the wine; add the whole together, and keep stirring it one way until it boils; then strain through muslin, and pour into cups or moulds that have been well rinsed in cold water.

FIGS A LA GENEVIEVE.

DISSOLVE two ounces of best sugar in half a pint of cold water in an enameled stewpan, with half the very thin rind of a large lemon; when this is done, put into it half a pound of Turkey figs, and put the stewpan either over a moderate

fire or on a stove, so that the figs may stew very
slowly; when quite soft, add one glassful of common port or any other wine and the strained juice
of half a lemon; serve them hot for second course.
They are very good cold for dessert. About two
hours or two hours and a half is the average time
for stewing the figs, and the flavor may be varied
by using orange peel and juice instead of lemon,
and by boiling two or three bitter almonds in the
syrup.

SNOW CREAM.—A VERY SIMPLE DISH.

No sweet dish is more agreeable or easily made
for small balls or parties than the following snow
cream. If the recipe is closely followed, any family
may enjoy it at a trifling expense, and it is really
worthy the table of an epicure. Put in a stewpan
four ounces of ground rice, two ounces of sugar, a
few drops of the essence of almonds or any other
essence you choose, with two ounces of fresh
butter; add one quart of milk; boil from fifteen
to twenty minutes till it forms a smooth substance,
though not too thick; then pour into a mould
previously buttered, and serve when cold and well
set. If the mould be dipped in warm water, the

cream will turn out like a jelly. If no mould, put either in cups or a pie-dish. The rice had better be done a little too much than under.

THE HIDDEN MOUNTAIN.—A PRETTY DISH.

Six eggs, a few slices of citron, sugar to taste, three-quarters of a pint of cream, a layer of any kind of jam; beat the whites and yolks of the eggs separately; then mix them and beat well again, adding a few thin slices of citron, the cream and sufficient pounded sugar to sweeten it nicely; when the mixture is well beaten, put it into a buttered pan, and fry the same as pancake, but it should be three times the thickness of an ordinary pancake; cover it with jam, and garnish with slices of citron and holly leaves. This dish is served cold.

COMPOTE AUX COMFITURES.

Peel some apples, leave them whole, but take out the cores; put a little water in the preserving-pan, and let the apples cook with a large lump of sugar, taking great care that they do not break; place the apples in a glass dish, and when they are cold, fill the centre of each with apricot jam

31 *

or any *recherche* preserve; boil the liquid until it jellies; pour it into a dish that it may take its form, let it cool, and then put it over the apples without breaking it. The French recipe adds that the jelly will leave the dish easily if it be dipped for an instant into hot water, but as this would be likely to dull the jelly, it is a better plan to just dip shape, jelly and all into cold water, a plan followed by good confectioners.

ITALIAN CREAM.

PUT two pints of cream into two bowls; with one bowl mix six ounces of powdered loaf sugar, the juice of two large lemons and two glassesful of white wine; then add the other pint of cream, and stir the whole very hard; boil two ounces of isinglass with four small teacupsful of water till reduced to one-half; then stir the isinglass luke-warm in the other ingredients; put them in a glass dish to congeal.

BURNT CUSTARD.

BOIL one quart of milk; when cold, mix with it the yolks of eight eggs; stir them together over the fire a few minutes; sweeten to your taste; put some slices of Savoy cake in the bottom of a deep dish, and pour on the custard; whip the whites of the eggs to a strong froth; lay it lightly on top; sift some sugar over it, and hold a very hot iron over it until it is a light brown; garnish the top with raspberry marmalade or any kind of preserved fruit.

FROZEN CUSTARD.

SWEETEN one quart of cream or rich milk with half a pound of sugar, and flavor to taste; put it over the fire in a farina kettle; as soon as it begins to boil, stir into it a tablespoonful of corn-starch or rice flour which has been previously mixed smooth with a little milk; after it has boiled a few minutes, take it off the fire and stir in very gradually six eggs which have been beaten until thick; when quite cold, freeze it as ice cream.

ORANGE SALAD.

TAKE off the outer rinds and remove the thick inside skin of some fine, clear oranges; slice them, taking out the seeds, and strew them very thickly with powdered sugar; drop upon this a little lemon juice, and over the whole pour a cupful of currant shrub.

APPLE TOAST.

CUT six apples in four quarters each; take the core out, peel and cut them in slices; put in a saucepan one ounce of butter, then throw over the apples about two ounces of white pounded sugar and two tablespoonsful of water; put the saucepan on the fire, let it stew quickly, toss them up, or stir with a spoon: a few minutes will do them; when tender, cut two or three slices of bread half an inch thick, put in a frying-pan two ounces of butter, put on the fire; when the butter is melted, put in your bread, which fry of a nice yellowish color; when nice and crisp, take them out, place them on a dish, a little white sugar over, the apples about one inch thick; serve hot.

LEMON CUP CUSTARD.

TAKE four large ripe lemons and roll them; squeeze them in a bowl; mix with the juice a very small teacupful of cold water; add gradually sugar enough to make it very sweet; beat twelve eggs very light and stir into the mixture; beat thoroughly, put into cups, bake; grate nutmeg over when cold and serve; may be eaten with jelly or preserves.

FINE ICE-CREAMS.

Two quarts of new unskimmed milk (or good cream is better), two pounds (or less to taste) of powdered loaf sugar, eight eggs, a pinch of salt; dissolve the sugar in the milk; beat the eggs to a froth and add to the milk and sugar; strain and set on fire till thoroughly hot through, but not quite boiling: be very careful not to scorch; flavor with vanilla, lemon, orange or rose to taste (below we give the methods for flavoring with fruits); then put it in a tin freezer, which should be not more than one-half full, and pack the freezer in a deep tub with broken ice and salt, and whirl the freezer rapidly till the cream has the proper consistency, occasionally scraping down from the inside. The number of eggs may be reduced to suit taste and purse.

STRAWBERRY.—Mash one pint of fresh ripe strawberries with a spoon; sprinkle on half a pound of fine sugar and let it stand about an hour; press through a fine sieve or through a cloth, and if the sugar is not all dissolved, stir it well in; add a little water, and stir this juice into the milk or cream prepared as above, and freeze.

RASPBERRY.—Made the same as strawberry; a delicate dish, and pink.

BLACKBERRY.—Made the same as strawberry; as healthy a cream as made.

WHORTLEBERRY.—Made the same as strawberry; fine purple.

GOOSEBERRY.—Same as strawberry; fine green.

RED CURRANT.—Made same as strawberry; fine pink.

PEACH.—Take fine ripe freestone peaches; pare, chop fine, mash, and work as strawberry.

PINE APPLE.—Pare, shred fine.

COCOANUT.—Shell, grate fine and work as strawberry; a very little lemon juice is an improvement.

ALMOND.—Mash five-sixths sweet to one-sixth bitter almonds, putting in just enough rose-water to prevent oiling.

WALNUT.—Same as almond.

GRAPE.—Stew not too much; sweeten while stewing; when cold, strain out seeds and skins. The Delaware and other rich sorts are best.

TOMATO.—Pare and slice very ripe tomatoes; sift sugar over to taste; in preparing the milk or cream use rather less sugar; a little lemon is a decided improvement.

In substantially the same way ice-cream may be made of almost any flavor desired. Be sure to make the fruit very smooth before putting it in the cream.

WATER ICES.

ORANGE.—Take one dozen of oranges, the skin grated and juice squeezed out, six quarts of water, ten ounces of white sugar to each quart of water; mix well and put into **freez**er. Be careful to stir steadily while freezing or it will cake into lumps or be crusty. A little arrowroot is considered an improvement by many. The amount of sugar and of orange juice may be varied to suit taste.

OTHER FLAVORS may be made in the same way, varying the flavoring to taste.

FROZEN FRUITS.

THE above recipes, increasing quantity of peaches, raspberries or whatever fruit you may use, and adding a small amount of rich cream, make fine frozen fruits. The fruit should be mashed to a smooth pulp, but not thinned too much. In freezing, you must be especially careful to prevent its getting lumpy.

How to Cook Eggs.

GENERAL REMARKS.

THE French have nearly, if not quite, seven hundred ways of dressing eggs. In this country we have a few hundred less, and as a rule scarce one well understood or practiced by the "general public." An egg is truly a wonderful thing— rich, delicate and quite full of nutriment, if rightly used. Its value as an article of food is much enhanced by the ease and quickness with which it can be prepared and served.

If perfectly fresh eggs are not obtainable, great care should be taken in the use of doubtful ones. One test of their fitness is to drop them into cold water; the stale or addled ones will float on the water, or at least rise on end.

BOILED EGGS.

THE fresher eggs are, the more time will be required for boiling; to have them soft and tender, drop them in water at a boiling point, and let them stand from five to seven minutes, without boiling. If desired for salad, boil them for ten minutes; then throw them in cold water; roll gently on a table or board, and the shell is easily removed. Egg racks, to set in boiling hot water, are convenient.

FRIED EGGS.

To fry eggs to accompany ham or bacon, put some sweet, clean lard in a perfectly clean frying-pan, and when boiling hot, slip in the eggs, having broken each one separately in a saucer; do not turn them over, but keep dipping the hot lard over them with an iron spoon; they require about three minutes; take them out with an egg-slice, trim off the discolored parts, put them on a hot plate, drain off the grease, and send to the table hot. Some place them on slices of ham. The whites should be transparent, so that the yolk will shine through. To accompany the eggs, slice ham very thin, and soak the slices in hot water for about an hour, changing the water several times, and always pouring it on boiling hot; this process extracts the superfluous salt, as well as makes the meat tender; after soaking, dry

32

the slices with a cloth and broil over a clear fire; cold boiled ham may be sliced and broiled, and served with eggs—of course the slices need no soaking. Try this method, and see if it be not a great improvement upon the ordinary method of "fried" ham, and the eggs fried in the ham gravy.

POACHED EGGS.

To have perfect success choose eggs that are not less than two days old, yet they must be fresh; quite fresh eggs are too milky; the beauty of a poached egg, like a fried one, consists in having the white just sufficiently hardened to form a transparent veil for the yolk; strain as much boiling water as you need through a clean cloth into a stewpan; break the eggs separately into a cup or saucer, and when the water boils, remove the pan from the heat, and gently slip the eggs in; when the white is set, replace the pan over the fire (which should be moderate), and as soon as the water boils, the eggs are done; remove them with a slice and trim off the ragged edges; if served on toast, cut the bread in pieces a little larger than the egg, and about quarter of an inch thick; toast only on one side, and just enough to give a yellow color. The toast may be moistened with a little hot water; some sprinkle on it a few drops of vinegar, lemon juice or essence of anchovy sauce.

POACHED EGGS WITH HAM SAUCE.

MINCE fine two or three slices of boiled ham, a morsel of onion, a little parsley, pepper and salt; stew all together quarter of an hour; put the poached eggs in a dish, squeeze over them the juice of half an orange or lemon, and pour over this the sauce about half boiling.

OMELETTES.

A PERFECT omelette is neither greasy, burnt, nor overdone; the fire should not be too hot, as it is an object to have the whole substance heated without much browning; the perfect omelette is not thin, like a piece of fried leather, but it is thick, in order to be full and moist; the richness may be modified by beating two or three table-spoonsful of mashed potatoes with six eggs, or some corn-starch; beat them well with a fork or egg-beater and add a saltspoonful of salt; put two ounces of butter in the frying-pan; when melted, pour in the beaten eggs, stir with a spoon until it begins to set, then turn it up all around the edges, and when it is of a nice brown, it is done; to take it out, turn a hot plate over the omelette, and turn the pan upside down; double it over like a turn-over, and serve hot; if not sufficiently brown on the top, brown with a salamander or a heated shovel; to have the omelettes particularly fine, about as many whites as yolks should be used. Omelettes are sometimes served with gravy, which should be flavored with sweet herbs and onions, and thickened with potato, corn-starch or arrow-root; never with wheat flour. Omelettes are called by the name of what is added to give them flavor—a ham or tongue omelette, a veal kidney omelette (which is a great favorite with a French-man, on account of its delicacy); after the kidney is boiled, cut it into and beat with the eggs; in the same manner, ham, anchovies or tongue, shred small, makes a delicately flavored dish; some onion, parsley or a clove of eschalot minced very finely; some chop oysters.

How to Make Beverages.

GENERAL REMARKS.

THIS head includes Coffee, Tea, etc., and Light Wines, Beer, etc. To many persons a really good cup of coffee at their morning meal is not only a luxury but at the same time an essential part of the meal, and yet there are few, even among the most expert housewives, who quite understand the *art;* nothing but repeated efforts and constant care can give proficiency, though the instructions below will be found a valuable help. Tea, too, is often spoiled in the making; the quantity of tea used is important, but the manner of making is more so.

For dinner, lunch and at evening social companies home-made wines, beer, etc., are often found convenient and acceptable, and are far safer and preferable to the wines, cordials, brandies and other alcoholic stuffs which have done such incalculable harm and are so pernicious and baneful in the family circle.

32*

TEA.

TAKE sufficient tea, green or black or mixed, to taste; moisten in cold water; strain off the cold water and put the moist leaves in your tea-pot (earthen is best) and pour on boiling water; let it stand a few minutes near enough to the fire to keep hot, but not to boil at all; then pour off into a warm clean pot.

COFFEE.

NEVER buy your coffee ground, but grind it yourself immediately before using it; keep your coffee-pot, whatever kind you may use, wiped clean and dry inside; a damp tea or coffee-pot acquires a musty flavor that spoils the best tea or coffee. Put your freshly ground coffee into the coffee-pot previously made warm, and pour water upon it actually boiling; set the pot on the fire for a few seconds, but do not let it boil up, then pour a cupful out and return it back again to the pot in order to clear it; having done this let it stand on the hob or centre to settle, and in less than five minutes a transparent, strong, aromatic cup of coffee may be poured out. The proportions of coffee (which should not be too finely ground) recommended, are an ounce to a pint or pint and a half of water.

The milk used with coffee should always be boiled and used as hot as possible; the boiling of milk imparts a peculiar and exceedingly pleasant flavor to the coffee. White sugar is recommended, as the molasses-like flavor of moist sugar quite overpowers the delicate aroma.

SUBSTITUTES FOR COFFEE.

THOSE who are not particular as to quality, but only want something that looks like coffee, will find the following among the best of the many subtitutes: Roasted acorns, chick peas, beans, rye, cocoa shells, burned wheat bread, dried and roasted turnip, carrot and dandelion root. We do not recommend any substitute.

STRAWBERRY DRINK.

PUT to one pint of water one pound of strawberries, which you are to bruise or mash in the water; then put in quarter of a pound or five ounces of sugar, and squeeze into it the juice of a lemon, and suffer it to cool before you drink it. If the lemon be full, it will serve two pints.

CHOCOLATE.

CHIP one small square of chocolate, such as are marked on the half pounds; put this into a bowl, pour some boiling water, and mix it very smooth; then put it into a kettle or sauce-pan, and add to it one pint of boiling water; let it boil a few minutes, then add half a pint of boiling milk; boil the whole ten or fifteen minutes longer.

COCOA.

GRIND one teacupful of cocoa in a coffee-mill; put it in a small bag made of very thin muslin, tie it close; put it in a pot with three half pints of boiling water and one pint of boiling milk; boil the whole for half an hour, then put it into another pot and send it to table.

This will be found to suit delicate stomachs better than chocolate, as it is not so rich.

BOTTLED LEMONADE.

TAKE two quarts of hot water, two lemons, sliced, half a pound of loaf sugar and quarter of an ounce of gum arabic; strain through a flannel bag and bottle off.

SODA WATER POWDERS.

TAKE one ounce of tartaric acid, one and a half ounces of carbonate of soda; divide it into sixteen portions, wrap up the acid in white paper and the soda in blue; dissolve the soda in a tumblerful of water, put in the acid, and drink immediately. Citric acid may be used instead of the tartaric, and will be found an improvement.

SODA WATER.

DISSOLVE one ounce of the carbonate of soda in one gallon of water; put it into bottles, in the quantity of a tumblerful or half a pint to each; having the cork ready, drop into each bottle half a drachm of tartaric or citric acid in crystals; cork and wire it immediately, and it will be ready for use at any time.

APPLEADE.

SLICE some apples, put them in a deep pan and pour enough boiling water over them to cover them; place the cover on the pan, and when cold, strain the liquid; sweeten it, and flavor with a little lemon.

ORANGEADE.

A PLEASANT and antiseptic and anti-diarrhœa summer beverage is thus composed: Take of dilute sulphuric acid, contrated infusion of orange-peel, each twelve drachms, syrup of orange-peel five fluid ounces; add same to two imperial gallons of water. A large wineglassful is taken for a draught, mixed with more or less water, according to taste. Try it.

CRANBERRYADE.

POUR boiling water upon bruised cranberries, let them stand for a few hours, strain off the liquor and sweeten to the taste. This forms an agreeable and refreshing beverage.

CREAM BEER.

Two and one-fourth pounds of white sugar, two ounces of tartaric acid, juice of one lemon and three pints of water; boil together five minutes; when nearly cold, add the whites of three eggs beaten to a froth, half a cupful of flour well beaten with the egg and half an ounce of wintergreen essence or any other kind preferred; bottle, and keep in a cool place.

LEMONADE.

SIX lemons, one quart of boiling water, one or two ounces of clarified sugar.

TOMATO BEER.

A VERY healthy and palatable beer can be made in this wise: Gather ripe, sound tomatoes; mash, strain through a coarse linen bag, and to every gallon of juice add one pound of good, moist brown sugar; let it stand nine days; pour off and bottle closely; the longer kept the better. When used, fill nearly full a pitcher with sweetened water, add lemon juice to suit taste, and to this some of the preparation described, and you will find it equal to the best lemonade. To half a gallon of sweetened water add one tumblerful of beer.

BLACK OR WHITE ELDER WINE.

GATHER the elderberries ripe and dry, pick them and bruise them with your hands and strain them; set the liquor by in glazed earthen vessels for twelve hours to settle; put to every pint of juice one pint and a half of water, and to every gallon of this liquor three pounds of moist sugar;

set it in a kettle over the fire, and when it is ready to boil, clarify it with the whites of four or five eggs; let it boil one hour, and when it is almost cold, work it with strong ale yeast, and turn it, filling up the vessel from time to time with the same liquor, saved on purpose, as it sinks by working. In a month's time, if the vessel holds about eight gallons, it will be fine and fit to bottle, and after bottling will be fit to drink in twelve months; but if the vessel be larger, it must stand longer in proportion, three or four months at least for a hogshead. All liquors must be fined before they are bottled, or else they will grow sharp and ferment in the bottles. Add to every gallon of this liquid one pint of strong mountain wine, but not such as has the *borachio* or nag's-skin flavor. This wine will be very strong and pleasant.

Home-made wine may be made in a similar way with other berries or fruit substituted for the elderberries.

GINGER BEER.

PUT into any vessel two gallons of boiling water, two pounds of common loaf sugar, two ounces of best ginger (bruised), two ounces of cream of tartar, or else a lemon sliced; stir them up until the sugar is dissolved, let it rest until about as warm as new milk, then add two tablespoonsful of good yeast, pour on to a bit of bread put to float on it; cover the whole over with a cloth, and suffer it to remain undisturbed twenty-four hours; then strain it, and put it into bottles, observing not to put more in than will occupy three-quarters full; cork the bottles well, and tie the corks, and in two days, in warm weather, it will be fit to drink. If not to be consumed until a week or a fortnight after it is made, a quarter of the sugar may be spared.

In substantially the same way beer may be made of any desired flavor by using the appropriate fruit, etc.

CIDER KEPT SWEET ALL THE WINTER.

BRUISE one pound of white mustard seed and add two eggs well beaten and one pint of fresh milk; when the cider is in a condition for drinking, pour in the above mixture, shake the barrel well and bung tightly; the cider can be used when it settles. This recipe has been found to answer the purpose.

33

MULLED ALE.

BOIL one quart of good ale with some nutmeg; beat up six eggs and mix them with a little cold ale; then pour the hot ale to it, and return it several times to prevent it curdling; warm, and stir it till sufficiently thick; add a piece of butter or a glass of brandy, and serve it with dry toast.

CHERRY BOUNCE.

MIX together six pounds of morello cherries and six pounds of large black-heart cherries; put them in a wooden bowl and mash them with a pestle to mash the stones; mix with the cherries three pounds of loaf sugar and put them into a demijohn or large stone jar; pour on two gallons of best rectified whisky; stop the vessel closely and let it stand three months; shake it every day the first month; at the end of three months it is fit for use.

How to Can Fruits.

GENERAL REMARKS.

THE best method to preserve fruit with all its original flavor is by hermetically sealing it from the air in cans prepared for the purpose, and these should be of glass or stoneware, as the acids of fruit act chemically on tin or other metals, often destroying the flavor of the fruit, and sometimes rendering it very unwholesome. Either self-sealing cans, or those which require wax, may be used successfully, but probably the former are best for those of little experience, and they are unquestionably more convenient. Of these there are several claimants for public favor, all of them highly recommended, and doubtless all of them good. Our own experience favors the "Valve Jar," the "Mason" and the "Hero."

THE SELECTION OF FRUIT.—This should be done with the greatest care. Some varieties cannot be preserved at all, unless canned when perfectly fresh, and success is more certain with all kinds if this particular is regarded. The fruit should be nearly or quite ripe, but not over-ripe, and any which bears signs of decay must be carefully excluded.

COOKING THE FRUIT.—Nearly all varieties are better steamed than stewed or boiled, and this for three reasons: 1. The fruit is not so badly broken and mashed; 2. It retains more of its original flavor; 3. Little or no water is required to be added, and it is therefore cooked in its own juice.

Almost every family has conveniences for steaming on a small scale, either with the common tin steamer or the elevated platform, which can be used in a common kettle. To those who wish for more ample facilities we would recommend the following cheap and simple method: Take a common wash-boiler, and have fitted into it a horizontal platform of sheet-iron, perforated freely with half-inch holes so as to allow the free passage of steam. Have it mounted upon legs so it will stand clear from the water, which should be only a few inches deep in the bottom of the boiler.

Have your fruit carefully picked over and placed in a clean tin or earthen dish, with a cover over it to prevent the condensed steam from dropping into it. No sugar is required with any kind of fruit. We are informed by one who is always successful in this business that the flavor of the fruit is better preserved without sugar, and she never lost a can. If sugar must be used, it can be added when the cans are opened for the table.

Place your dish of fruit on the platform of your steamer, having sufficient water in the bottom, but not too much. Then cover the whole closely, and steam until thoroughly scalded. Some kinds of fruit require a longer time than others, and judgment must be exercised in regard to the matter. It should not be cooked so as to fall to pieces, but care should be taken to have it thoroughly scalded.

While the fruit is cooking, the cans should be prepared. Several methods have been recommended, but perhaps the following is the best: Have your cans thoroughly cleansed, and pour into each a small quantity of tepid water. Shake thoroughly until the can is of a uniform temperature. Then add a little warm water, shaking as before; then a little hot water, and so on until the can is hot. This is one of the best safeguards against breakage, and nearly as expeditious as any method. This should be done just in time,

33 *

so that the cans will be all ready for the fruit as
soon as done. While placing the fruit in the
cans be careful to protect them from currents
of air, as they are frequently broken by a simple
draught of cold air.

The fruit may now be poured into the cans.
Peaches, pears, or other large fruit, may be tastily
arranged in the cans with a fork, piece by piece, and
the boiling juice added afterward to cover them.
When the can is full, shake it, and incline it
back and forth, so as to cause the air to rise to
the top, if any should be among the fruit. Be
sure that the can is full to the brim, and then
screw on the cover, or if not a self-sealing can,
put in the cork and cover with melted sealing
wax. The following recipe makes good wax:
One pound of rosin, two ounces of beeswax, one
and a half ounces of mutton tallow. Melt and
mix.

All the above work should be performed expe-
ditiously. The cans may then be set away to
cool, and should be kept in a cool, dark place
and closely watched for a few days, to see that the
sealing is perfect. If the fruit shows signs of not
being perfectly sealed, it should be at once taken
out, scalded and sealed again.

Tomatoes, berries and small fruits may be preserved in stone jugs. Observe the same rules in preparation, heating the jugs thoroughly before putting in the fruit. When filled, place one or two thicknesses of cloth over the mouth and then put in the cork, covering the whole with wax.

By close attention to particulars and the exercise of good judgment, success is almost certain.

ANOTHER METHOD.

THE following is recommended by a neighbor who has had much successful experience: To can peaches, I allow half a pound or less of sugar to one pound of peaches. Make a syrup of the sugar by adding a pint of water to one pound of sugar, and boiling for a time. Pare and halve the peaches; drop them into the syrup and boil for ten minutes. Put into the cans—glass ones—and seal tightly. Any other kind of fruit may be preserved in the same manner. They will keep equally well without sugar, but it is usually quite as convenient to add the sugar when canned. Some add a few peach kernels blanched. For convenience and safety's sake, place the can, being filled with hot fruit, on a wet napkin or towel folded a number of times. Some varieties of pears require longer cooking, while some other varieties of fruit need less. The cans should be filled to the top.

CANNED GRAPES.

THERE is no fruit so difficult to can nicely as the grape; by observing the following instructions you will find the grapes rich and tender a year from putting up. Squeeze the pulp from the skin, as the seeds are objectionable; boil the pulp until the seeds begin to loosen, having the skins boiling in a little water, hard, as they are tough. When the pulp seems tender, put it through the sieve; then add the skins, if tender, with the water they boil in, if not too much. We use a large coffeecupful of sugar for a quart can; boil until thick, and can in the usual way.

PRESERVES, JELLIES, ETC.

GENERAL REMARKS.

IN selecting fruit for preserves it should always
be the finest and least defective, and much care
taken to remove all the bruised or decayed parts;
by allowing them to remain they darken the syrup,
and consequently the beauty of the preserve is
lost. The best loaf sugar should always be used,
unless for immediate use; it requires less skimming, and is not so apt to ferment. The Russian
isinglass, as also the white of egg, may be used for
clearing. The former should be prepared some
hours previous to using by pouring boiling water
over and allowing it to stand until wanted.

Glass tumblers are decidedly preferable to larger
vessels for all kinds of jellies and preserves, for
by frequent opening they very soon spoil. A
paper well saturated with brandy should be placed
on each, and a thick piece pasted over the top to
exclude the air. They should always be kept in
a dry, cool place.

393

SYRUP FOR PRESERVES.

To every pound of sugar add one gill of water, and let it stand until it is dissolved. For every twelve pounds of sugar allow half an ounce of Russian isinglass. Dissolve the isinglass by pouring over it a little boiling water. Put it in with the sugar; when cold, place the whole over the fire, and as soon as it begins to boil, skim it until no more scum will rise. The syrup is then ready for any kind of fruit which you may wish to preserve.

PINE APPLE PRESERVES.

CHOOSE your pine apples as ripe as you can get them. Pare and cut them into thin slices, weigh them, and allow one pound of the best double-refined loaf sugar to each pound of fruit. Take a deep china bowl or dish, and in it put a layer of fruit and sugar alternately, observing to put a coating of sugar on the top, and let it stand all night.

In the morning take out the fruit and put the syrup into a preserving-kettle. Boil and skim it until it is perfectly clear; whilst it is boiling hot pour it over the fruit, and let it stand uncovered until it becomes entirely cold.

If it is covered, the steam falls into the syrup and thins it. Put your fruit in glass jars or tumblers, and cover it close by pasting paper over the top.

PEACH PRESERVES.

TAKE fine large peaches, pare them and remove the pits. Weigh the fruit, and allow an equal quantity of the best loaf sugar. Put the peaches into a large dish and strew one-half of the sugar over them. Cover the dish and let it stand till next morning. Then take all the juice from the fruit, put it into a preserving-kettle with the remaining sugar, and when it is cold, put in some isinglass or the white of egg beaten.

In like manner quince, plum, apricot, apple, cherry, green gage and other fruit preserves are made; in every case fine large fruit should be taken, free from imperfections, and the slightest bruise or other fault should be removed.

CRANBERRY PRESERVES.

PICK, wash and weigh your cranberries; to each pound of fruit allow a pound of sugar. Dissolve the sugar in as small a quantity of water as

possible; put it over the fire in a preserving-
kettle, let it boil, and skim until it is perfectly
clear; then put in your cranberries, boil them
until they are quite soft and clear. Pour them
warm into your glasses; paste or tie paper over
when cold.

TOMATO PRESERVES.

WASH, bruise them and put in a boiler over a
fire; boil half an hour and strain; boil the juice
until reduced one-half; cool, put in jars, and seal;
then place the jars in a boiler of cold water, with
straw or rags to prevent breakage; boil twenty
minutes; when perfectly cold, place the jars in a
cool, dark cellar. They will keep for years. Add
seasoning when brought on the table.

WATERMELON RIND PRESERVES.

SELECT your rind, firm, green and thick; cut
them in any fanciful shape, such as leaves, stars,
diamonds, etc. When cut, weigh, and to each
pound of rind allow one and a half pounds of
loaf sugar. To green them take a brass or
copper kettle, and to a layer of grape vine leaves,
which should be well washed, add a layer of the

rind, and so on until the last, which should be a
thick layer of the leaves and well covered with a
coarse linen cloth. To each pound of the rind
add a piece of alum the size of a pea; then fill up
with warm water sufficient to cover the whole, and
let it stand upon the stove, where it will steam,
but not boil, until the greening is completed,
which will be in two or three hours. When green,
lay them in clear, cold water and commence your
syrup. To each pound of sugar add one and a
half pints of water; clarify, put in your rind;
have ready sliced some lemons, two to each pound
of rind, and when about half done, add the lemons.
Boil until the rind is perfectly transparent. If
you like the taste of ginger, add a few pieces of
the root, which will impart a high flavor, and is
very pleasant when blended with the lemons.
This preserve when candied is a very good substitute for citron in fruit cake and mince pies.

GARDEN CITRON PRESERVES.

AFTER having cut your citron in fanciful
shapes, place them in a jar of salt water and let
them remain three days and nights, then in fresh
water two days and nights, and the same length

34

of time in alum water. Scald them well in the alum water, drop them into fresh water, and let them remain one night, then boil in fresh water until transparent; cover them while boiling with grape leaves. Then make a syrup, allowing two pounds of loaf sugar to one of citron, and boil like preserves.

BLACKBERRY JAM.

CHOOSE large blackberries which are fully ripe, weigh them and allow one pound of sugar to a pound of fruit. Mash the fruit and sugar together; put the whole in a preserving-kettle; skim it while boiling, and stir it frequently; let it boil about one hour; when done, put in small pots or glasses, and when it becomes cold, cover with brandy paper and paste or tie them close.

WHOLE STRAWBERRY PRESERVES.

CHOOSE the largest scarlet strawberries, not too ripe. For every pound of fruit weigh a pound of double-refined sugar. Spread the fruit on large dishes and sprinkle over it half the sugar finely pulverized; shake the dish gently, so that the sugar ay come in contact with the under side of the fruit.

On the following day make a thin syrup with the
remaining half of the sugar, and allow one pint
of red currant juice to every three pounds of
strawberries. Mix the sugar and currant juice
together, and in this syrup simmer the strawberries until sufficiently jellied. When done,
place them in small glasses; when cold, cover
with brandied paper, and tie or paste paper over
each to exclude the air.

PUMPKIN PRESERVES.

SELECT a thick yellow pumpkin, take off the
rind and cut it into pieces of any form you may
fancy. Weigh the pumpkin, and for each pound
of fruit take a pound of loaf sugar. Allow one
wineglassful of lemon juice for each pound of
sugar; put the sugar over the pumpkin and pour
the juice over the whole. Cover it, and let it
stand all night. The next day add the parings
of one or two lemons, according to the quantity of
fruit, and boil the pumpkin long enough to make
it tender and clear, without being broken. Take
out the fruit, place it on broad dishes to cool.
Put it in jars or tumblers, and pour the syrup
over; when cold, cover with brandy paper and
tie close, or paste paper over.

QUINCE MARMALADE.

CHOOSE very ripe quinces; wash, pare and core them; to each pound of fruit allow one pound of loaf sugar. Boil the parings and cores together, with water enough to cover them, till quite soft; strain the liquid into the preserving-kettle with the fruit and sugar. Boil the whole over a slow fire, stirring it frequently until it becomes a thick mass. When cold, put in tumblers or glass jars. Cover with brandy paper and tie or paste paper over each, and keep in a dry, cool place.

Other fruit marmalades are made in like manner.

ORANGES IN JELLY.

TAKE the smallest sized oranges; boil them in water until a straw will easily penetrate them; clarify half a pound of sugar for each pound of fruit; cut them in halves or quarters, put them into the syrup, and simmer them until the fruit becomes clear; then take out the oranges and put them into a deep dish. Stir into the syrup an ounce or more of Russian isinglass, and let it boil a short time; if the syrup should not be thick enough, put in sufficient isinglass. As soon as you have a perfect jelly, strain it hot over the oranges.

PEACH JAM.

LET your peaches be quite ripe, pare and cut them in small pieces; to every pound of fruit add one pound of sugar; put the fruit and sugar into a preserving-kettle, mash all together, place it over the fire, and when it begins to cook, stir it until it becomes quite thick. Then take it from the fire, put it in glasses, and when cold, tie closely.

CRANBERRY JELLY.

TAKE two ounces of isinglass, boil it in one pint of water; when cold, mix with it double its quantity of cranberry juice. To every pint of this mixture add one pound of double refined sugar, and boil until it jellies. If for immediate use, rinse your forms with cold water, pour in the jelly while warm, and when perfectly cold it will turn out readily.

APPLE JELLY.

PARE, core and slice your apples; place them in a pan, and pour in water enough to cover them; stew them gently until they are soft, then turn them into a jelly-bag; let all of the syrup

34 *

run through without pressing it; then to each pint of this juice put one pound of loaf sugar and boil it to a jelly.

CALF'S FEET JELLY.

WASH and prepare one set of feet, place them in four quarts of water, and let them simmer gently five hours. At the expiration of this time, take them out and pour the liquid into a vessel to cool. When cold, remove every particle of fat, replace the jelly into the preserving-kettle, and add one pound of loaf sugar, the rind and juice of two lemons; when the sugar has dissolved, beat two eggs with their shells in one gill of water, which pour into the kettle, and boil five minutes, or until perfectly clear; then add one gill of Madeira wine, and strain through a flannel bag into any form you like.

ORANGE SYRUP.

PARE the oranges, squeeze and strain the juice from the pulp. To one pint of juice allow one pound and three-quarters of loaf sugar. Put the juice and sugar together, boil and skim it until it is clear; then strain it through a flannel bag, and let it stand until it becomes cool, then put in bottles and cork tight.

Lemon syrup is made in the same way, except that you scald the lemons and squeeze out the juice; allow rather more sugar.

STRAWBERRIES IN WINE.

STEM the finest and largest strawberries; put them into wide-mouthed pint bottles. Put into each bottle four large tablespoonsful of pulverized loaf sugar; fill up the bottles with Madeira or Sherry wine. Cork them closely, and keep them in a cool place.

BRANDY PEACHES.

TAKE large juicy freestone peaches, not so ripe as to burst or mash on being handled. Rub off the down from every one with a clean thick flannel. Prick every peach down to the stone with a large silver fork, and score them all along the seam or cleft. To each pound of peaches allow a pound of double-refined loaf sugar, broken up small, and half a pint of water mixed with half a white of egg, slightly beaten. Put the sugar into a porcelain kettle and pour the water upon it. When it is quite melted, give it a stirring, set it over the fire, and boil and skim it till no more scum rises. Next put in the peaches, and let them cook (uncovered) in the syrup till they look clear, or for about half an hour, or till a straw will penetrate them. Then take the kettle off the fire. Having allotted a pint of the very best white brandy to each pound of peaches, mix it with the syrup, after taking out the fruit with a wooden spoon and draining it over the kettle. Put the peaches into a large tureen. Let the syrup remain in the kettle a little longer. Mix the brandy with it, and boil them together ten minutes or more. Transfer the peaches to large glass jars (two-thirds full), and pour the brandy and syrup over them, filling quite up to the top. When cool, cover them closely and tie some bladder over the lids.

GREEN GAGES

ARE brandied in the same manner. Also large egg-plums. Pears, also, having first peeled them. To pear sweetmeats always add lemon rind grated and lemon juice.

How to Make Pickles.

GENERAL REMARKS.

THIS important department of cookery requires but little instruction beyond the two essential points—be careful to select perfectly sound fruit or vegetables for pickling, and use none but the very best cider vinegar. Good white wine vinegar does well for some sorts of pickles, but be ever watchful against chemical preparations called vinegar, that destroy instead of preserving the articles put away in it. In the selection of spices there is so much diversity of taste that no general directions will be of practical value. Do not use brass or copper kettles.

CUCUMBER PICKLES.

WASH your cucumbers very clean; make a pickle of salt and water sufficiently strong to float an egg, and pour it over them. Put a weight on the top of the vessel to keep the cucumbers under the brine, and let them stand nine days; then take them out and wash them in fresh water. Line the bottom of your kettle with green cabbage leaves, put in your pickles and as much vinegar and water, mixed in equal quantities, as will cover them. Put a layer of cabbage leaves on the top. Hang them over a slow fire; let the water get hot, but do not allow them to simmer, as that would soften them. When they are perfectly green, take them out and let them drain. Wipe them dry, put them in jars with some allspice, cloves and a few small onions or cloves of garlic. A piece of alum in each jar will keep them firm. Cover your pickles with the best cider vinegar; tie them close and keep them in a cool, dry place. By adding one tablespoonful of sugar it will be found a great improvement.

PICKLED MANGOES.

WASH your mangoes and rub them until they are smooth. Cut a piece out of the side of each one, take out all the seeds; then replace the piece and tie it closely with a thread. Make a pickle of salt and water strong enough to float an egg. Put in the mangoes, and place a cover over them and a weight upon it, in order to keep them entirely under the brine.   Let them remain nine or ten days; then take them out and wash them in clear water.   Line the bottom of your kettle with leaves, put in your mangoes, cover them with water and put a layer of cabbage leaves over them; place them over a slow fire, keep them scalding hot, but do not let them simmer.   As soon as they become of a fine green, take them out and wipe them dry.   Stir together some scraped horseradish, mustard seed, cloves, allspice, coriander seed and garlic; fill your mangoes with this mixture, tie on the piece again and lay them in the jars with the cut side up.   A little sugar may be added to the vinegar, of which pour over a sufficient quantity to cover the pickles.   Tie them closely.

They are not fit for use until they become soft.

PICKLED PEPPERS.

To one hundred peppers put three half pints of salt and as much scalding water as will cover them. It is best to put a weight over to keep them under the water.   Let them remain in the salt and water two days; then take them out and let them drain.

Make a small opening in the side to let out the water. Wipe them, put them in a stone jar with half an ounce of cloves, half an ounce of allspice and a small lump of alum. Cover them with cold vinegar.

When done in this way they do not change color.

ONION PICKLES.

SELECT small white onions, put them over the fire in cold water with a handful of salt. When the water becomes scalding hot, take them out and peel off the skins, lay them in a cloth to dry; then put them in a jar. Boil half an ounce of allspice and half an ounce of cloves in a quart of vinegar. Take out the spice and pour the vinegar over the onions while it is hot. Tie up the jar when the vinegar is cold, and keep it in a dry place.

CHOU CHOU.

To one peck of green tomatoes add three good-sized onions, six peppers with the seeds taken out; chop together, and boil three minutes in three quarts of vinegar. Throw this vinegar away after straining. Then to three quarts of new vinegar, when scalding hot, add two cupsful of sugar, one cupful of mixed mustard, one table-spoonful of cloves, one tablespoonful of allspice, two tablespoonsful of cinnamon, three tablespoons-ful of salt. Pour over the tomatoes hot.

PICKLED PEACHES.

TAKE hard ripe peaches, wipe off the down, stick a few cloves in them, and lay them in cold spiced vinegar. In three months they will be fit for use.

PICKLED RED CABBAGE.

SLICE it into a colander, and sprinkle each layer with salt; let it drain two days, then put it into a jar and pour boiling vinegar enough to cover, and put in a few slices of red beet-root. Observe to choose the purple red cabbage. Cauli-flower cut in bunches, and thrown in after being salted, will look of a beautiful red.

PICKLED MUSHROOMS.

RUB the buttons with flannel and salt, throw them in a stewpan, with a little salt over them; sprinkle them with some pepper and a small quantity of mace; as the liquor comes out shake

35

them well, and keep them over a gentle fire until all is dried into them again; then put as much vinegar into the pan as will cover them; give it a scald, and pour the whole into bottles.

WALNUTS.

THEY must be gathered when young enough to prick with a pin readily; pour on them boiling salt and water, and let them remain covered with it nine days, changing it every three days; take out and lay on dishes in open air a few minutes, taking care to turn them over; this will make them black sooner; put them in a pot; strew over them some whole peppers, cloves, a little garlic, mustard seed and horseradish scraped and dried. Cover with strong cold vinegar.

INDIA PICKLE.

FIFTEEN old cucumbers; pare, seed and cut them in thin strips; spread them on a board strewn thickly with salt; let them stand twelve hours; then expose them to the sun, turning until perfectly dry, avoiding the night air; wash them in vinegar; put a layer of mustard seed, onions, a stick of grated horseradish. Simmer in one quart of vinegar, half an ounce of tumeric, half an ounce of race ginger (both tied in a bag), allspice whole, a few cloves and cinnamon. When cool, pour it over the cucumbers.

SWEET PICKLES.

VARIOUS fruit, such as peaches, plums, cherries, grapes, etc., are very nice sweet pickled. The process is the same as for other light pickles, except you sweeten the vinegar to taste. Watermelon rind makes a nice sweet pickle; flavor with green ginger.

TOMATO CATSUP.

WASH and boil one bushel of tomatoes. When soft, pass the whole through a colander, mashing the mass till it has ceased to drip. There will be about eleven quarts of juice. Put this in a china-lined kettle, and add four tablespoonsful of salt, two tablespoonsful of allspice, three of ground mustard, one and a half teaspoonsful of ground black pepper, one of cayenne. Boil this two hours; if you wish it thick, three or four hours. Bottle, putting a little sweet oil on the top of each, to exclude air. Seal, and it is ready for use in two weeks.

COOKERY FOR THE SICK.

LIEBIG'S BROTH FOR THE SICK.—For one portion of broth take half a pound of freshly-killed meat (beef or chicken), cut it into small pieces and add to it one and one-eighth pounds of pure water to which have been added four drops of muriatic acid and one-half to one drachm of salt; mix them well together. After standing an hour, the whole is strained through a hair sieve, allowing it to pass through without pressing or squeezing. The portion passing through first being cloudy, it is again poured through the sieve, and this process is repeated until it becomes perfectly clear. Upon the residue of meat remaining in the sieve, half a pound of pure water is poured, in small portions. In this manner, about one pound of liquid (cold extract of meat) is obtained, of a red color and a pleasant meat-broth taste. It is administered to the sick, cold, by the cupful, according to their inclination. It must not be heated, as it becomes cloudy thereby, and a thick coagulum

412

is deposited. A great hindrance to the employment of this broth is, in summer, its liability to change in warm weather; it commences regularly to ferment, like sugar water with yeast, without the usual odor. On account of this, the meat must be extracted with perfectly cold water and in a cool place. Ice water and refrigeration with ice completely remove this difficulty. Most important of all is it that the meat should be perfectly fresh. This broth is now in use in the hospitals, and in the private practice of several of the most distinguished physicians of Munich.

A VEGETABLE SOUP.—Take an onion, a turnip, two pared potatoes, a carrot (a head of celery or not); boil them in three pints of water till the vegetables are cooked; add a little salt; have a slice of bread, toasted and buttered, put into a bowl, and pour soup over. When in season, tomatoes, or okra, or both, improve this.

GUM WATER.—Half an ounce to one ounce dissolved in one quart of cold water. Sweeten it.

COFFEE.—Sick persons should have their coffee made separate from the family, as standing in the tin pot spoils the flavor. Put two teaspoonsful of ground coffee in a small mug, and pour boiling

35 *

water on it; let it set by the fire to settle, and pour it off in a cup, with sugar and cream. Care should be taken that there are no burnt grains.

CHOCOLATE.—To make a cup of chocolate, grate a large teaspoonful in a mug, and pour a teacupful of boiling water on it; let it stand covered by the fire a few minutes, when you can put in sugar and cream.

BLACK TEA.—Black tea is much more suitable than green for sick persons, as it does not affect the nerves. Put a teaspoonful in a pot that will hold about two cupsful, and pour boiling water on it. Let it set by the fire to draw five or ten minutes.

RYE MUSH.—This is a nourishing and light diet for the sick, and is by some preferred to mush made of Indian meal. Four large spoonsful of rye flour mixed smooth in a little water, and stirred in a pint of boiling water; let it boil twenty minutes, stirring frequently. Nervous persons who sleep badly rest much better after a supper of corn or rye mush than if they take tea or coffee.

BOILED CUSTARD.—Beat an egg with a heaped teaspoonful of sugar; stir it into a teacupful of boiled milk, and stir till it is thick; pour it in a bowl on a slice of toast cut up, and grate a little nutmeg over.

PANADA.—Put some crackers, crusts of dry bread or dried rusk in a saucepan with cold water and a few raisins; after it has boiled half an hour, put in sugar, nutmeg, and half a glass of wine if the patient has no fever. If you have dried rusk, it is a quicker way to put the rusk in a bowl with some sugar, and pour boiling water on it out of the tea-kettle. If the patient can take nothing but liquids, this makes a good drink when strained.

BARLEY-WATER.—Well wash two ounces of pearl barley; boil it a few minutes in half a pint of water, which is to be thrown away; then add four pints of boiling water; keep it boiling till two only are left, and strain. A small quantity of lemon-juice may be added.

MUCILAGINOUS BROTH.—Cut a young fowl into several parts, and wash them thoroughly; put these into a three-quart stewpan; add three pounds of the lean of white veal, a couple of turnips, a carrot and one head of celery, the whole to be cut into small pieces; fill the stewpan with water, and boil it, removing the scum as it rises to the surface. After the broth has thrown off the albumen of the meat in the shape of scum, add to it two ounces of best Ceylon moss, taking care to mix well the moss with the broth; keep it gently boiling for one hour and a quarter; skim it for use. This broth is very nutritious and cooling, and will prove beneficial in cases of sore throat.

PLAIN CHICKEN BROTH.—Cut into four parts a young fowl, wash them and put them into a stewpan with one quart of water and a little salt; set it to boil; skim it well, and then add the heart of a white cabbage lettuce and a handful of chervil; boil the broth an hour, and then strain it for use.

BEEF TEA.—Two pounds of the lean of beef; pare away carefully every portion of fat, skin or sinew, cut it into pieces the size of a nut; put it into a stewpan that will hold two quarts, and pour three pints of boiling water upon it; add a little salt; when it boils, skim it, and then remove it to the side of the stove to boil gently for an hour; skim it for use.

COOKERY AMERICANA
AN ARNO PRESS COLLECTION

Each of the following titles includes an Introduction and Revised Recipes by Chef Louis Szathmáry.

Along the Northern Border: Cookery in Idaho, Minnesota, and North Dakota. New York, 1973.

Cooking in Old Créole Days by Célestine Eustis. New York, 1904.

Cool, Chill, and Freeze: A New Approach to Cookery. New York, 1973.

Directions for Cookery, in Its Various Branches by Miss Eliza Leslie. 31st edition. Philadelphia, 1848.

Fifty Years of Prairie Cooking. New York, 1973.

Hand-Book of Practical Cookery by Pierre Blot. New York, 1869.

High Living: Recipes from Southern Climes. Compiled by L. L. McLaren. San Francisco, 1904.

Home Cookery & Ladies' Indispensable Companion: Cookery in Northeastern Cities. New York, 1973.

The Improved Housewife, or Book of Receipts by Mrs. A. L. Webster. 6th edition. Hartford, 1845.

The Kansas Home Cook-Book. Compiled by Mrs. C. H. Cushing and Mrs. B. Gray. 5th edition. Leavenworth, Kansas, 1886.

Midwestern Home Cookery. New York, 1973.

Mrs. Porter's New Southern Cookery Book by Mrs. M. E. Porter. Philadelphia, 1871.

One Hundred Recipes for the Chafing Dish by H. M. Kinsley. New York, 1894.

Six Little Cooks by Elizabeth Stansbury Kirkland. Chicago, 1879.

Southwestern Cookery: Indian and Spanish Influences. New York, 1973.

ARNO PRESS, 330 MADISON AVENUE, NEW YORK, N.Y. 10017